Adult Development

Adult Development

Nanak Chand

RANDOM

RANDOM PUBLICATIONS

NEW DELHI (INDIA)

Adult Development

ISBN 978-93-5111-958-6

Published in 2016 in India by

RANDOM PUBLICATIONS

4376-A/4B, Gali Murari Lal, Ansari Road
New Delhi-110 002
Phone : +9111-43580356, 011-23289044, 011-43142548
e-mail: sales@randompublications.com,
info@randompublications.com, randomexports@gmail.com

Type Setting by : Friends Media, Delhi-110089
Digitally Printed at : Replika Press Pvt. Ltd.

Preface

Adult development encompasses the changes that occur in biological, psychological, and interpersonal domains of human life from the end of adolescence until the end of one's life. These changes may be gradual or rapid, and can reflect positive, negative, or no change from previous levels of functioning.

The concept of adulthood has legal and socio-cultural definitions. The legal definition of an adult is a person who has reached the age at which they are considered responsible for their own actions, and therefore legally accountable for them.

This is referred to as the age of majority, which is age 18 in most cultures, although there is variation from 16 to 21. The socio-cultural definition of being an adult is based on what a culture normatively views as being the required criteria for adulthood, which in turn influences the life of individuals within that culture. This may or may not coincide with the legal definition. Current views on adult development in late life focus on the concept of successful aging, defined as "...low probability of disease and disease-related disability, high cognitive and physical functional capacity, and active engagement with life."

Developmental cognitive neuroscience is an interdisciplinary scientific field devoted to understanding psychological processes and their neurological bases in the developing organism. It examines how the mind changes as children grow up, interrelations between that and how the brain is changing, and environmental and biological influences on the developing mind and brain.

Adult development is a broad psychological area of study focusing on the psychological development of adults;it is a subfield of developmental psychology. This broad field is concerned with many aspects of adult psychology, such as dealing with the loss of parental influence, learning as an adult, and the connection between psychological and physical health in adults. People study adult development for many different reasons, ranging from the purely academic to those with practical workplace applications.

The knowledge gained through such research is often applied in the workplace, especially in training and preparing individuals for leadership positions within a company.

Present book has been complete to cater to the requirements of the teachers, researchers and students.

– Author

Contents

1

Introduction

Adult development encompasses the changes that occur in biological, psychological, and interpersonal domains of human life from the end of adolescence until the end of one's life. These changes may be gradual or rapid, and can reflect positive, negative, or no change from previous levels of functioning. Changes occur at the cellular level and are partially explained by biological theories of adult development and aging. Biological changes influence psychological and interpersonal/social developmental changes, which are often described by stage theories of human development. Stage theories typically focus on "age-appropriate" developmental tasks to be achieved at each stage. Erik Erikson and Carl Jung proposed stage theories of human development that encompass the entire life span, and emphasized the potential for positive change very late in life.

The concept of adulthood has legal and socio-cultural definitions. The legal definition of an adult is a person who has reached the age at which they are considered responsible for their own actions, and therefore legally accountable for them. This is referred to as the age of majority, which is age 18 in most cultures, although there is variation from 16 to 21. The socio-cultural definition of being an adult is based on what a culture normatively views as being the required criteria for adulthood, which in turn influences the life of individuals within that culture. This may or may not coincide with the legal definition. Current views on adult development in late life focus on the concept of successful aging, defined as "...low probability of disease and disease-related disability, high cognitive and physical functional capacity, and active engagement with life."

Biomedical theories hold that one can age successfully by caring for physical health and minimizing loss in function, whereas psychosocial theories posit that capitalizing upon social and cognitive resources, such as a positive attitude or social support from neighbours and friends, is key to aging successfully. Jeanne Louise Calment exemplifies successful aging as the longest living person, dying at the age of 122 years. Her long life can be attributed to her genetics (both parents lived into their 80s) and her active lifestyle and optimistic attitude.

She enjoyed many hobbies and physical activities and believed that laughter contributed to her longevity. She poured olive oil on all of her food and skin, which she believed also contributed to her long life and youthful appearance.

CONTEMPORARY AND CLASSIC THEORIES

Changes in adulthood have been described by a number of theories and metatheories, which serve as framework for adult development research.

LIFESPAN DEVELOPMENT THEORY

Life span development is an overarching framework that considers individual development (ontogeny) from conception to old age. The framework considers the lifelong accumulation of developmental gains and losses, with the relative proportion of gains to losses diminishing over an individual's life time. According to this theory, life span development has multiple trajectories (positive, negative, stable) and causes (biological, psychological, social, and cultural). Individual variation is a hallmark of this theory – not all individuals develop and age at the same rate and in the same manner.

ERIK ERIKSON'S THEORY OF PSYCHOSOCIAL DEVELOPMENT

Erik Erikson developed stages of ego development that extended through childhood, adolescence and adulthood. He was trained in psychoanalysis and was highly influenced by Freud, but unlike Freud, Erikson believed that social interaction is very important to the individual's psychosocial development. His stage theory consists of 8 stages in life from birth to old age, each of which is characterized by a specific developmental task. During each stage, one developmental task is dominant, but may be carried forward into later stages as well. According to Erikson, individuals may experience tension when advancing to new stages of development, and seek to establish equilibrium within each stage.

- Stage 1 – Trust vs. Mistrust (0 to 1.5 yrs)
- Stage 2 – Autonomy vs. Shame and Doubt (1.5 – 3 years)
- Stage 3 – Initiative vs. Guilt (3 - 6 yrs)
- Stage 4 – Industry vs. Inferiority (6 years to puberty)
- Stage 5 – Identity vs. Role Confusion (adolescence)
- Stage 6 – Intimacy vs. Isolation (early adulthood)
- Stage 7 – Generativity vs. Stagnation (middle adulthood)
- Stage 8 – Integrity vs. Despair

MICHAEL COMMONS'S THEORY

Michael Commons's Model of Hierarchical Complexity (MHC) is an enhancement and simplification of Inhelder and Piaget's developmental model. It offers a standard method of examining the universal pattern of development.

In order for one task to be more hierarchically complex than another, the new task must meet three requirements: 1) It must be defined in terms of the lower stage actions;2) it must coordinate the lower stage actions;3) it must do so in a non-arbitrary way

- 0 Calculatory
- 1 Sensory and Motor
- 2 Circular sensory-motor
- 3 Sensory-motor
- 4 Nominal
- 5 Sentential
- 6 Preoperational
- 7 Primary
- 8 Concrete
- 9 Abstract
- 10 Formal
- 11 Systematic
- 12 Metasystematic
- 13 Paradigmatic
- 14 Cross-paradigmatic
- 15 Meta-Cross-paradigmatic

CARL JUNG'S THEORY

Carl Jung, a Swiss psychoanalyst, formulated four stages of development and believed that development was a function of reconciling opposing forces.

- *Childhood:* (birth to puberty) Childhood has two substages. The archaic stage is characterized by sporadic consciousness, while the monarchic stage represents the beginning of logical and abstract thinking. The ego starts to develop.
- *Youth:* (puberty until 35 – 40) Maturing sexuality, growing consciousness, and a realization that the carefree days of childhood are gone forever. People strive to gain independence, find a mate, and raise a family.
- *Middle Life:* (40-60) The realization that you will not live forever creates tension. If you desperately try to cling to youth, you will fail in the process of self-realization. Jung believed that in midlife, one confronts one's shadow. Religiosity may increase during this period, according to Jung.
- *Old Age:* (60 and over) Consciousness is reduced. Jung thought that death is the ultimate goal of life. By realizing this, people will not face death with fear, but with a hope for rebirth.

DANIEL LEVINSON'S THEORY

Daniel Levinson's theory is a set of psychosocial 'seasons' through which adults must pass as they move through early adulthood and midlife. Each of these seasons is created by the challenges of building or maintaining a life structure, by the social norms that apply to particular age groups, particularly in relation to relationships and career. The process that underlies all these stages is individuation - a movement towards balance and wholeness over time.

The key stages that he discerned in early adulthood and midlife were as follows:

- Early Adult Transition (Ages 16–24)
- Forming a Life Structure (Ages 24–28)
- Settling down (Ages 29–34)
- Becoming One's Own Man (Ages 35–40)
- Midlife Transition (Early forties)
- Restabilization, into Late Adulthood (Age 45 and on)

A BIOPSYCHOSOCIAL METATHEORY OF ADULT DEVELOPMENT

The 'biopsychosocial' approach to adult development states that in order to understand human development in its fullness, biological, psychological and social levels of analysis must be included. There are a variety of biopsychosocial meta-models, but all entail a commitment to the following four premises:

1. Human development happens concurrently at biological, psychological and social levels throughout life, and a full descriptive account of development must include all three levels.
2. Development at each of these three levels reciprocally influences the other two levels;therefore nature (biology) and nurture (social environment) are in constant complex interaction, when considering how and why psychological development occurs.
3. Biological, psychological and social descriptions and explanations are all as valid as each other, and no level has causal primacy over the other two.
4. Any aspect of human development is best described and explained in relation to the whole person and their social context, as well as to their biological and cognitive-affective parts. This can be called a holistic or contextualist viewpoint, and can be contrasted with the reductionist approach to development, which tends to focus solely on biological or mechanistic explanations.

NORMATIVE PHYSICAL CHANGES IN ADULTHOOD

Physical development in midlife and beyond include changes at the biological level (senescence) and larger organ and musculoskeletal levels. Sensory changes and degeneration begin to be common in midlife. Degeneration can include the break down of muscle, bones and joints, leading to physical ailments such as sarcopenia orarthritis.

At the sensory level, changes occur to vision, hearing, taste, touch, and smell, and taste. Two common sensory changes that begin in midlife include our ability to see close objects and our ability to hear high pitches. Other developmental changes to vision might include cataracts, glaucoma, and the loss of central visual field with macular degeneration. Hearing also becomes impaired in midlife and aging adults, particularly in men. In the past 30 years, hearing impairment has doubled. Hearing aids as an aid for hearing loss still leave many individuals dissatisfied with their quality of hearing.

Olfaction can co-occur with changes in sense of taste. "Olfactory dysfunction can impair quality of life and may be a marker for other deficits and illnesses" and can also lead to decreased satisfaction in taste when eating. Losses to the sense of touch are usually noticed when there is a decline in the ability to detect a vibratory stimulus. The loss in sense of touch can harm a person's fine motor skills such as writing and using utensils. The ability to feel painful stimuli is usually preserved in aging, but the process of decline for touch is accelerated in those with diabetes.

Physical deterioration to the body begins to increase in midlife and late life, and includes degeneration of muscle, bones, and joints.Sarcopenia, a normal developmental change, is the degeneration of muscle mass, which includes both strength and quality. This change occurs even in those who consider themselves athletes, and is accelerated by physical inactivity. Many of the contributing factors that may cause sarcopenia include neuronal and hormonal changes, inadequate nutrition, and physical inactivity.

Apoptosis has also been suggested as an underlying mechanism in the progression of sarcopenia. The prevalence of sarcopenia increases as people age and is associated with the increased likelihood of disability and restricted independence among elderly people. Approaches to preventing and treating sarcopenia are being explored by researchers. A specific preventative approach includes progressive resistance training, which is safe and effective for the elderly.

Developmental changes to various organs and organ systems occur throughout life. These changes affect responses to stress and illness, and can compromise the body's ability to cope with demand on organs. The altered functioning of the heart, lungs, and even skin in old age can be attributed to factors like cell death or endocrine hormones. There are changes to the reproductive system in midlife adults, most notably menopause for women, the permanent end of fertility. In men, hormonal changes also affect their reproductive and sexual physiology, but these changes are not as extreme as those experienced by women.

ILLNESSES ASSOCIATED WITH AGING

As adult bodies undergo a variety of physical changes that cause health to decline, a higher risk of contracting a variety of illnesses, both physical and mental, is possible.

Cancer

Scientists have made a distinctive connection between aging and cancer. It has been shown that the majority of cancer cases occur in those over 50 years of age.

This may be due to the decline in strength of the immune system as one ages or co existing conditions. There a variety of symptoms associated with cancer, commonly growths or tumors may be indicators of cancer. Radiation, chemotherapy, and in some cases, surgery, is used to treat the cancer.

Arthritis

Osteoarthritis is one of the most commonly experienced illnesses in adults as they age. Although there are a variety of types of arthritis they all include very similar symptoms: aching joints, stiff joints, continued joint pain, and problems moving joints.

Cardiovascular Disease

It has been found that older age does increase the risk factor of contracting a cardiovascular disease. Hypertension and high cholesterol have also been found to increase the likelihood of acquiring a cardiovascular disease, which are also commonly found in older adults. Cardiovascular diseases include a variety of heart conditions that may induce a heart attack or other heart-related problems. Healthy eating, exercise, and avoiding smoking are usually used to prevent cardiovascular disease.

Immune System

Infection occurs more easily as one ages, as the immune system starts to slow and become less effective. Aging also changes how the immune system reacts to infection, making new infections harder to detect and attack. Essentially, the immune system has a higher chance of being compromised the older one gets.

ADULT NEUROGENESIS AND NEUROPLASTICITY

New neurons are constantly formed from stem cells in parts of the adult brain throughout adulthood, a process called adult neurogenesis. The hippocampus is the area of the brain that is most active in neurogenesis. Research shows that thousands of new neurons are produced in the hippocampus every day.

The brain constantly changes and rewires itself throughout adulthood, a process known as neuroplasticity. Evidence suggests that the brain changes in response to diet, exercise, social environment, exercise, stress and toxin intake. These same external factors also influence genetic expression throughout adult life - a phenomenon known as genetic plasticity.

NON-NORMATIVE COGNITIVE CHANGES IN ADULTHOOD

Dementia is characterized by persistent, multiple cognitive deficits in the domains including, but not limited to, memory, language, and visuospatial skills and can result from central nervous system dysfunction. Two forms of dementia exist: degenerative and non-degenerative.

The progression of non-degenerative dementias, like head trauma and brain infections, can be slowed or halted but degenerative forms of dementia, like Parkinson's disease, Alzheimer's disease, and Huntington's are irreversible and incurable.

ALZHEIMER'S DISEASE

Fig. A time lapse showing the advancement of plaques and tangles in Alzheimer's disease tissue.

Alzheimer's disease (AD) was discovered in 1907 by Dr. Alois Alzheimer, a German neuropathologist and psychiatrist. Physiological abnormalities associated with AD include neurofibrillary plaques and tangles. Neuritic plaques, that target the outer regions of the cortex, consist of withering neuronal material from a protein, amyloid-beta.

Neurofibrillary tangles, paired helical filaments containing over-phosphorylated tau protein, are located within the nerve cell. Early symptoms of AD include difficulty remembering names and events, while later symptoms include impaired judgement, disorientation, confusion, behaviour changes, and difficulty speaking, swallowing, and walking. After initial diagnosis, a person with AD can live, on average, an additional 3 to 10 years with the disease. In 2013, it was estimated that 5.2 million Americans of all ages had AD. Environmental factors such as head trauma, high cholesterol, and type 2 diabetes can increase the likelihood of AD.

HUNTINGTON'S DISEASE

Huntington's disease (HD) named after George Huntington is a disorder that is caused by an inherited defect in a single gene on chromosome 4, resulting in a progressive loss of mental faculties and physical control. HD affects muscle coordination (involuntary writhing) and leads to cognitive decline and psychiatric issues. Symptoms usually appear between the ages of 30-50 but can occur at any age, including adolescence. There is currently no cure for HD and treatments focus on managing symptoms and quality of life. Current estimates claim that 1 in 10,000 Americans have HD, however, 1 in 250,000 are at-risk of inheriting it from a parent. Most individuals with HD live 10 to 20 years after a diagnosis.

PARKINSON'S DISEASE

Parkinson's disease (PD) was first described by James Parkinson in 1817. It typically affects people over the age of 50. PD is related to damaged nerve cells that producedopamine. Common symptoms experienced by people with PD include trembling of the hands, arms, legs, jaw, or head;rigidity (stiffness in limbs and the midsection);bradykinesia;and postural instability, leading to impaired balance and/or coordination. PD cannot be cured, but diagnosis and treatment can help relieve symptoms. Treatment options include medications like Carbidopa/Levodopa (L-dopa), that reduce the severity of motor symptoms in patients. Alternative treatment options include non-pharmacological therapy. Surgery (pallidotomy, thalamotomy) is often viewed as the last viable option.

MENTAL HEALTH IN ADULTHOOD AND OLD AGE

Older adults represent a significant proportion of the population, and this proportion is expected to increase with time. Mental health concerns of older adults are important at treatment and support levels, as well as policy issues. The prevalence of suicide among older adults is higher than in any other age group.

DEPRESSION

Depression is one of the most common disorders that presents in old age and is comorbid with other physical and psychiatric conditions, perhaps due to the stress induced by these conditions. In older adults, depression presents as impairments already associated with age such as memory and psychomotor speed. Research indicates that higher levels of exercise can decrease the likelihood of depression in older adults even after taking into consideration factors such as chronic conditions, body mass index, and social relationships. In addition to exercise, behavioural rehabilitation and prescribed antidepressants, which is well tolerated in older adults, can be used to treat depression.

ANXIETY

Anxiety is a relatively uncommon diagnosis in older adults and it difficult to determine its prevalence. Anxiety disorders in late life are more likely to be under-diagnosed because of medical comorbidity, cognitive decline, and changes in life circumstances that younger adults do not face. However, in the Epidemiological Catchment Area Project, researchers found that 6-month prevalence rates for anxiety disorders were lowest for the 65 years of age and older cohort. A recent study found that the prevalence of general anxiety disorder (GAD) in adults aged 55 or older in the United States was 33.7per cent with an onset before the age of 50.

ATTENTION DEFICIT HYPERACTIVITY DISORDER (ADHD)

ADHD is generally believed to be a children's disorder and is not commonly studied in adults. However, ADHD in adults results in lower household incomes, less educational achievement as well as a higher risk of marital issues and substance abuse. Activities such as driving can be affected;adults who suffer from inattentiveness due to ADHD experience increased rates of car accidents. Adults with ADHD tend to be more creative, vibrant, aware of multiple activities, and are able to multitask when interested in a certain topic.

OTHER MENTAL DISORDERS

The impact of mental disorders such as schizophrenia, other forms of psychosis, and bipolar disorder in adulthood is largely mediated by the environmental context. Those in hospitals and nursing homes differ in risk for a multitude of disorders in comparison to community-dwelling older adults. Differences in how these environments treat mental illness and provide social support could help explain disparities and lead to better knowledge of how these disorders are manifested in adulthood.

OPTIMIZING HEALTH AND MENTAL WELL-BEING IN ADULTHOOD

Exercising four to six times a week for thirty to sixty minutes has physical and cognitive effects such as lowering blood sugar and increasing neural plasticity. Physical activity reduces loss of function by 10per cent each decade after the age of 60 and active individuals drop their rate of decline in half. Cardio activities like walking promote endurance while strength, flexibility, and balance can all be improved through Tai Chi, yoga, and water aerobics. Diets containing foods with calcium, fibre, and potassium are especially important for good health while eliminating foods with high sodium or fat content. A well-balanced diet can increase resistance to disease and improve management of chronic health problems thus making nutrition an important factor for health and well-being in adulthood.

Fig. An older adult performing a recommended exercise for aging individuals.

Mental stimulation and optimism are vital to health and well-being in late adulthood. Adults who participate in intellectually stimulating activities every day are more likely to maintain their cognitive faculties and are less likely to show a decline in memory abilities. Mental exercise activities such as crossword puzzles, spatial reasoning tasks, and other mentally stimulating activities can help adults increase their brain fitness. Additionally, researchers have found that optimism, community engagement, physical activity and emotional support can help older adults maintain their resiliency as they continue through their life span.

MANAGING STRESS AND DEVELOPING COPING STRATEGIES

Fig. Older adults doing Tai Chi.

Cognitive, physical, and social losses, as well as gains, are to be expected throughout the lifespan. Older adults typically self-report having a higher sense of well-being than their younger counterparts because of their emotional self-regulation. Researchers use Selective Optimization with Compensation Theory to explain how adults compensate for changes to their mental and physical abilities, as well as their social realities. Older adults can use both internal and external resources to help cope with these changes.

The loss of loved ones and ensuing grief and bereavement are inevitable parts of life. Positive coping strategies are used when faced with emotional crises, as well as when coping with everyday mental and physical losses. Adult development comes with both gains and losses, and it is important to be aware and plan ahead for these changes in order to age successfully.

PERSONALITY IN ADULTHOOD

Personality change and stability occur in adulthood. For example, self-confidence, warmth, self-control, and emotional stability increase with age, whereas neuroticism and openness to experience tend to decline with age.

PERSONALITY CHANGE IN ADULTHOOD

Two types of statistics are used to classify personality change over the life span. Rank-order change refers to a change in an individual's personality trait relative to other individuals. Mean-level change refers to absolute change in the individual's level of a certain trait over time.

CONTROVERSY

The plaster hypothesis refers to personality traits tending to stabilize by age 30. Stability in personality throughout adulthood has been observed in longitudinal and sequential research. However, personality also changes. Research on the Big 5 Personality traits include a decrease in openness and extraversion in adulthood;an increase of agreeableness with age;peak conscientiousness in middle age;and a decrease of neuroticism late in life. The concepts of both adjustment and growth as developmental processes help reconcile the large body of evidence for personality stability and the growing body of evidence for personality change. There are normative adjustments in personality with increasing age, but personality is largely stable throughout adulthood.

INTELLIGENCE IN ADULTHOOD

According to the lifespan approach, intelligence is a multidimensional and multidirectional construct characterized by plasticity and interindividual variability. Intellectual development throughout the lifespan is characterized by decline as well as stability and improvement. Mechanics of intelligence, the basic architecture of information processing, decreases with age. Pragmatic intelligence, knowledge acquired through culture and experience, remains relatively stable with age. The psychometric approach assesses intelligence based on scores on standardized tests such as the Wechsler Adult Intelligence Scale and Stanford Binet for children. The Cognitive Structural approach measures intelligence by assessing the ways people conceptualize and solve problems, rather than by test scores.

DEVELOPMENTAL TRENDS IN INTELLIGENCE

Primary mental abilities are independent groups of factors that contribute to intelligent behaviour and include word fluency, verbal comprehension, spatial visualization, number facility, associative memory, reasoning, and perceptual speed. Primary mental abilities decline around the age of 60 and may interfere with life functioning. Secondary mental abilities include crystallized intelligence (knowledge acquired through experience) and fluid intelligence (abilities of flexible and abstract thinking). Fluid intelligence declines steadily in adulthood while crystallized intelligence increases and remains fairly stable with age until very late in life.

RELATIONSHIPS

A combination of friendships and family are the support system for many individuals and an integral part of their lives from young adulthood to old age.

FAMILY

Fig. Ties to family become increasingly important in old age.

Family relationships tend to be some of the most enduring bonds created within one's lifetime. As adults age, their children often feel a sense of filial obligation, in which they feel obligated to care for their parents. This is particularly prominent in Asian cultures. Marital satisfaction remains high in older couples, oftentimes increasing shortly after retirement. This can be attributed to increased maturity and reduced conflict within the relationship. However, when health problems arise, the relationship can become strained. Studies of spousal caregivers of individuals with Alzheimer's disease show marital satisfaction is significantly lower than in couples who are not afflicted.Most people will experience the loss of a family member by death within their life time. This life event is usually accompanied by some form of bereavement, or grief. There is no set time frame for a mourning period after a loved one passes away, rather every person experiences bereavement in a different form and manner.

FRIENDS

Friendships, similar to family relationships, are often the support system for many individuals and a fundamental aspect of life from young adulthood to old age. Social friendships are important to emotional fulfillment, behavioural adjustment, and cognitive function. Research has shown that emotional closeness in relationships greatly increases with age even though the number of social relationships and the development of new relationships begin to decline. In young adulthood, friendships are grounded in similar aged peers with similar goals, though these relations might be more transitory. In older adulthood, friendships have been found to be much deeper and longer lasting. While small in number, the quality of relationships is generally thought to be much stronger for older adults.

RETIREMENT

Retirement, or the point in which a person stops employment entirely, is often a time of psychological distress or a time of high quality and enhanced subjective well-being for individuals. Most individuals choose to retire between the ages of 50 to 70, and researchers have examined how this transition affects subjective well-being in old age. One study examined subjective well-being in retirement as a function of marital quality, life course, and gender. Results indicated a positive correlation between well-being for married couples who retire around the same time compared to couples in which one spouse retires while the other continues to work.

RETIREMENT COMMUNITIES

Retirement communities provide for individuals who want to live independently but do not wish to maintain a home. They can maintain their autonomy while living in a community with individuals who are similar in age as well as within the same stage of life.

LONG TERM CARE

Assisted living facilities are housing options for older adults that provide a supportive living arrangement for people who need assistance with personal care, such as bathing or taking medications, but are not so impaired that they need 24-hour care. These facilities provide older adults with a home-like environment and personal control while helping to meet residents' daily routines and special needs.

Fig. Resident in assisted living facility.

Adult day care is designed to provide social support, companionship, health care, and other services for adult family members who may pose safety risks if left at home alone while another family member, typically a care giver, must work or otherwise leave the home. Adults who have cognitive impairments should be carefully introduced to adult day care.

Nursing home facilities provide residents with 24-hour skilled medical or intermediate care. A nursing home is typically seen as a decision of last resort for many family members. While the patient is receiving comprehensive care, the cost of nursing homes can be very high with few insurance companies choosing to cover it.

ERIKSON'S STAGES OF PSYCHOSOCIAL DEVELOPMENT

Erikson's stages of psychosocial development, as articulated by Erik Erikson, in collaboration with Joan Erikson, is a comprehensive psychoanalytic theory that identifies a series of eight stages, in which a healthy developing individual should pass through from infancy to late adulthood. All stages are present at birth but only begin to unfold according to both a natural scheme and ones ecological and cultural upbringing.

In each stage, the person confronts, and hopefully masters, new challenges. Each stage builds upon the successful completion of earlier stages. The challenges of stages not successfully completed may be expected to reappear as problems in the future.

However, mastery of a stage is not required to advance to the next stage. The outcome of one stage is not permanent and can be modified by later experiences. Erikson's stage theory characterizes an individual advancing through the eight life stages as a function of negotiating his or her biological forces and sociocultural forces. Each stage is characterized by a psychosocial crisis of these two conflicting forces. If an individual does indeed successfully reconcile these forces (favoring the first mentioned attribute in the crisis), he or she emerges from the stage with the corresponding virtue. For example, if an infant enters into the toddler stage (autonomy vs. shame and doubt) with more trust than mistrust, he or she carries the virtue of hope into the remaining life stages.

STAGES

Approxime Age	Virtues	Psychosocial crisis	Significant relationship	Existential question	Examples
Infancy 0-2 years	Hope	Basic trust vs. mistrust	Mother	Can I trust the world?	Feeding, abandonment
Early childhood 2–4 years	Will	Autonomy vs. shame and doubt	Parents	Is it okay to be me?	Toilet training, clothing themselves
Preschool age 4–5 years	Purpose	Initiative vs. guilt	Family	Is it okay for me to do, move, and act?	Exploring, using tools or making art
School age 5–12 years	Competene	Industry vs. inferiority	Neighbors, school	Can I make it in the world of people and things?	School, sports
Adolescenc e 13–19 years	Fidelity	Identity vs. role confusion	Peers, role model	Who am I? Who can I be?	Social relationships
Early adulthood 20–39 years	Love	Intimacy vs. isolation	Friends, partners	Can I love?	Romantic relationships
Adulthood 40–64 years	Care	Generativity vs. stagnation	Household, workmates	Can I make my life count?	Work, parenthood
Maturity 65-death	Wisdom	Ego integrity vs. despair	Mankind, my kind	Is it okay to have been me?	Reflection on life

HOPE: TRUST VS. MISTRUST (ORAL-SENSORY, INFANCY, 0–2 YEARS)

Existential Question: Can I Trust the World?

The first stage of Erik Erikson's theory centers around the infant's basic needs being met by the parents and this interaction leading to trust or mistrust.

Trust as defined by Erikson is "an essential truthfulness of others as well as a fundamental sense of one's own trustworthiness." The infant depends on the parents, especially the mother, for sustenance and comfort. The child's relative understanding of world and society come from the parents and their interaction with the child.

A child's first trust is always with the parent or caregiver;whomever that might be;however, even the caregiver is secondary where as the parents are primary in the eyes of the child. If the parents expose the child to warmth, regularity, and dependable affection, the infant's view of the world will be one of trust. Should the parents fail to provide a secure environment and to meet the child's basic needs;a sense of mistrust will result. Development of mistrust can lead to feelings of frustration, suspicion, withdrawal, and a lack of confidence.According to Erik Erikson, the major developmental task in infancy is to learn whether or not other people, especially primary caregivers, regularly satisfy basic needs. If caregivers are consistent sources of food, comfort, and affection, an infant learns trust- that others are dependable and reliable.

If they are neglectful, or perhaps even abusive, the infant instead learns mistrust- that the world is an undependable, unpredictable, and possibly a dangerous place. While negative, having some experience with mistrust allows the infant to gain an understanding of what constitutes dangerous situations later in life, yet being at the stage of infant or toddler;it is a good idea not to put them in situations of mistrust, the child's number one needs are to feel safe, comforted, and well cared for..

WILL: AUTONOMY VS. SHAME AND DOUBT (MUSCULAR-ANAL, EARLY CHILDHOOD, 2–4 YEARS)

Existential Question: Is It Okay to Be Me?

As the child gains control over eliminative functions and motor abilities, they begin to explore their surroundings. The parents still provide a strong base of a security from which the child can venture out to assert their will. The parents' patience and encouragement helps foster autonomy in the child. Children at this age like to explore the world around them and they are constantly learning about their environment. Caution must be taken at this age while children may explore things that are dangerous to their health and safety.

At this age children develop their first interests. For example, a child who enjoys music may like to play with the radio. Children who enjoy the outdoors may be interested in animals and plants. Highly restrictive parents, however, are more likely to instill in the child a sense of doubt, and reluctance to attempt new challenges. As they gain increased muscular coordination and mobility, toddlers become capable of satisfying some of their own needs. They begin to feed themselves, wash and dress themselves, and use the bathroom.

If caregivers encourage self-sufficient behaviour, toddlers develop a sense of autonomy—a sense of being able to handle many problems on their own. But if caregivers demand too much too soon, refuse to let children perform tasks of which they are capable, or ridicule early attempts at self-sufficiency, children may instead develop shame and doubt about their ability to handle problems.

PURPOSE: INITIATIVE VS. GUILT (LOCOMOTOR-GENITAL, PRESCHOOL, 4–5 YEARS)

Existential Question: Is it Okay for Me to Do, Move, and Act?

Initiative adds to autonomy the quality of undertaking, planning and attacking a task for the sake of just being active and on the move. The child is learning to master the world around them, learning basic skills and principles of physics.

Things fall down, not up. Round things roll. They learn how to zip and tie, count and speak with ease. At this stage, the child wants to begin and complete their own actions for a purpose. Guilt is a confusing new emotion. They may feel guilty over things that logically should not cause guilt. They may feel guilt when this initiative does not produce desired results.

The development of courage and independence are what set preschoolers, ages three to six years of age, apart from other age groups. Young children in this category face the challenge of initiative versus guilt. As described in Bee and Boyd (2004), the child during this stage faces the complexities of planning and developing a sense of judgement. During this stage, the child learns to take initiative and prepare for leadership and goal achievement roles. Activities sought out by a child in this stage may include risk-taking behaviours, such as crossing a street alone or riding a bike without a helmet;both these examples involve self-limits.

Within instances requiring initiative, the child may also develop negative behaviours. These behaviours are a result of the child developing a sense of frustration for not being able to achieve a goal as planned and may engage in behaviours that seem aggressive, ruthless, and overly assertive to parents. Aggressive behaviours, such as throwing objects, hitting, or yelling, are examples of observable behaviours during this stage.

Preschoolers are increasingly able to accomplish tasks on their own, and can start new things. With this growing independence comes many choices about activities to be pursued. Sometimes children take on projects they can readily accomplish, but at other times they undertake projects that are beyond their capabilities or that interfere with other people's plans and activities. If parents and preschool teachers encourage and support children's efforts, while also helping them make realistic and appropriate choices, children develop initiative- independence in planning and undertaking activities. But if, instead, adults discourage the pursuit of independent activities or dismiss them as silly and bothersome, children develop guilt about their needs and desires.

COMPETENCE: INDUSTRY VS. INFERIORITY (LATENCY, SCHOOL AGE, 5–12 YEARS)

Existential Question: Can I Make it in the World of People and Things?

The aim to bring a productive situation to completion gradually supersedes the whims and wishes of play. The fundamentals of technology are developed. The failure to master trust, autonomy, and industrious skills may cause the child to doubt his or her future, leading to shame, guilt, and the experience of defeat and inferiority. "Children at this age are becoming more aware of themselves as individuals." They work hard at "being responsible, being good and doing it right."

They are now more reasonable to share and cooperate. Allen and Marotz (2003) also list some perceptual cognitive developmental traits specific for this age group. Children grasp the concepts of space and time in more logical, practical ways. They gain a better understanding of cause and effect, and of calendar time.

At this stage, children are eager to learn and accomplish more complex skills: reading, writing, telling time. They also get to form moral values, recognize cultural and individual differences and are able to manage most of their personal needs and grooming with minimal assistance. At this stage, children might express their independence by talking back and being disobedient and rebellious. Erikson viewed the elementary school years as critical for the development of self-confidence.

Ideally, elementary school provides many opportunities for children to achieve the recognition of teachers, parents and peers by producing things-drawing pictures, solving addition problems, writing sentences, and so on. If children are encouraged to make and do things and are then praised for their accomplishments, they begin to demonstrate industry by being diligent, persevering at tasks until completed, and putting work before pleasure. If children are instead ridiculed or punished for their efforts or if they find they are incapable of meeting their teachers' and parents' expectations, they develop feelings of inferiority about their capabilities.

At this age, children start recognizing their special talents and continue to discover interests as their education improves. They may begin to choose to do more activities to pursue that interest, such as joining a sport if they know they have athletic ability, or joining the band if they are good at music. If not allowed to discover their own talents in their own time, they will develop a sense of lack of motivation, low self-esteem, and lethargy. They may become "couch potatoes" if they are not allowed to develop interests.

FIDELITY: IDENTITY VS. ROLE CONFUSION (ADOLESCENCE, 13–19 YEARS)

Existential Question: Who Am I and What Can I Be?

The adolescent is newly concerned with how they appear to others. Superego identity is the accrued confidence that the outer sameness and continuity prepared in the future are matched by the sameness and continuity of one's meaning for oneself, as evidenced in the promise of a career. The ability to settle on a school or occupational identity is pleasant. In later stages of Adolescence, the child develops a sense of sexual identity. As they make the transition from childhood to adulthood, adolescents ponder the roles they will play in the adult world. Initially, they are apt to experience some role confusion—mixed ideas and feelings about the specific ways in which they will fit into society—and may experiment with a variety of behaviours and activities (*e.g.* tinkering with cars, baby-sitting for neighbours, affiliating with certain political or religious groups). Eventually, Erikson proposed, most adolescents achieve a sense of identity regarding who they are and where their lives are headed.

Erikson is credited with coining the term "Identity Crisis." Each stage that came before and that follows has its own 'crisis', but even more so now, for this marks the transition from childhood to adulthood. This passage is necessary because "Throughout infancy and childhood, a person forms many identifications. But the need for identity in youth is not met by these."

This turning point in human development seems to be the reconciliation between 'the person one has come to be' and 'the person society expects one to become'. This emerging sense of self will be established by 'forging' past experiences with anticipations of the future. In relation to the eight life stages as a whole, the fifth stage corresponds to the crossroads: What is unique about the stage of Identity is that it is a special sort of synthesis of earlier stages and a special sort of anticipation of later ones. Youth has a certain unique quality in a person's life;it is a bridge between childhood and adulthood. Youth is a time of radical change—the great body changes accompanying puberty, the ability of the mind to search one's own intentions and the intentions of others, the suddenly sharpened awareness of the roles society has offered for later life.

Adolescents "are confronted by the need to re-establish [boundaries] for themselves and to do this in the face of an often potentially hostile world." This is often challenging since commitments are being asked for before particular identity roles have formed.

At this point, one is in a state of 'identity confusion', but society normally makes allowances for youth to "find themselves," and this state is called 'the moratorium': The problem of adolescence is one of role confusion—a reluctance to commit which may haunt a person into his mature years. Given the right conditions—and Erikson believes these are essentially having enough space and time, a psychosocial moratorium, when a person can freely experiment and explore—what may emerge is a firm sense of identity, an emotional and deep awareness of who he or she is.

As in other stages, bio-psycho-social forces are at work. No matter how one has been raised, one's personal ideologies are now chosen for oneself. Often, this leads to conflict with adults over religious and political orientations. Another area where teenagers are deciding for themselves is their career choice, and often parents want to have a decisive say in that role. If society is too insistent, the teenager will acquiesce to internal wishes, effectively forcing him or her to 'foreclose' on experimentation and, therefore, true self-discovery. Once someone settles on a worldview and vocation, will he or she be able to integrate this aspect of self-definition into a diverse society? According to Erikson, when an adolescent has balanced both perspectives of "What have I got?" and "What am I going to do with it?" he or she has established their identity: Dependent on this stage is the ego quality of fidelity—the ability to sustain loyalties freely pledged in spite of the inevitable contradictions and confusions of value systems. (Italics in original)

Given that the next stage (Intimacy) is often characterized by marriage, many are tempted to cap off the fifth stage at 20 years of age. However, these age ranges are actually quite fluid, especially for the achievement of identity, since it may take many years to become grounded, to identify the object of one's fidelity, to feel that one has "come of age."

In the biographies Young Man Luther and Gandhi's Truth, Erikson determined that their crises ended at ages 25 and 30, respectively: Erikson does note that the time of Identity crisis for persons of genius is frequently prolonged. He further notes that in our industrial society, identity formation tends to be long, because it takes us so long to gain the skills needed for adulthood's tasks in our technological world. So... we do not have an exact time span in which to find ourselves. It doesn't happen automatically at eighteen or at twenty-one. A very approximate rule of thumb for our society would put the end somewhere in one's twenties.

LOVE: INTIMACY VS. ISOLATION (EARLY ADULTHOOD, 20-39 YEARS)

Existential Question: Can I Love?

The Intimacy vs. Isolation conflict is emphasized around the age of 30. At the start of this stage, identity vs. role confusion is coming to an end, though it still lingers at the foundation of the stage (Erikson, 1950). Young adults are still eager to blend their identities with friends. They want to fit in. Erikson believes we are sometimes isolated due to intimacy.

We are afraid of rejections such as being turned down or our partners breaking up with us. We are familiar with pain and to some of us rejection is so painful that our egos cannot bear it. Erikson also argues that "Intimacy has a counterpart: Distantiation: the readiness to isolate and if necessary, to destroy those forces and people whose essence seems dangerous to our own, and whose territory seems to encroach on the extent of one's intimate relations" (1950).

Once people have established their identities, they are ready to make long-term commitments to others. They become capable of forming intimate, reciprocal relationships (*e.g.* through close friendships or marriage) and willingly make the sacrifices and compromises that such relationships require. If people cannot form these intimate relationships – perhaps because of their own needs – a sense of isolation may result;arousing feelings of darkness and angst.

CARE: GENERATIVITY VS. STAGNATION (ADULTHOOD, 40–64 YEARS)

Existential Question: Can I Make My Life Count?

Generativity is the concern of guiding the next generation. Socially-valued work and disciplines are expressions of generativity. The adult stage of generativity has broad application to family, relationships, work, and society. "Generativity, then is primarily the concern in establishing and guiding the next generation... the concept is meant to include... productivity and creativity."

During middle age the primary developmental task is one of contributing to society and helping to guide future generations. When a person makes a contribution during this period, perhaps by raising a family or working towards the betterment of society, a sense of generativity- a sense of productivity and accomplishment- results. In contrast, a person who is self-centered and unable or unwilling to help society move forward develops a feeling of stagnation- a dissatisfaction with the relative lack of productivity.

Central tasks of middle adulthood

- Express love through more than sexual contacts.
- Maintain healthy life patterns.
- Develop a sense of unity with mate.
- Help growing and grown children to be responsible adults.
- Relinquish central role in lives of grown children.
- Accept children's mates and friends.
- Create a comfortable home.
- Be proud of accomplishments of self and mate/spouse.
- Reverse roles with aging parents.
- Achieve mature, civic and social responsibility.

- Adjust to physical changes of middle age.
- Use leisure time creatively.

WISDOM: EGO INTEGRITY VS. DESPAIR (MATURITY, 65 – DEATH)

Existential Question: Is it Okay to Have Been Me?

As we grow older and become senior citizens we tend to slow down our productivity and explore life as a retired person. It is during this time that we contemplate our accomplishments and are able to develop integrity if we see ourselves as leading a successful life. If we see our life as unproductive, or feel that we did not accomplish our life goals, we become dissatisfied with life and develop despair, often leading to depression and hopelessness.

The final developmental task is retrospection: people look back on their lives and accomplishments. They develop feelings of contentment and integrity if they believe that they have led a happy, productive life. They may instead develop a sense of despair if they look back on a life of disappointments and unachieved goals. This stage can occur out of the sequence when an individual feels they are near the end of their life (such as when receiving a terminal disease diagnosis).

NINTH STAGE

Psychosocial Crises: All First Eight Stages in Reverse Quotient Order

Joan M. Erikson, who married and collaborated with Erik Erikson, added a ninth stage in The Life Cycle Completed: Extended Version. Living in the ninth stage, she wrote, "old age in one's eighties and nineties brings with it new demands, re-evaluations, and daily difficulties." Addressing these new challenges requires "designating a new ninth stage." Erikson was ninety-three years old when she wrote about the ninth stage.

Joan Erikson showed that all the eight stages "are relevant and recurring in the ninth stage." In the ninth stage, the psychosocial crises of the eight stages are faced again, but with the quotient order reversed. For example, in the first stage (infancy), the psychosocial crisis was "Trust vs. Mistrust" with Trust being the "syntonic quotient" and Mistrust being the "diatonic." Joan Erikson applies the earlier psychosocial crises to the ninth stage as follows.

"Basic Mistrust vs. Trust: Hope"

In the ninth stage, "elders are forced to mistrust their own capabilities" because one's "body inevitably weakens." Yet, Joan Erikson asserts that "while there is light, there is hope" for a "bright light and revelation."

"Shame and Doubt vs Autonomy: Will"

Ninth stage elders face the "shame of lost control" and doubt "their autonomy over their own bodies." So it is that "shame and doubt challenge cherished autonomy."

"Inferiority vs. Industry: Competence"

Industry as a "driving force" that elders once had is gone in the ninth stage. Being incompetent "because of aging is belittling" and makes elders "like unhappy small children of great age."

"Identity Confusion vs. Identity: Fidelity"

Elders experience confusion about their "existential identity" in the ninth stage and "a real uncertainty about status and role."

"Isolation vs. Intimacy: Love"

In the ninth stage, the "years of intimacy and love" are often replaced by "isolation and deprivation." Relationships become "overshadowed by new incapacities and dependencies."

"Stagnation vs, Generativity: Care"

The generativity in the seventh stage of "work and family relationships," if it goes satisfactorily, is "a wonderful time to be alive." In one's eighties and nineties, there is less energy for generativity or caretaking. Thus, "a sense of stagnation may well take over."

"Despair and Disgust vs. Integrity: Wisdom"

Integrity imposes "a serious demand on the senses of elders." Wisdom requires capacities that ninth stage elders "do not usually have." The eighth stage includes retrospection that can evoke a "degree of disgust and despair." In the ninth stage, introspection is replaced by the attention demanded to one's "loss of capacities and disintegration." Living in the ninth stage, Joan Erikson expressed confidence that the psychosocial crisis of the ninth stage can be met as in the first stage with the "basic trust" with which "we are blessed."

DEVELOPMENT OF POST-FREUDIAN THEORY

Erikson was a student of Anna Freud, the daughter of Sigmund Freud, whose psychoanalytic theory and psychosexual stages contributed to the basic outline of the eight stages, at least those concerned with childhood. Namely, the first four of Erikson's life stages correspond to Freud's oral, anal, phallic, and latency phases, respectively. Also, the fifth stage of adolescence is said to parallel the genital stage in psychosexual development: Although the first three phases are linked to those of the Freudian theory, it can be seen that they are conceived along very different lines. Emphasis is not so much on sexual modes and their consequences as on the ego qualities which emerge from each stages. There is an attempt also to link the sequence of individual development to the broader context of society.

Erikson saw a dynamic at work throughout life, one that did not stop at adolescence. He also viewed the life stages as a cycle: the end of one generation was the beginning of the next. Seen in its social context, the life stages were linear for an individual but circular for societal development: In Freud's view, development is largely complete by adolescence. In contrast, one of Freud's students, Erik Erikson (1902-1994) believed that development continues throughout life. Erikson took the foundation laid by Freud and extended it through adulthood and into late life.

CRITIQUE

Erikson's theory may be questioned as to whether his stages must be regarded as sequential, and only occurring within the age ranges he suggests. There is debate as to whether people only search for identity during the adolescent years or if one stage needs to happen before other stages can be completed. However, Erikson states that each of these processes occur throughout the lifetime in one form or another, and he emphasizes these "phases" only because it is at these times that the conflicts become most prominent. Most empirical research into Erikson has related to his views on adolescence and attempts to establish identity. His theoretical approach was studied and supported, particularly regarding adolescence, by James E. Marcia. Marcia's work has distinguished different forms of identity, and there is some empirical evidence that those people who form the most coherent self-concept in adolescence are those who are most able to make intimate attachments in early adulthood. This supports Eriksonian theory, in that it suggests that those best equipped to resolve the crisis of early adulthood are those who have most successfully resolved the crisis of adolescence.

2

Neuroscience as a Basis for Adult Development

DEVELOPMENTAL COGNITIVE NEUROSCIENCE

Developmental cognitive neuroscience is an interdisciplinary scientific field devoted to understanding psychological processes and their neurological bases in the developing organism. It examines how the mind changes as children grow up, interrelations between that and how the brain is changing, and environmental and biological influences on the developing mind and brain.

Developmental cognitive neuroscience is at the boundaries of neuroscience (behavioural, systems, and cognitive neuroscience), psychology (developmental, cognitive, and biobehavioural/ physiological psychology), developmental science (which includes sociology, anthropology, and biology in addition to psychology and neuroscience), cognitive science(which includes computer science, philosophy, dynamical systems, and linguistics in addition to psychology), and even includes socio-emotional development and developmental aspects of social neuroscience and affective neuroscience.

The scientific interface between cognitive neuroscience and human development has evoked considerable interest in recent years, as technological advances make it possible to map in detail the changes in brain structure that take place during development. Developmental cognitive neuroscience overlaps somewhat with fields such as developmental psychology, developmental neuropsychology, developmental psychopathology, and developmental neuroscience, but is distinct from each of them as well.

Developmental cognitive neuroscience is concerned with the brain bases of the phenomena that developmental psychologists study. Developmental neuropsychology and developmental psychopathology are both devoted primarily to studying patients, whereas developmental cognitive neuroscience is concerned with studying both typical and atypical development. Developmental neuroscience is devoted entirely to the study of developmental processes in the brain, and primarily during the prenatal period. Developmental cognitive neuroscience, on the other hand, is concerned with interrelations between psychological and biological development. Developmental cognitive neuroscientists study brain development and cognitive, social, and emotional development from the prenatal period through adulthood.

More recently, developmental cognitive neuroscience is interested in the role of genes in development and cognition. Thus, developmental cognitive neuroscience may shed light on nature versus nurture debates as well as constructivism and neuroconstructivism theories. Developmental cognitive neuroscience research provides data that alternately blends together, clarifies, challenges, and causes revisions in developmental, cognitive, and neuroscientific theories.

ORIGINS OF THE DISCIPLINE

The origin of the discipline of developmental cognitive neuroscience can be traced back to conference held in Philadelphia in 1989 co-funded by NICHD and NIMH, organized by Adele Diamond, that started the process of developmental psychologists, cognitive scientists, and neuroscientists talking with one another. To bridge the communication gaps, researchers were invited from different fields who were either using the same experimental paradigms to study the same behaviours or were investigating related scientific questions in complementary ways—though they were unaware of one another's work.

They used different words to talk about their work and had different ways of thinking about it, but the concrete, observable behaviours, and the precise experimental conditions under which those behaviours occurred, served to make translation possible. Participants were a small Who's Who of leaders in developmental science, behavioural neuroscience, and cognitive science. Several new cross-disciplinary collaborations resulted from it, and it is a testament to the value of what came out of the meeting that Oxford University Press tried to acquire the rights to re-issue the book of the meeting's proceedings 10 years later—The Development and Neural Basis of Higher Cognitive Functions. (The original printing sold out faster than any other New York Academy of Science Annals issue has before or since.)

Developmental psychologists and neuroscientists used to know little of one another's work. There was so little communication between those fields that for 50 years scientists in both fields were using essentially the same behavioural assay but they did not know it. (Developmental psychologists called the measure the A-not-B task but neuroscientists called it the delayed response task.) In the early 1980s, Diamond not only showed these two tasks showed the identical developmental progression and rely on the same region of prefrontal cortex but through a systematic series of studies in human infants, and infant and adult monkeys with and without lesions to different brain regions.That work was absolutely pivotal in launching the field of developmental cognitive neuroscience because it established the very first strong link between early cognitive development and the functions of a specific brain region. That gave encouragement to others that rigorous experimental work addressing brain-behaviour relations was possiblein infants. It also fundamentally altered the scientific understanding of prefrontal cortex early in development;clearly it was not silent as accepted wisdom had held. Mark Johnson's 1997 text Developmental Cognitive Neuroscience was seminal in coining the field's name.

TOOLS AND TECHNIQUES EMPLOYED

Absolutely critical to being able to understand brain function in children have been neuroimaging techniques, first EEG & ERPs, then fMRI, and more recently NIRS, MEG, & TMS that look at function and MRI, DTI, & MRS that look at structure, connectivity, and metabolism. Before functional neuroimaging techniques scientists were constrained to trying to understand function from dysfunction (*i.e.*, trying to understand how the brain works from seeing what deficits occur when the brain is damaged or impaired). It is difficult to understate how important technological advances have been to the emerging field of developmental cognitive neuroscience.

EDUCATIONAL NEUROSCIENCE

Educational neuroscience (or neuroeducation, a component of Mind Brain and Education) is an emerging scientific field that brings together researchers in cognitive neuroscience, developmental cognitive neuroscience, educational psychology, educational technology, education theory and other related disciplines to explore the interactions between biological processes and education. Researchers in educational neuroscience investigate the neural mechanisms of reading, numerical cognition, attentionand their attendant difficulties including dyslexia, dyscalculia and ADHD as they relate to education.

Researchers in this area may link basic findings in cognitive neuroscience with educational technology to help in curriculum implementation for mathematics education and reading education. The aim of educational neuroscience is to generate basic and applied research that will provide a new transdisciplinary account of learning and teaching, which is capable of informing education. A major goal of educational neuroscience is to bridge the gap between the two fields through a direct dialogue between researchers and educators, avoiding the "middlemen of the brain-based learning industry". These middlemen have a vested commercial interest in the selling of "neuromyths" and their supposed remedies.

The potential of educational neuroscience has received varying degrees of support from both cognitive neuroscientists and educators. Davis argues that medical models of cognition, "...have only a very limited role in the broader field of education and learning mainly because learning-related intentional states are not internal to individuals in a way which can be examined by brain activity." Pettito and Dunbar on the other hand, suggest that educational neuroscience "provides the most relevant level of analysis for resolving today's core problems in education."

Howard-Jones and Pickering surveyed the opinions of teachers and educators on the topic, and found that they were generally enthusiastic about the use of neuroscientific findings in the field of education, and that they felt these findings would be more likely to influence their teaching methodology than curriculum content. Some researchers take an intermediate view and feel that a direct link from neuroscience to education is a "bridge too far", but that a bridging discipline, such as cognitive psychology or educational psychology can provide a neuroscientific basis for educational practice. The prevailing opinion, however, appears to be that the link between education and neuroscience has yet to realise its full potential, and whether through a third research discipline, or through the development of new neuroscience research paradigms and projects, the time is right to apply neuroscientific research findings to education in a practically meaningful way.

Several academic institutions around the world are beginning to devote resources and energy to the establishment of research centres focused on educational neuroscience research. For example, the Centre for Educational Neuroscience in London UK is an inter-institutional project between University College, London, Birkbeck and the Institute of Education. The centre brings together researchers with expertise in the fields of emotional, conceptual, attentional, language and mathematical development, as well as specialists in education and learning research with the aim of building a new scientific discipline (Educational Neuroscience) in order to ultimately promote better learning.

THE NEED FOR A NEW DISCIPLINE

The emergence of educational neuroscience has been born out of the need for a new discipline that makes scientific research practically applicable in an educational context. Addressing the broader field of "mind, brain and education", Kurt Fischer states, "The traditional model will not work. It is not enough for researchers to collect data in schools and make those data and the resulting research papers available to educators", as this method excludes teachers and learners from contributing to the formation of appropriate research methods and questions.

Learning in cognitive psychology and neuroscience has focused on how individual humans and other species have evolved to extract useful information from the natural and social worlds around them. By contrast, education, and especially modern formal education, focuses on descriptions and explanations of the world that learners cannot be expected to acquire by themselves. In this way, learning in the scientific sense, and learning in the educational sense can be seen as complementary concepts.

This creates a new challenge for cognitive neuroscience to adapt to the real world practical requirements of educational learning. Conversely, neuroscience creates a new challenge for education, because it provides new characterizations of the current state of the learner – including brain state, genetic state, and hormonal state - that could be relevant to learning and teaching. By providing new measures of the effects of learning and teaching, including brain structure and activity, it is possible to discriminate different types of learning method and attainment. For example, neuroscience research can already distinguish learning by rote from learning through conceptual understanding in mathematics.

The United States National Academy of Sciences published an important report, stressing that, "Neuroscience has advanced to the point where it is time to think critically about the form in which research information is made available to educators so that it is interpreted appropriately for practice—identifying which research findings are ready for implementation and which are not."

In their book The Learning Brain, researchers from London's "Centre for Educational Neuroscience", Blakemore and Frith outline the developmental neurophysiology of the human brain that has given rise to many theories regarding educational neuroscience. One of the fundamental pillars supporting the link between education and neuroscience is the ability of the brain to learn. Neuroscience is developing and increasing our understanding of early brain development, and how these brain changes might relate to learning processes.

EARLY BRAIN DEVELOPMENT

Almost all of the neurons in the brain are generated before birth, during the first three months of pregnancy, and the newborn child's brain has a similar number of neurons to that of an adult. Many more neurons form than are needed, and only those that form active connections with other neurons survive. In the first year after birth the infant brain undergoes an intense phase of development, during which excessive numbers of connections between neurons are formed, and many of these excess connections must be cut back through the process of synaptic pruning that follows.

This pruning process is just as important a stage of development as the early rapid growth of connections between brain cells. The process during which large numbers of connections between neurons are formed is called synaptogenesis. For vision and hearing (visual and auditory cortex), there is extensive early synaptogenesis. The density of connections peaks at around 150per cent of adult levels between four and 12 months, and the connections are then extensively pruned. Synaptic density returns to adult levels between two and four years in the visual cortex.

For other areas such as prefrontal cortex (thought to underpin planning and reasoning), density increases more slowly and peaks after the first year. Reduction to adult levels of density takes at least another 10–20 years;hence there is significant brain development in the frontal areas even in adolescence. Brain metabolism (glucose uptake, which is an approximate index of synaptic functioning) is also above adult levels in the early years. Glucose uptake peaks at about 150per cent of adult levels somewhere around four to five years.

By the age of around ten years, brain metabolism has reduced to adult levels for most cortical regions. Brain development consists of bursts of synaptogenesis, peaks of density, and then synapse rearrangement and stabilisation. This occurs at different times and different rates for different brain regions, which implies that there may be different sensitive periods for the development of different types of knowledge. Neuroscience research into early brain development has informed government education policy for children under three years old in many countries including the USA and the United Kingdom. These policies have focused on enriching the environment of children during nursery and preschool years, exposing them to stimuli and experiences thought to maximise the learning potential of the young brain.

CAN NEUROSCIENCE INFORM EDUCATION?

Although an increasing number of researchers are seeking to establish educational neuroscience as a productive field of research, debate still continues with regards to the potential for practical collaboration between the fields of neuroscience and education, and whether neuroscientific research really has anything to offer educators.

Daniel Willingham states that "whether neuroscience can be informative to educational theory and practice is not debatable-it has been." He draws attention to the fact that behavioural research alone was not decisive in determining whether developmental dyslexia was a disorder of primarily visual or phonological origin. Neuroimaging research was able to reveal reduced activation for children with dyslexia in brain regions known to support phonological processing, thus supporting behavioural evidence for the phonological theory of dyslexia.

While John Bruer suggests that the link between neuroscience and education is essentially impossible without a third field of research to link the two, other researchers feel that this view is too pessimistic. While acknowledging that more bridges must be built between basic neuroscience and education, and that so called neuromyths must be deconstructed, Usha Goswami suggests that cognitive developmental neuroscience has already made several discoveries of use to education, and has also led to the discovery of 'neural markers' that can be used to assess development. In other words, milestones of neural activity or structure are being established, against which an individual can be compared in order to assess their development. For example, event-related potential (ERP) research has uncovered several neural signatures of language processing, including markers of semantic processing (*e.g.* N400), phonetic processing and syntactic processing (*e.g.* P600). Goswami points out that these parameters can now be investigated longitudinally in children, and that certain patterns of change may indicate certain developmental disorders.

Furthermore, the response of these neural markers to focused educational interventions may be used as a measure of the intervention's effectiveness. Researchers such as Goswami assert that cognitive neuroscience has the potential to offer various exciting possibilities to education. For special education, these include the early diagnosis of special educational needs;the monitoring and comparison of the effects of different kinds of educational input on learning;and an increased understanding of individual differences in learning and the best ways to suit input to learner.

A potential application of neuroimaging highlighted by Goswami is in differentiating between delayed development and atypical development in learning disorders. For instance, is a given child with dyslexia developing reading functions in a totally different way from typical readers, or is he/she developing along the same trajectory, but just taking longer to do so? Indeed, evidence already exists to suggest that in children with specific language impairments and dyslexia the development of the language system is delayed rather than fundamentally different in nature. In disorders such as autism however, brain development may be qualitatively different, showing a lack of development in brain regions associated with a "theory of mind".

Goswami also suggests that neuroimaging could be used to assess the impact of particular training programmes, such as the Dore, an exercise based programme based on the cerebellar deficit hypothesis that aims to improve reading through a series of balance exercises. Some brain imaging research is beginning to show that for children with dyslexia who receive targeted educational interventions, their brain activation patterns begin to look more like those of people without reading disorders, and in addition, that other brain regions are acting as compensatory mechanisms. Such findings may help educators understand that, even if dyslexic children show behavioural improvement, the neural and cognitive mechanisms by which they process written information may still be different, and this may have practical implications for the ongoing instruction of these children.

Neuroscience research has evidenced its ability to reveal 'neural markers' of learning disorders, most notably in the case of dyslexia. EEG studies have revealed that human infants at risk of dyslexia (*i.e.* with immediate family members who suffer from dyslexia) show atypical neural responses to changes in speech sounds, even before they are able to understand the semantic content of language. Not only does such research allow for the early identification of potential learning disorders, but it further supports the phonological hypothesis of dyslexia in a manner unavailable to behavioural research. Many researchers advocate a cautious optimism with regards to the marriage between education and neuroscience, and believe that to bridge the gap between the two, the development of new experimental paradigms is necessary and that these new paradigms should be designed to capture the relationships between neuroscience and education across different levels of analysis (neuronal, cognitive, behavioural).

NEUROSCIENCE AND EDUCATION: SAMPLE CASES

LANGUAGE AND LITERACY

Human language is a unique faculty of the mind and the ability to understand and produce oral and written language is fundamental to academic achievement and attainments. Children who experience difficulties with oral language raise significant challenges for educational policy and practice;National Strategies, Every Child a Talker, 2008). The difficulties are likely to persist during the primary school years where, in addition to core deficits with oral language, children experience problems with literacy, numeracy and behaviour and peer relations. Early identification and intervention to address these difficulties, as well as identification of the ways in which learning environments can support atypical language development are essential. Untreated speech and language needs result in significant costs both to the individual and to the national economy (ICAN, 2006).

Over the last decade, there has been a significant increase in neuroscience research examining young children's processing of language at the phonetic, word, and sentence levels. There are clear indications that neural substrates for all levels of language can be identified at early points in development. At the same time, intervention studies have demonstrated the ways in which the brain retains its plasticity for language processing. Intense remediation with an auditory language processing programme has been accompanied by functional changes in left temporo-parietal cortex and inferior frontal gyrus. However, the extent to which these results generalize to spoken and written language is debated.

The relationships between meeting the educational needs of children with language difficulties and the findings of neuroscience studies are not yet established. One concrete avenue for progress is to use neuroscientific methods to address questions that are significant to practice in learning environments. For example, the extent to which language skills are attributable to a single common trait, and the consistency of such a trait over development, are matters of debate. However, direct assessments of brain activity can inform these debates. A detailed understanding of the sub-components of the language system, and the ways these change over time may inevitably yield implications for educational practice.

MATHEMATICS

Mathematical skills are important not only for the national economy but also for an individual's life chances: low numeracy increases the probability of arrest, depression, physical illnesses, unemployment. One of the main causes of low numeracy is a congenital condition called dyscalculia. As the Foresight report on Mental Capital and Wellbeing puts it, "Developmental dyscalculia – because of its low profile but high impacts, its priority should be raised. Dyscalculia relates to numeracy and affects between 4-7per cent of children.

It has a much lower profile than dyslexia but can also have substantial impacts: it can reduce lifetime earnings by £114,000 and reduce the probability of achieving five or moreGCSEs (A*-C) by 7–20 percentage points. Home and school interventions have again been identified by the Project. Also, technological interventions are extremely promising, offering individualised instruction and help, although these need more development." Understanding typical and atypical mathematical development is a crucial underpinning for the design of both the mainstream mathematics curriculum and for helping those who fail to keep up. Over the past ten years, a brain system for simple number processing has been identified and a handful of studies of children's brains that throw a little light on its development.

An increasing convergence of evidence suggests that dyscalculia may be due to a deficit in an inherited core system for representing the number of objects in a set, and how operations on sets affect number and in the neural systems that support these abilities. This core deficit affects the learner's ability to enumerate sets and to order sets by magnitude, which in turn make it very difficult to understand arithmetic, and very hard to provide a meaningful structure for arithmetical facts. Twin and family studies suggest that dyscalculia is highly heritable, and genetic anomalies, such as Turner's Syndrome, indicate an important role for genes in thc X chromosomc.

This suggestion that dyscalculia is caused by a deficits in a core deficit in number sense is analogous to the theory that dyslexia is due to a core deficit in phonological processing. Despite these similarities in terms of the scientific progress, public awareness of dyscalculia is much lower than it is for dyslexia. The UK's Chief Scientific Advisor,John Beddington, notes that, "developmental dyscalculia is currently the poor relation of dyslexia, with a much lower public profile. But the consequences of dyscalculia are at least as severe as those for dyslexia."

The application of neuroscience to understanding mathematical processing has already resulted in understanding beyond the early cognitive theories. Cognitive neuroscience research has revealed the existence of an innate 'number sense' system, present in animals and infants as well as adults, that is responsible for basic knowledge about numbers and their relations. This system is located in the parietal lobe of the brain in each hemisphere.

This parietal system is active in children and adults during basic numerical tasks, but over the course of development it appears to become more specialised. Furthermore, children with mathematical learning disabilities (dyscalculia) show weaker activation in this region than typically developing children during basic number tasks. These results show how neuroimaging can provide important information about the links between basic cognitive functions and higher level learning, such as those between comparing two numbers and learning arithmetic.

In addition to this basic number sense, numerical information can be stored verbally in the language system, a system that neuroscience research is beginning to reveal as qualitatively different at the brain level to the number sense system. This system also stores information about other well learned verbal sequences, such as days of the week, months of the year and even poetry, and for numerical processing it supports counting and the learning of multiplication tables. While many arithmetic problems are so over learned that they are stored as verbal facts, other more complex problems require some form of visuo-spatial mental imagery. Showing that these subsets of arithmetic skills are supported by different brain mechanisms offers the opportunity for a deeper understanding of the learning processes required to acquire arithmetic proficiency.

Neuroimaging studies of mathematical learning disabilities are still rare but dyscalculia is an area of increasing interest for neuroscience researchers. Since different neural mechanisms contribute to different elements of mathematical performance, it may be that children with dyscalculia show variable patterns of abnormality at the brain level.

For example, many children with dyscalculia also have dyslexia, and those that do may show different activation of the verbal networks that support maths, while those who have dyscalculia only, may show impairments of the parietal number sense system. Indeed, the few studies carried out on children with dyscalculia only point to a brain level impairment of the number sense system.

Such evidence is beginning to contribute to a theoretical debate between researchers who believe that dyscalculia is caused by a brain level deficit of the number sense and those who believe that the disorder stems from a problem in using numerical symbols to access the number sense information. With the continued development of theoretical models of dyscalculia that generate explicit testable hypotheses, progress should be rapid in developing research which investigates the link between mathematical learning disorders and their neural correlates.

SOCIAL AND EMOTIONAL COGNITION

In the last 10 years, there has been an explosion of interest in the role of emotional abilities and characteristics in contributing to success in all aspects of life. The concept ofEmotional Intelligence (EI) has gained wide recognition and is featured in the Foresight report on Mental Capital and Wellbeing. Some have made influential claims that EI is more important than conventional cognitive intelligence, and that it can more easily be enhanced. Systematic research has yet to provide much support for these claims, although EI has been found to be associated with academic success and there is some evidence that it may be of particular importance for groups at-risk of academic failure and social exclusion. In spite of the weak evidence base, there has been a focus on promoting the social and emotional competence, mental health and psychological wellbeing of children and young people, particularly in schools as the result of the investment in universal services, prevention and early intervention.

The neural basis of emotional recognition in typically developing children has been investigated, although there is little neuroimaging work on atypically developing children who process emotions differently. Males are commonly over-represented in these atypically developing populations and a female advantage is commonly reported both on EI measures and on most areas of emotion processing. In processing facial expressions the female advantage appears best explained by an integrated account considering both brain maturation and social interaction.

Prefrontal brain damage in children affects social behaviour causing insensitivity to social acceptance, approval or rejection. These brain areas process social emotions such as embarrassment, compassion and envy. Moreover, such damage impairs cognitive as well as social decision making in real world contexts supporting the Vygotskian view that social and cultural factors are important in cognitive learning and decision making. This view emphasizes the importance of bringing together neuroscientific and social constructionist perspectives, in this case in examining the influence of emotion on transferable learning.

However, there are currently many gaps in the attempt to bring together developmental science and neuroscience to produce a more complete understanding of the development of awareness and empathy. Educational research relies on pupil's accurate self-report of emotion, which may not be possible for some pupils, *e.g.*, those with alexithymia—a difficulty in identifying and describing feelings, which is found in 10per cent of typical adults. Emotional awareness can be measured using neuroimaging methodsthat show that differing levels of emotional awareness are associated with differential activity in amygdala, anterior insular cortex, and the medial prefrontal cortex. Studies of brain development in childhood and adolescence show that these areas undergo large-scale structural changes. Hence, the degree to which school-age children and young adults are aware of their emotions may vary across this time period, which may have an important impact on classroom behaviour and the extent to which certain teaching styles and curriculum approaches might be effective.

Neuroimaging work is also beginning to help in the understanding of social conduct disorders in children. For example, callous-unemotional traits in children are a particularly difficult problem for teachers to deal with, and represent a particularly serious form of conduct disturbance. Jones et al. (2009) showed that children with callous-unemotional traits revealed less brain activation in the right amygdala in response to fearful faces, suggesting that the neural correlates of that type of emotional disturbance are present early in development.

Researchers from the Centre for Educational Neuroscience in London have been instrumental in developing a research body that investigates how social cognition develops in the brain. In particular, Sarah-Jayne Blakemore, co-author of "The Learning Brain", has published influential research on brain development related to social cognition during adolescence. Her research, suggests that activity in brain regions associated with emotional processing undergo significant functional changes during adolescence.

ATTENTION AND EXECUTIVE CONTROL

Attention refers to the brain mechanisms that allow us to focus on particular aspects of the sensory environment to the relative exclusion of others. Attention modulates sensory processing in "top-down" fashion. Maintaining selective attention towards a particular item or person for a prolonged period is clearly a critical underpinning skill for the classroom. Attention is the key cognitive skill impaired in ADHD resulting in difficulty in completing tasks or attending to details. Aspects of attention may also be atypical in children showing anti-social behaviour and conduct disorders. From the perspective of basic neuroscience, recent evidence suggests that attention skills may be one of the human brain functions that respond best to early intervention and training.

Further, from a neuroconstructivist perspective attention is a vital mechanism through which the child can actively select particular aspects of their environment for further learning. Executive functions include the abilities to inhibit unwanted information or responses, to plan ahead for a sequence of mental steps or actions, and to retain task-relevant and changing information for brief periods (working memory). Like attention, executive function abilities provide a critical platform for the acquisition of domain-specific knowledge and skills in an educational context. Further, recent studies show that preschool training of executive skills may prevent early school failure.

Children with ADHD, anti-social behaviour, conduct disorders and autism can all show atypical patterns of executive function. Basic neuroscience studies have identified the primary brain structures and circuits involved in executive functions, including the prefrontal cortex, in adults. However, much research remains to be done to understand the development of this circuitry, and the genetic and neural bases of individual differences in executive function. Foresight Mental Capital and Wellbeing Project specifically identifies and highlights the importance of attention and executive function skills in the future challenges for difficulties in learning.

NEUROSCIENCE AND EDUCATION: A BRIDGE TOO FAR?

Despite optimism from many who believe that neuroscience can make a meaningful contribution to education and that the potential exists for the establishment of a research field of educational neuroscience, some researchers believe that the differences between the two disciplines are too great for them to ever be directly linked in a practically meaningful way. In 1997 John Bruer published a major critique of what he called the "Neuroscience and education argument".

The 'neuroscience and education argument' as Bruer defines it, stems from three major findings in developmental neurobiology.

1. Early childhood is characterised by rapid growth in the number of synapses in the brain (synaptogenesis), and this expansion is followed by a pruning period.
2. There are so called experience dependant critical periods during which the developing brain is best suited to develop certain sensory and motor skills.
3. A stimulus rich environment causes greater synaptogenesis. The essential argument is that children are capable of learning more at an early age when they have an excess of synaptic growth and peak brain activity.

The knowledge of early brain development afforded by neurobiology has been used to support various arguments with regards to education. For example, the idea that any subject can be taught to young children in some intellectually honest form, due to the great adaptability and learning potential of the young brain.

Alternatively, the idea that critical periods exist for learning certain skills or knowledge sets appeals to the fact that in animal studies, if the developing brain is deprived of certain sensory inputs, the brain areas responsible for processing those inputs fail to develop fully later in development, and thus "if you miss the window, you are playing with a handicap".

One of Bruer's major points of contention with reports in favour of neuroscience and education is the lack of actual neuroscience evidence. Reports such as Years of Promise: A Comprehensive Learning Strategy for America's Children (Carnegie Corporation of New York, 1996) cite many cognitive and behavioural psychology studies, but no more than a handful of brain based studies, and yet draws dramatic inferences with regards to the role of the brain in learning.

Bruer argues that behavioural science can provide a basis for informing educational policy, but the link to neuroscience is "a bridge too far", and the limitations of the application of neuroscience to education stem from the limitations of neuroscience knowledge itself. Bruer supports his critique by arguing the limitations of current knowledge regarding the three key tenets of the neuroscience and education argument.

Another problem is the discrepancy between spatial resolution of imaging methods and the spatial resolution of synaptic changes that are suggested to underlie learning processes. A similar problem is true with regards to the temporal resolution. This makes it hard to relate subcomponents of cognitive skills to brain function. However, the primary flaw of the education neuroscience argument in Bruer's opinion is that it attempts to link what happens at the synaptic level to higher order learning and instruction. The terminology, "Mind, brain and education" alludes to the idea that if we cannot bridge education and neuroscience directly, then we can use two existing connections to inform education. These are the link between cognitive psychology and education, and between cognitive psychology and neuroscience.

Bruer contends that neuroscience in its current form has little to offer educators at the practical level. Cognitive science on the other hand, can serve as a basis for the development of an applied science of learning and education. Other researchers have suggested alternative bridges to the cognitive psychology suggested by Bruer.Mason suggests that the gap between education and neuroscience can be best bridged by educational psychology, which she outlines as being concerned with "developing descriptive, interpretive and prescriptive models of student learning and other educational phenomena".

CHALLENGES TO EDUCATIONAL NEUROSCIENCE

Despite Willingham's assertion that the potential for neuroscience to contribute to educational practice and theory is already beyond doubt, he highlights three challenges that must be overcome to marry the two disciplines effectively.

The Goals Problem: Willingham suggests that education is a so-called "artificial science" that seeks to construct an 'artifact', in this case a set of pedagogic strategies and materials. Neuroscience, on the other hand is a so-called "natural science", concerned with the discovery of natural principles that describe neural structure and function. This difference means that some goals set by education are simply impossible to answer using neuroscience research, for example, the building of character or aesthetic sense in children.

The Vertical Problem: Levels of analysis: Willingham suggests that the highest level of analysis employed by neuroscientists is the mapping of brain structure and activity onto cognitive function, or even the interaction of cognitive functions (*i.e.* the impact of emotion on learning). Within neuroscience research these functions are studied in isolation for the sake of simplicity, and the nervous system as a whole, functioning in its entirety with all its huge composition of functional interactions, is not considered. For educators, on the other hand, the lowest level of analysis would be the mind of a single child, with levels increasing to incorporate the classroom, neighbourhood, country etc.

Thus, importing research about a single cognitive factor in isolation, into a field in which context is essentially important creates an inherent difficulty. For example, while rote learning may be shown to improve learning in the research laboratory, the teacher cannot implement that strategy without considering the impact on the child's motivation. In return, it is difficult for neuroscientists to characterize such interactions in a research setting.

The Horizontal Problem: Translating research findings: While education theory and data are almost exclusively behavioural, findings from neuroscience research can take on many forms (*e.g.* electrical, chemical, spatial, temporal etc.). The most common form of data taken from neuroscience to education is the spatial mapping of brain activation to cognitive function. Willingham (2009) highlights the difficulty in applying such spatial information to educational theory. If a certain brain region is known to support a cognitive function relevant for education, what can actually be done with that information? Willingham suggests that this 'horizontal problem' can be solved only when a rich body of behavioural data and theories already exist, and points out that such methods have already been successful in identifying subtypes of dyslexia.

Willingham suggests that what is essential for a successful union of neuroscience and education is that both fields have realistic expectations of one another. For example, educators should not expect that neuroscience will provide prescriptive answers for educational practice, answers for educational goals that are incompatible with neuroscientific methods (*e.g.* aesthetic training), or levels of analysis beyond the individual level. Finally Willingham suggests that neuroscience will only be useful to educators when targeted at a specific problem at a fine grained level of analysis, such as how people read, but that these data will only be useful in the context of well developed behavioural theories.

Other researchers, such as Katzir and Pareblagoev have pointed out that neuroimaging methodology as it stands may not be suitable for the examination of higher level cognitive functions, because it relies primarily on the 'subtraction method'. By this method, brain activity during a simple control task is subtracted from that of a 'higher order' cognitive task, thus leaving the activation that is related specifically to the function of interest. Katzir and Pareblagoev suggest that while this method may be very good for examining low level processing, such as perception, vision and touch, it is very hard to design an effective control task for higher order processing, such as comprehension in reading and inference making. Thus, some researchers argue that functional imaging technologies may not be best suited for the measurement of higher order processing.

Katzir and Pareblagoev, suggest that this may not be a deficit of the technology itself, but rather of the design of experiments and the ability to interpret the results. The authors advocate using experimental measures in the scanner for which the behavioural data is already well understood, and for which there exists a strong theoretical framework.

TRANSFORMING CHALLENGES INTO OPPORTUNITIES

Another recent review of the educational neuroscience debate by Varma, McCandliss and Schwartz focuses on eight primary challenges, divided into scientific challenges and practical challenges, facing the field, and attempts to transform those challenges into opportunities.

SCIENTIFIC CHALLENGES

Methods

Neuroscience methods create artificial environments and thus cannot provide useful information about classroom contexts. Furthermore, the concern is that if neuroscience begins to influence educational practice too heavily, there may be a de-emphasis of contextual variables, and solutions to educational problems may become primarily biological rather than instructional.

However, Varma et al. argue that novel experimental paradigms create the opportunity to investigate context, such as brain activation following different learning procedures and that neuroimaging can also allow for the examination of strategic/mechanistic developmental changes that cannot be tapped by reaction time and behavioural measures alone. Furthermore, Varma et al. cite recent research that shows that the effects of cultural variables can be investigated using brain imaging, and the results used to draw implications for classroom practice.

Data

Knowing the brain region that supports an elementary cognitive function tells us nothing about how to design instruction for that function. However,

Varma et al. suggest that neuroscience provide the opportunity for a novel analyses of cognition, breaking down behaviour into elements invisible at the behavioural level. For example, the question of whether different arithmetic operations show different speed and accuracy profiles is the result of different efficiency levels within one cognitive system versus the use of different cognitive systems.

Reductionist Theories

Applying neuroscience terminology and theory to educational practice is a reduction and is of no practical use to educators. Nothing is gained be redescribing a behavioural deficit in neuroscientific terms. Varma et al. point out that reductionism is a mode by which sciences are unified, and that the co-opting of neuroscience terminology does not necessitate the elimination of education terminology, it simply provides the opportunity for interdisciplinary communication and understanding.

Philosophy

Education and neuroscience are fundamentally incompatible, because attempting to describe behavioural phenomena in the classroom by describing physical mechanisms of the individual brain is logically wrong. However, neuroscience may help to resolve internal conflicts within education resulting from differing theoretical constructs and terminologies used within subfields of education by providing a measure of uniformity with regards to results reporting.

PRAGMATIC CONCERNS

Costs

Neuroscience methods are highly expensive, and the expected outcomes do not justify the costs. However, Varma et al. point out that educationally relevant neuroscience may attract addition funding to education research rather than usurping resources. The essential claim of educational neuroscience is that the two fields are interdependent and that a portion of the funding allocated collectively to the two fields should be directed towards shared questions.

Timing

Neuroscience, while expanding rapidly, is still in relative infancy with regards to the non-invasive study of healthy brains, and thus education researchers should wait until more data is collected and distilled into succinct theories. Contrary to this, Varma et al. argue that some success is already evident. For example, studies examining the success of dyslexia remediation programmes have been able to reveal the impact of these programmes on the brain networks supporting reading. This in turn leads to the generation of new research questions.

Control

If education allows neuroscience in the door, theories will increasingly be cast in terms of neural mechanisms and debates will rely increasingly on neuroimaging data. Neuroscience will cannibalise resources and education research will lose its independence. Varma et al. argue that the assumption of an asymmetric relationship between the two fields is unnecessary. Education has the potential to influence neuroscience, directing future research into complex forms of cognition and education researchers can help Educational Neuroscience to avoid naïve experiments and repetition of earlier mistakes.

Neuromyths

Thus far most of the neuroscience findings applied to education have turned out to be neuromyths, irresponsible extrapolations of basic research to education questions. Furthermore, such neuromyths have escaped beyond academia and are being marketed directly to teachers, administrators and the public. Varma et al. respond that the existence of neuromyths reveals a popular fascination with brain function. Appropriate translation of educational neuroscience results and well established collaborative research can decrease the likelihood of neuromyths.

A BIDIRECTIONAL RELATIONSHIP

Researchers such as Katzir and Pareblagoev and Cacioppo and Berntson (1992) argue that as well as neuroscience informing education, the educational research approach can contribute to the development of new experimental paradigms in neuroscience research. Katzir and Pareblagoev (2006) suggest the example of dyslexia research as a model of how this bidirectional collaboration might be achieved.

In this case, theories of reading processes have guided both the design and interpretation of neuroscience research, but the existing theories were developed primarily from behavioural work. The authors suggest that the establishment of theories, which delineate required skills and subskills for educationally relevant tasks, is an essential requirement for educational neuroscience research to be productive. Furthermore, such theories need to suggest empirically testable connections between educationally relevant behaviours and brain function.

THE ROLE OF EDUCATORS

Kurt Fischer, director of Harvard University's Mind, Brain and Education graduate programme states "One of the reasons there is so much junk out there is that there are so few people who know enough about education and neuroscience to put the thing together". Educators have been reliant upon others' expertise for the interpretations from Neuroscience hence have not been able to discern whether the claims made are valid or invalid representations of the research. Without a direct access to the primary research educators may be at risk of misusing results from neuroscience research. The need for so called 'middlemen' in the translation of research to practice has led to a situation where the application of cognitive neuroscience research findings is running ahead of the research itself. In order to negate the need for middlemen, some researchers have suggested the need to developed a group of neuro-educators, a specially trained class of professionals whose role would be to guide the introduction of cognitive neuroscience into educational practice in a sensible and ethical manner. Neuro-educators would play a pivotal role in assessing the quality of evidence purporting to be relevant to education, assessing who is best placed to employ newly developed knowledge, and with what safeguards, and how to deal with unexpected consequences of implemented research findings.

Byrnes and Fox (1998) have suggested that developmental psychologists, educational psychologists and teachers generally fall into one of four orientations with respect to neuroscientific research "(1) those who readily accept (and sometimes over interpret) the results of neuroscientific studies;(2) those who completely reject the neuroscientific approach and consider the results of neuroscientific studies meaningless;(3) those who are unfamiliar with and indifferent towards, neuroscientific research;and (4) those who cautiously accept neuroscientific findings as being a proactive part of the total pattern of findings that have emerged from different corners of the cognitive and neural sciences". Greenwood (2009) suggests that as the body of knowledge available to educators increases, and the ability to be expert in all areas diminishes, the most productive standpoint would the fourth outlined by, that of cautious acceptance of neuroscientific findings and proactive collaboration.

Bennett and Rolheiser-Bennett (2001) point out that "teachers must be aware of and act on the science within the art of teaching". They suggest that educators must become aware of other methods and incorporate them into their practice. Furthermore, Bennett and Rolheiser-Bennett suggest that specific bodies of knowledge will play an important role in informing educators when making important decisions with regards to the "design of learning environments". The bodies of knowledge discussed include multiple intelligences, emotional intelligences, learning styles, the human brain, children at risk and gender. As the authors explain these and other areas are just "lenses designed to extend teachers' understanding of how students learn, and from that understanding, to make decisions about how and when to select, integrate, and enact items in the ... list".

Mason supports calls for a two-way constructive collaboration between neuroscience and education, whereby, rather than neuroscience research simply being applied to education, findings from neuroscience research would be used to constrain educational theorizing. In return, education would influence the types of research questions and experimental paradigms used in neuroscience research. Mason also gives the example that while pedagogical practice in the classroom may give rise to educational questions regarding the emotional bases of performance on school tasks, neuroscience has the potential to reveal the brain basis of higher-order thinking processes and thus may help to understand the role that emotion plays in learning and open new areas of study of emotional thought in the classroom.

NEUROMYTHS

The term "neuromyths" was first coined by an OECD report on understanding the brain. The term refers to the translation of scientific findings into misinformation regarding education. The OECD report highlights three neuromyths for special attention, although several others have been identified by researchers such as Usha Goswami.

1. The belief that hemispheric differences relate to different types of learning (*i.e.* left brain versus right brain).
2. The belief that the brain is plastic for certain types of learning only during certain "critical periods", and therefore that learning in these areas must occur during these periods.
3. The belief that effective educational interventions have to coincide with periods of synaptogenesis. Or in other words, children's environments should be enriched during the periods of maximal synaptic growth.

LEFT VERSUS RIGHT BRAIN

The idea that the two hemispheres of the brain may learn differently has virtually no grounding in neuroscience research. The idea has arisen from the knowledge that some cognitive skills appear differentially localised to a specific hemisphere (*e.g.*, language functions are typically supported by left hemisphere brain regions in healthy right handed people). However, massive amount of fibre connections link the two hemispheres of the brain in neurologically healthy individuals. Every cognitive skill that has been investigated using neuroimaging to date employs a network of brain regions spread across both cerebral hemispheres, including language and reading, and thus no evidence exists for any type of learning that is specific to one side of the brain.

CRITICAL PERIODS

The critical periods neuromyth is an overextension of certain neuroscience research findings primarily from research into the visual system, rather than cognition and learning. Although sensory deprivation during certain time periods can clearly impede the development of visual skills, these periods are sensitive rather than critical, and the opportunity for learning is not necessarily lost forever, as the term "critical" implies. While children may benefit from certain types of environmental input, for example, being taught a second language during the sensitive period for language acquisition, this does not mean that adults are unable to acquire foreign language skills later in life.

The idea of critical periods comes primarily from the work of Hubel and Wiesel. Critical periods generally coincide with periods of excess synapse formation, and end at around the same time that synaptic levels stabilise. During these periods of synaptic formation, some brain regions are particularly sensitive to the presence or absence of certain general types of stimuli. There are different critical periods within specific systems, *e.g.* visual system has different critical periods for ocular dominance, visual acuity and binocular function as well as different critical periods between systems, for example, the critical period for the visual system appears to end around the age of 12 years, while that for acquiring syntax ends around 16 years.

Rather than talking of a single critical period for general cognitive systems, neuroscientists now perceive sensitive periods of time during which the brain is most able to be shaped in a subtle and gradual fashion. Furthermore, critical periods themselves may be divided into three phases. The first, rapid change, followed by continued development with the potential for loss or deterioration, and finally a phase of continued development during which the system can recover from deprivation. Although there is evidence for sensitive periods, we do not know whether they exist for culturally transmitted knowledge systems such as educational domains like reading and arithmetic. Further, we do not know what role synaptogenesis plays in the acquisition of these skills.

ENRICHED ENVIRONMENTS

The enriched environment argument is based on evidence that rats raised in complex environments perform better on maze tasks and have 20-25per cent more synaptic connections than those raised in austere environments. However, these enriched environments were in laboratory cages, and did not come close to replicating the intensely stimulating environment a rat would experience in the wild. Furthermore, the formation of these additional connections in response to novel environmental stimuli occurs throughout life, not just during a critical or sensitive period. For example, skilled pianists show enlarged representations in the auditory cortex relating specifically to piano tones, while violinists have enlarged neural representations for their left fingers.

Even London taxi drivers who learn the London street map in intense detail develop enlarged formations in the part of the brain responsible for spatial representation and navigation. These results show that the brain can form extensive new connections as the result of focused educational input, even when this input is received solely during adulthood. Greenough's work suggests a second type of brain plasticity. Whereas synaptogenesis and critical periods relate to experience-expectant plasticity, synaptic growth in complex environments relates to "experience-dependent" plasticity. This type of plasticity is concerned with environment specific learning, and not to features of the environment that are ubiquitous and common to all members of the species, such as vocabulary.

Experience dependent plasticity is important because it does potentially link specific learning and brain plasticity, but it is relevant throughout the lifetime, not just in critical periods. "Experience-expectant plasticity", suggests that the environmental features necessary for fine tuning sensory systems are ubiquitous and of a very general nature. These kinds of stimuli are abundant in any typical child's environment. Thus, experience-expectant plasticity does not depend on specific experiences within a specific environment, and therefore cannot provide much guidance in choosing toys, preschools, or early childcare policies. The link between experience and brain plasticity is intriguing. No doubt learning affects the brain, but this relationship does not offer guidance on how we should design instruction.

Bruer also warns of the dangers of enriching environments on the basis of socio-economic value systems, and warns of a tendency to value typically middle class pursuits as more enriching than those associated with a working class lifestyle, when there is no neuroscientific justification for this.

SYNAPTOGENESIS

In addition some critics of the Educational Neuroscience approach have highlighted limitations in applying the understanding of early physiological brain development, in particular synaptogenesis to educational theory. Synaptogenesis research has primarily been carried out on animals (*e.g.* monkeys and cats). Measures of synaptic density are aggregate measures, and it is known that different types of neuron within the same brain region differ in their synaptic growth rates. Secondly, the purported "critical period" of birth to three years is derived from research on rhesus monkeys, who reach puberty at the age of three, and assumes that the period of synaptogenesis in humans exactly mirrors that of monkeys. It may be more reasonable to assume that this period of neural growth actually lasts until puberty, which would mean until early teenage years in humans.

Periods of intense synaptogenesis are typically correlated with the emergence of certain skills and cognitive functions, such as visual fixation, grasping, symbol use and working memory. However, these skills continue to develop well after the period that synaptogenesis is thought to end. Many of these skills continue to improve even after synaptic density reaches adult levels, and thus the most we can say is that synaptogenesis may be necessary for the emergence of these skills, but it cannot account entirely for their continued refinement. Some other form of brain change must contribute to ongoing learning. Additionally, the types of cognitive changes usually seen to correlate with synaptogenesis revolve around visual, tactile, movement and working memory. These are not taught skills but rather skills that are usually acquired independent of schooling, even though they may support future learning. How these skills relate to later school learning is, however, unclear. We know that synaptogenesis occurs, and that the pattern of synaptogenesis is important for normal brain function. However, what is lacking is the ability of neuroscience to tell educators what sort of early childhood experiences might enhance children's cognitive capacities or educational outcomes.

MALE VERSUS FEMALE BRAIN

The idea that a person can have a "male" brain or "female" brain is a misinterpretation of terms used to describe cognitive styles by when attempting to conceptualise the nature of cognitive patterns in people with autism spectrum disorder. Baron-Cohen suggested that while men were better "systemisers" (good at understanding mechanical systems), women were better "empathisers" (good at communicating and understanding others), therefore he suggested that autism could be thought of as an extreme form of the "male brain". There was no suggestion that males and females had radically different brains or that females with autism had a male brain.

LEARNING STYLES

A common myth in the field of education is that individuals have different learning styles, such as 'visual' or 'kinesthetic'. Many individuals will state preferences for the way in which they want to learn, but there is no evidence that matching a teaching technique to a preferred style will improve learning, despite this hypothesis being tested multiple times. There may even be harms associated with the use of learning styles, wherein learners become 'pigeonholed', perceiving that they may not be suited to types of learning that are not matched to their 'learning style' (*e.g.* so-called visual learners may not wish to learn music). Despite this lack of evidence, a 2012 study demonstrated that a belief in the use of learning styles is widespread amongst teachers, and a 2015 study showed that the majority of research papers in higher education research mistakenly endorse the use of learning styles.

CONVERGING EVIDENCE FOR COGNITIVE CONSTRUCTS

To date, cognitive neuroscience studies of aging have been primarily cross-sectional, focusing on differences between younger adults, aged 18–30, and older adults, aged 60–80. Functional magnetic resonance imaging (fMRI), which measures changes in blood flow to index localized changes in neural activity, has largely replaced positron emission tomography (PET) as the dominant brain imaging methodology.

In the 1980s and 1990s, behavioural approaches to cognitive aging implicated four major domains of age-related decline—working memory, inhibitory control, processing speed, and long-term memory. Here, we consider how imaging research provides converging support and mechanistic insight into age effects in each domain. Critically, neuroscience evidence reveals that each domain is associated with age-related alterations indicating that no single cognitive mechanism or unitary account proposed to date will suffice to explain cognitive aging.

WORKING MEMORY

Working memory, the cognitive system that actively maintains several pieces of information in mind for immediate use in higher-order processing tasks, has figured prominently in cognitive theories of aging, and is a central focus of neuroscience research on aging as well.

Performance differences between younger and older adults are generally minimal on simple span tasks (*i.e.*, digit span) or item recognition that require only rote rehearsal, whereas differences are pronounced when executive functions such as memory updating, reordering, or inhibition are added to the task. Imaging studies of item recognition, however, reveal pronounced activation differences, despite age-equivalent recognition accuracy, especially in regions of prefrontal cortex.

Varying memory load parametrically reveals that both age groups generally recruit the same brain regions but older adults recruit more (stronger activation, more sites of activation or both) at lower objective memory loads compared with younger adults. This pattern of prefrontal overactivation suggests that older adults are engaging additional "executive" resources to support short-term memory maintenance.

This interpretation gains support from the finding that younger adults also recruit these additional prefrontal sites, but at higher objective memory loads. Indeed, as load increases (*e.g.*, greater than four items), older adults typically perform more poorly than younger adults, and this behavioural decline is accompanied by less prefrontal activation for older compared with younger adults—a pattern referred to as underactivation—suggesting a resource ceiling has been reached.

For complex working memory tasks like operation span and N-back, older adults also show overactivation in dorsolateral prefrontal regions under conditions of age-equivalent performance. With increasing demand, older adults shift to underactivation coupled with performance that falls below their younger counterparts. Taken together, these results suggest frontally mediated executive processes may be flexibly recruited to support working memory performance in older adults but are more resource dependent and resource limited.

INHIBITORY CONTROL

Hasher and Zacks (1988) proposed that excitatory or activational aspects of attention are preserved in older adults, whereas inhibitory processes are deficient. Their view focused on the role of inhibition in controlling the contents of working memory by keeping out irrelevant information, and deleting no-longer relevant contents. Although the ubiquity of inhibitory dysfunction has been challenged, brain imaging has documented specific inhibitory impairment in older adults. For example, during item recognition, they are more vulnerable than young adults to interference from distractors appearing in the retention interval. Gazzaley, Cooney, Rissman, and D'Esposito (2005) demonstrated these effects using faces as the memoranda, and natural scenes such as distractors, or vice versa. These classes of stimuli are advantageous because they activate distinct localized regions making it possible to separate the brain's response to the memoranda and the distractors. Older and younger adults show equivalent activation for the to-be-remembered items;however, older adults showed more distractor-related activity than younger adults and distractor-related activation was correlated inversely with memory performance.

Other work suggests that activational aspects of attentional selection may also be compromised with age. Johnson, Mitchell, Raye, and Greene (2004)have shown that the simple instruction to selectively activate or refresh a representation in working memory can improve subsequent memory for that item and activates a region of left dorsolateral prefrontal cortex. Older adults show neither the behavioural benefit nor the neural correlate of the refresh operation suggesting that this activational process is deficient.

Inhibitory deficit theory also proposes that older adults are deficient in the deletion of no-longer relevant information, as evident in greater proactive interference (PI) for older than younger adults. Greater PI in older adults is associated with impaired activation in a region of left inferior frontal gyrus that has been linked specifically to interference control. Thus, brain-based measures indicate several correlates of inhibitory dysfunction with age that involve altered engagement of prefrontal control processes and impaired top-down control at earlier stages of input processing.

Processing Speed

Evidence for age-related slowing is pervasive in the cognitive aging literature. A variety of analytic behavioural approaches demonstrate a prominent, although not exclusive, role of processing speed in age-related declines. Nevertheless, speed deficits with age are clearly associated with age differences in brain-based measures that provide a reasonable proxy of neural transmission. These include measures of white matter volume and microstructure. Localized white matter deficits mediate the relationship between speed and memory retrieval. However, different cognitive measures (*e.g.*, processing speed, episodic memory, working memory, inhibition, and attention) have been associated with different localized regions or networks of white matter decline. Such regional specificity suggests that age-related effects on different cognitive processes depend on the integrity of different neural substrates, supporting the conclusion that one unitary cause of cognitive decline with age is unlikely.

Long-Term Memory

Aging is thought to have its greatest effect on long-term episodic memory. Accordingly, the Web of Science indicates that the majority of publications on imaging and cognitive aging focus on memory, posing a considerable challenge for a succinct summary of this area. We focus here on studies illuminating two major questions: What might be going wrong in the older brain when memory is poor? And likewise, what neural processes can be linked to successful memory performance in the older brain?

Poor memory in older adults stems, in part, from deficient encoding, which is unlikely to be effortful or strategic unless specific encoding instructions are provided. Environmental support can improve memory and minimize age differences. Brain imaging supports these statements. With minimal instruction, older adults show less activation than young adults in left inferior prefrontal regions that mediate semantic encoding operations. With the help of cues or encoding strategies, older adults show improved performance and a corresponding "increase" in left prefrontal activation.

The neural correlates of memory success have been productively investigated by classifying trials from the encoding phase of an experiment based on their memory outcome. These "subsequent memory" effects permit comparisons between encoding activity that leads to remembering versus forgetting. Based on this approach, older adults often show weaker activation in regions of the medial temporal lobe ([MTL] including hippocampus and parahippocampus), but "increased" activation in prefrontal regions compared with younger adults. It is tempting to interpret prefrontal overactivations as compensatory because they are associated with successful memory.

Episodic memory decline with age has also been attributed to impaired binding—the association of an item or event and its context. Associative memory decline is related to volumetric decreases in MTL regions, which are particularly vulnerable to age-related shrinkage. Moreover, binding deficits are associated with MTL and prefrontal activity reductions, along with weaker correlations between these regions, indicative of reduced functional connectivity. Older adults who perform well on tasks requiring memory for context show additional involvement of prefrontal regions that may compensate for binding deficiencies.

The proposal that aging spares automatic processing but not effortful processing also receives neuroscientific support. First, preventing younger adults from allocating full attention to memory encoding creates activation patterns resembling older brains under full attention conditions. Second, familiarity-based memory, which is preserved in older adults, can be accompanied by prefrontal overactivation and increased connectivity with certain MTL regions, suggesting compensatory circuitry. In contrast, recollective memory, which is especially poor in older adults, leads to pronounced underactivation in MTL consistent with processing deficiency. Third, implicit memory, as reflected in priming, is relatively preserved and associated with age-equivalent activation patterns, particularly involving left inferior prefrontal regions associated with semantic processing. In short, brain imaging supports a number of hypothesized mechanisms for memory decline in older age.

NEUROIMAGING DISCOVERIES ABOUT AGING

This chapter examines four discoveries about aging brain function that have emerged from brain imaging research. We begin with the finding of more widespread activation in older than younger adults. Although underactivation in older adults is also a common pattern, overactivation has been a particularly unexpected and intriguing result making it the topic of other recent reviews and debate. Here, we present some highlights of these issues.

Overactivation

Early PET studies first reported that older adults activated more and different brain areas than younger adults. The tasks used were either perceptual or memory based, and overactivity emerged in posterior and anterior brain regions. These results challenged the traditional doctrine of "localization of function"—the idea that brain functions were mediated by and localized to specific brain regions.

Further challenge arose when left hemisphere dominance for verbal processing and right hemisphere dominance for spatial processing were found lacking in the brain activation patterns of older adults. So, like age-related overactivation generally, this age-related alteration in hemispheric specialization, a pattern dubbed "hemispheric asymmetry reduction in older adults" or HAROLD, means that cognitive neuroscience studies of brain aging are raising new questions with broad neuroscientific implications.

But could such effects be due to age differences in neurovascular coupling on which both PET and fMRI depend (*i.e.*, the blood-oxygenation level dependent or BOLD response)? Indeed, cerebrovascular aging probably underlies the decreased signal-to-noise ratio, amplitude reduction, and increased lag of the hemodynamic response in healthy older adults. Yet, despite these changes, the shape, summation, and refractory properties of the hemodynamic response do not differ due to age, nor are the findings of "greater" activation in older adults readily explained by alterations in neurovascular coupling.

So, if frank age-related confounds are not at play, what is the functional significance of age-related overactivation? One plausible interpretation is that overactivation is a neural correlate of cognitive decline. This possibility is consistent with results from simple motor tasks, and some measures of verbal fluency where greater activation of the non-dominant hemisphere predicts poorer performance. However, evidence to the contrary from complex motor tasks and other cognitive domains, especially memory, finds overactivation in higher performing seniors, and in association with processes that lead to successful performance.

These latter brain-behaviour relations lead instead to the alternative popular view, which is that age-related overactivation indicates compensatory processing. By compensation, we mean that compared with younger adults, older adults are performing the same task using different neural circuitry, which in turn optimizes their performance. Older adults could be using additional brain regions to implement the same cognitive strategies as young adults or they could be using these brain regions to implement different strategies. Current evidence is insufficient to decide which interpretation is correct, and most likely a single account will not suffice for all tasks and all performance levels. Nevertheless, a compensation account is favored for at least some overactivation patterns in some cognitive domains. Also, overactivation could mediate "successful compensation" in that it supports performance equivalent to younger adults or in the upper range of an age-matched cohort, or "attempted compensation" that is insufficient to bring performance to such high levels. Moreover, as we discuss below, compensatory recruitment may have a cost.

Dedifferentiation

The concept of dedifferentiation originated in behavioural research with older adults but has gained prominence through neuroimaging. In the neural context, dedifferentiation refers to the loss of regional specialization or specificity.

Dedifferentiation connotes negative plasticity in older adults resulting in a breakdown of functional specificity, and therefore needs to be distinguished from beneficial or compensatory overrecruitment. As noted earlier, ventral visual cortex has functionally distinct subregions that respond selectively to categories or domains of visual input, such as faces, places/landmarks, and alphanumeric characters. Park and colleagues have documented declining specificity in older adults for whom face regions are also more responsive to places than in young adults where regions respond discriminatively to one category. Ventral visual dedifferentiation in older adults during working memory encoding together with prefrontal overactivation raises the possibility that frontal activity may compensate for lost perceptual specificity. Although much work remains to be done concerning the circuit changes and ubiquity of dedifferentiation, there are initial indications that it is greater in individuals with greater general reduction in cortical gray matter.

Frontal Compensation

Prefrontal overactivation is a paradoxical result in the cognitive neuroscience of aging. The paradox is because prefrontal regions are susceptible to considerable age-related atrophy and have been implicated in an array of age-related deficits. Nevertheless, medial, lateral, and anterior prefrontal overactivation are prevalent in older adults across a range of tasks. Importantly, prefrontal overactivation is often associated with underactivation in more posterior regions, including MTL and ventral visual cortex, as well as with improved performance. The two findings, referred to as posterior–anterior shift in aging, jointly support the interpretation that these regions are compensating for processing deficiencies elsewhere.

Default Network Alterations

The default network includes medial prefrontal, medial, and lateral parietal brain regions that have highly correlated activity and tend to be more active at rest than during task-related cognition. The prevailing view is that this network mediates cognitions associated with self-focus, reflective memories, and ambient attention to the environment. The default network was discovered first in healthy younger adults, but was soon found to be age sensitive with older adults showing greater default activation during cognitive tasks and less default suppression with greater task demand. Older adults also show less connectivity among default regions. Heightened frontal activation is associated with inefficient default activity in older adults during semantic retrieval and measures of subsequent memory. These results support the proposal that age-associated dysregulation of default activity may promote compensatory overactivation elsewhere.

NEURALLY BASED THEORIES OF COGNITIVE AGING

Cognitive neuroscience has given rise to new theories of cognitive aging that focus on functional or structural mechanisms to explain both deficient and preserved cognitive performance in older adults. Here, we briefly review a few of these new theoretical accounts that integrate brain imaging data with "cognitive behavioural effects" that accompany aging. Moving away from the "lesion models" of aging, the new generation of cognitive neuroscience theories incorporate constructs of plasticity and compensation as critical factors in understanding the aging mind.

Increased Noise

Li and her colleagues have proposed a model of aging that is based on age-related alterations in neural transmission, particularly related to dopaminergic decline. This theory and its computational implementation propose that aging is associated with decreased signal-to-noise ratio, which leads to less distinct neural representations;these effects may be exacerbated in pathological aging. The proposed mechanism is one that fits well with observations suggesting that some processes in the aging brain such as representational operations in ventral visual cortex can be characterized by dedifferentiation.

Proactive Versus Reactive Control

This theoretical proposal advanced by Braver, Paxton, Locke, and Barch (2009) focuses on the temporal dynamics of executive control of information processing operations.

Proactive control is preparatory, taking advantage of cuing and other contextual information that permits selective processing prior to the imperative events, whereas reactive control occurs later in the processing sequence, typically in response to or succeeding the imperative events. This dual mechanism view was proposed to account for imaging and behavioural results across a variety of tasks that permit different forms of control. Measures of memory and executive function indicate that altered prefrontal function in older adults is associated with poor proactive control, causing greater reliance on reactive control than in younger adults. These theoretical proposals are also reminiscent of the idea discussed previously that older adults are impaired at effortful, self-initiated processes.

CRUNCH

The compensation-related utilization of neural circuits hypothesis (CRUNCH) was proposed to account for patterns of overactivation and underactivation in older adults. The CRUNCH model posits that declining neural efficiency leads older adults to engage more neural circuits than young adults to meet task demands.

Therefore, older adults are likely to show overactivation, including frontal or bilateral recruitment, at lower levels of cognitive demand where younger adults show more focal activations. However, as load increases, younger adults may shift to an overactive or bilateral pattern to address task demands, whereas older adults, who may have already maxed out their neural resources at the lower load, show underactivation and performance decline.

The predictions of the CRUNCH model have been upheld in several studies of working memory. This model meshes well with the notion of "reserve" in that individuals with more reserve may reach their resource limit at higher load levels, making overactivation less likely at lower loads. This may be why longitudinal work has found that overactivation predicted subsequent cognitive decline. CRUNCH is also compatible with Scaffolding Theory of Aging and Cognition because compensatory activations may provide scaffolding to support aging cognition. Furthermore, CRUNCH is reminiscent of resource accounts of cognitive aging, which propose resource deficits as a basis for poorer performance of older adults.

Scaffolding Theory of Aging and Cognition

The STAC model provides the most integrative account of the theories reviewed here. The STAC model integrates the major findings from the cognitive neuroscience of aging and addresses both neurocognitive decline as well as neuroplasticity of the aging mind. STAC posits that the aging brain is subject to a range of neural challenges to which it must adapt. These challenges include amyloid deposition, atrophy, white matter deterioration, and dopamine receptor depletion. Such "hardware" changes are accompanied by the kinds of functional alterations reviewed above including dedifferentiation, default network dysregulation, and decreased activation of MTL structures. According to STAC, the brain responds to this corpus of neural burden by forging alternative neural circuitry (scaffolds) that may operate less efficiently than the focal, well-honed networks of young adulthood.

The scaffolding process permits individuals to maintain a high level of cognitive function at advanced ages and is represented by patterns of overactivation, primarily in the frontal cortex, but may include areas of parietal, mediotemporal, and occipital regions. Although the capacity for neurogenesis, synaptogenesis, and angiogensis decline with aging, the model posits that all mechanisms remain functional and provide plausible means for forging alternative neural circuitry.

Importantly, compensatory scaffolding is affected by experiences, so that new learning, enhanced cardiovascular health, sustained engagement in a mentally challenging activity, and cognitive training might all operate to enhance the brain's ability to build effective new scaffolding to maintain a high level of cognitive function that can no longer be supported by deteriorating structures and older functional networks. The magnitude of the neural deterioration combined with the effectiveness of new compensatory scaffolds operates to predict overall level of cognitive function.

One key idea in STAC is that scaffolding is not a process that simply begins in older age. Rather, across the life span, the individual is confronted with cognitive challenges to which the brain must adapt. Throughout childhood, existing circuitry must be harnessed and used to scaffold the forging of new circuitry to support the acquisition of new cognitive skills. Likewise, scaffolding supports new skill acquisition in adulthood. Early phases of new learning are often accompanied by high levels of activation and increased reliance on prefrontal circuitry.

The proposed continuity of scaffolding across the life span corresponds with the parallel between the sequence of neural development in childhood and age-related neuroanatomical decline, which follows a "last in, first out" progression: the regions that are later to myelinate developmentally are the first to decline in older age.

Thus, aspects of neural decline may recapitulate earlier developmental states, and thereby revisit scaffolding solutions that originally aided in the acquisition of cognitive abilities in early development. So, scaffolding is a lifelong process that is relied upon continually and increasingly in the later stages of life.

NEW DIRECTIONS IN THE PSYCHOLOGICAL NEUROSCIENCE OF AGING

A number of rapidly developing domains of neuroscientific enquiry are beginning to influence understanding of the aging mind and are likely to constitute new frontiers in the field. Continued research on emotional regulation, affect, and aging is fundamental to understanding the aging mind. Abundant behavioural evidence shows decreased negative affect and a bias to process and remember positive information in older adults. These biases are reflected in electrophysiological indices, greater amygdala response for positive stimuli, and increased fronto-limbic connectivity in older compared with younger adults. Likewise, aging may positively impact decision making along with representations of self and other, pointing to important frontiers for a social neuroscience of aging.

Affective regulation may also play an important role in the development of neural scaffolds in that poor emotional regulation could have deleterious effects on the ability to develop compensatory scaffolding. Another topic of increasing interest is the universality of patterns of neurocognitive aging, given evidence that cultural environments sculpt cognitive processes. Cross-cultural studies of the aging brain have the potential to reveal what aspects of the aging brain are biologically programmed and what aspects are more affected by the environment.

Evidence favoring continued neural plasticity into older age has energized the investigation of the effects of exercise, engagement, and cognitive training on neurocognitive function in older adults.

Although the potential for cognitive plasticity in older adults has been recognized for decades, the use of neural measures to identify mechanisms and correlates of improved performance is stimulating innovative and promising research. Current evidence is fairly conclusive that enhanced cardiovascular health is associated with better neurocognitive function. Moreover, there are strong correlations between an engagement in intellectual pursuits and later onset of Alzheimer's disease, although the causal relationship has not been determined. Critically, certain forms of cognitive training appear to change cognitive and even neural function, which can sometimes be sustained, but the demonstration of generalized improvement in cognitive function has proven more elusive.

Finally, over the next decade, the availability of new biological methods for genotyping and imaging destructive brain proteins such as beta amyloid which figures prominently in Alzheimer's disease will transform our understanding of the relationship between healthy and pathological life span trajectories, and help to harness the full potential for successful aging.

CONCLUSIONS

This review highlights three core contributions that have emerged from the cognitive neuroscience approaches to aging. The first pertains to the benefits of converging evidence: decades of behavioural aging research identified fundamental mechanisms that have garnered support from brain-based methods. Neuroimaging methods are promoting new neurally informed mechanistic accounts of cognitive decline and the realization that adverse effects of aging are unlikely to stem from a unitary or dominant cognitive mechanism.

The second contribution is evidence favoring enduring plasticity. From imaging, to animal models, to interventions, brain-based discoveries are revealing that psychological aging results from the combined effects of both negative and positive plasticity. The capacity for positive plasticity and compensation are proving more prevalent and integral to the aging mind than previously recognized. Human neuroscience and genetic approaches hold great promise for discovering the bases for successful aging and new ways to promote positive plasticity.

Third, brain-based studies of cognitive aging have broader human neuroscientific implications. Evidence for altered lateralization, changing specificity of visual cortex, and the pervasive recruitment of prefrontal areas indicate the dynamic nature of functional brain organization that can be relevant to compensatory and recovery processes across the life span.

Moreover, brain-based approaches to aging suggest continuities across the life span whereby investments made earlier in life, in the form of intellectual, social, and physical enrichment, may increase neural reserve and potential for effective scaffolding as people meet increasing challenges in later life.

In conclusion, the combined use of behavioural and biologically-based approaches to studying the aging mind has proven to be far more fruitful than either alone. We hope this review will further disseminate information about the new synthesis of psychological and brain science to study human aging and thereby energize new research that will be celebrated in future anniversary issues of this and other journals in the field.

3

Theories of Adult Development

ADULT DEVELOPMENT

In the discipline of psychology and sociology, a lot of time is spent exploring child and adolescent development, but we must not forget about the critical development of adults, as well. This lesson will identify and explore three theories of adult development that all have a unique perspective and similarities regarding adult development.

We will explore:

- Daniel Levinson's Seasons of Life Theory
- George Vaillant's Adult Tasks Theory
- Bernice Neugarten's Social Clock Theory

LEVINSON'S THEORY

Psychologist Daniel Levinson developed a comprehensive theory of adult development, referred to as the Seasons of Life theory, which identified stages and growth that occur well into the adult years.

His theory is comprised of sequence-like stages. Each stage is shaped by an event or action that leads into the next stage. The stages are:

1. Early Adult Transition (Age 17-22). This is the stage in which a person leaves adolescence and begins to make choices about adult life. These include choosing to go to college or enter the workforce, choosing to enter a serious relationship, and choosing to leave home.
2. Entering the Adult World (Age 22-28). This is the stage in which a person makes more concrete decisions regarding their occupation, friendships, values, and lifestyles.
3. Age 30 Transitions (Age 28-33). In this stage, there are often lifestyle changes that could be mild or more severe. For example, marriage or having children impact one's lifestyle, and these changes have differing consequences on how a person develops depending on how they embrace the event.
4. Settling Down (Age 33-40). In this stage, one often begins to establish

a routine, makes progress on goals for the future, and begins behaving like an adult. People in this stage are often parents or have more responsibilities.

5. Mid-Life Transition (Age 40-45). This time period is sometimes one of crisis. A person begins to evaluate his or her life. Values may change, and how society views these people may change also. Some people make drastic life changes, such as divorce or a career change. At this point, people begin thinking about death and begin to think about leaving a legacy.
6. Entering Middle Adulthood (Age 45-50). In this stage, choices must be made about the future and possibly retirement. People begin to commit to new tasks and continue to think about the legacy they are leaving.
7. Late Adulthood (Age 60+). In this stage, one begins to reflect on life and the decisions they have made.

Levinson also indicated that each stage consists of two types of periods:

- The Stable Period, in which a person makes crucial choices in life.
- The Transitional Period, in which one stage ends and another begins.

VAILLANT'S THEORY

Psychiatrist George Vaillant spent most of his career researching and charting adult development. His work is based on research of over 800 men and women spanning 60 years. Vaillant identified six adult life tasks that must be successfully accomplished in order for a person to mature as an adult.

The tasks are:

1. Developing an Identity. Vaillant explained that an adolescent must establish an identity that allows a separation from parents. This identity is made up of one's values, passions, and beliefs.
2. Development of Intimacy. This allows a person to have reciprocal relationships with another person. This task involves expanding one's sense of self to include another person.
3. Career Consolidation. In this task, the person finds a career that is valuable to society and to him or herself. According to Vaillant, a job turns into a career once one has contentment, compensation, competence, and commitment. He notes that such a career could be that of a spouse or stay-at-home parent as well.
4. Generativity. This involves the unselfish will and capacity to give. Generativity means being in a relationship in which one gives up much of the control. For example, serving as a consultant or mentor to others would help establish generativity.
5. Becoming Keeper of the Meaning. This task involves passing on the traditions of the past to the next generation.

6. Achieving Integrity. This task involves achieving a sense of peace and unity with respect to one's life and to the world itself.

THEORY OF DEVELOPMENT

Most theories of development and of intelligence seek to explain new problem-solving or concept-formation behaviour by the influence of acquired experience, that is, as a function of external reinforcements;and they seek to explain the formation of logical structures by the influence of language. In this double perspective, knowledge tends to be considered as a kind of "copy" of reality: either as a sensorimotor copy, because the "associations" on which the learning is based are seen to be in one-toone correspondence with a series of relationships already existing in the external world, or as a verbal copy, because language simply describes a reality that is considered ready-made.

Without denying the fundamental importance of both acquired experience and language, I would include, in addition, the following three central notions:

1. Knowledge of an object does not consist of having a static mental copy of the object but of effecting transformations on it and reaching some understanding of the mechanisms of these transformations. An intelligent act consists above all of coordinating operations, uniting, ordering (in the sense of introducing order), etc. These operations, which derive from the subject's internalization of his own actions, are the instruments of the transformations that knowledge is concerned with.
2. Logical relationships are, first and above all, operational structures. Although their most advanced forms are certainly expressed by language, their origins are found in the coordination of the subject's own actions. Even at the sensorimotor, preverbal level, a child is involved in activities that include uniting, ordering, introducing correspondences, etc.;and these activities are the source of operations and logico-mathematical structures.
3. Knowledge is not determined strictly by the knower, or by the objects known, but by exchanges or interactions between the knower and the objects (between the organism and the environment). The fundamental relation is not one of simple association but of assimilation and accommodation;the knower assimilates objects to the structures of his actions (or of his operations), and at the same time he accommodates these structures (by differentiating them) to the unforeseen aspects of the reality he encounters.

It is with this emphasis on the subject's own activities and transformational operations that I look at the stages of mental development and the progressive formation of intelligence. In a word, a ready-made object knowledge is not assumed, because we must transform it in order to know it;nor is a fully formed knowing subject assumed, because the subject must elaborate his own structures through transforming objects.

SENSORIMOTOR INTELLIGENCE

Even at the sensorimotor level, before the emergence of language, we can see this two-sided development—the child's thought structures develop in the very process of his "construction of reality." Infants assimilate situations into their repertory of actions;they find out about new things by acting on them in the ways they are capable of, such as sucking and grasping. By repetition, coordination, and generalization, these actions engender a system of "schemas of assimilation."

For example, a child who already pulls things and places things comes to coordinate these actions in the form of pulling a little rug towards himself in order to reach something placed on it. On the other hand, as part of this same development, this intelligence structures reality. For instance, at first, objects have no permanence;the universe is one of moving tableaux that appear and disappear and are without spatial localization once they have disappeared. But with the coordination of actions, a "schema of the permanent object" develops: an object is sought after it has disappeared, and it thus continues to exist in the sense of its having a spatial localization even when it is actually outside the field of perception and action.

Another basic schema, which, at the practical level, is closely tied to the schema of the permanent object, is that of the coordination of positions and changes of position, what geometers term "the displacement group"—the coordination of movements from positions with the possibility of a return to the point of departure and of the use of detours or alternate routes to get to the same point. There is even a sensorimotor schema of causality. First, this consists of attributing phenomena to the subject's own actions, without taking account of physical or spatial contact. Then, as causality is attributed to relations between objects themselves and some physical interaction is found necessary, there emerges progressive objectivation and spatialization of causal relations.

Sensorimotor intelligence thus makes two fundamental advances. (1) Actions are coordinated;and this is the source of later logic and operations, when these schemas will be internalized and restructured at the representational level. (2) From the point of view of structuring reality, the substructure is provided for certain fundamental concepts—object permanence, causality, space, and temporal succession.

FIGURATIVE AND OPERATIVE SYMBOLIC FUNCTIONS

At about one and a half or two years of age, there emerge the beginnings of the symbolic function and representational evocation, or "thought" (or, again, internalized intelligence). Knowing consists necessarily of a system of signification, and signification consists necessarily of a signifier and something signified. At the early sensorimotor level, the sensorimotor, perceptual, and postural actions upon objects—the schemas— are the things signified, and the signifiers are some aspect of these very schemas. Such signifiers are the cues or signals of conditioning, and at this early stage they are still relatively undifferentiated from what they signify.

By contrast, the symbolic function has its beginning (at around one and a half or two years) with the development of signifiers that are differentiated from the schemas that they signify;that is, some-thing can be evoked or represented by something other than a part of itself. Such signifiers may be symbols that bear some resemblance to what they stand for or signs that are arbitrary conventions.

Language and Imitation

The words of a language are signs. In children, at the same time the language sign system appears other aspects of functioning, which are based on symbols rather than signs, emerge: deferred imitation, symbolic (or fictional) play, and mental imagery (which is internalized imitation). All of these are alternate ways of evoking situations and objects in their absence.

Imitation is the medium by which the child progresses from sensorimotor to representational functions. A form of imitation is already present at the sensorimotor stage. This is a material, or active, representation and takes place only in the presence of the model being imitated. It is non-deferred imitation (even though it may keep going for a while after the model has disappeared). It does not imply any form of mental representation, and it does not necessarily result in any. On the other hand, deferred imitation (imitation that starts in the absence of the model) does lead to representation, as is clear in the case of symbolic play. It then becomes internalized as a mental image, which permits the acquisition of language. (Language is based on this deferred imitation, not only on conditioning;otherwise it would develop much earlier.)

Thought is made possible by the emergence of the symbolic function, through the internalization of sensorimotor actions and through the reconstruction of the early structures on the level of representational signification. But before looking more closely at this reconstruction, we must introduce an essential, although often overlooked, distinction. The recent research of Piaget and Inhelder reveals this distinction more and more clearly.

Figurative and Operative Aspects of Thought

At the heart of cognitive processes are two aspects— not separated sectors, but different poles: the figurative aspect and the operative aspect. The figurative aspect deals with static configurations of reality and provides adequate figural representations of these states. This aspect is predominant in perception, in imitation, and in mental imagery that is a form of internalized imitation. The operative aspect, on the other hand, deals with transformations of these states. This aspect is predominant in actions in general and, in the special case of operations, in internalized actions that have become reversible. The operations of adding and subtracting, for instance, are products of the actions of uniting and separating.

The term "operative" refers to both actions and operations, while the term "operational" refers to operations alone.

This distinction between the figurative and the operative aspects is an important one from the point of view of the development of intelligence. In adults, the figurative is subordinated to the operative;that is, states are seen as the result of one transformation and the starting point for another. However, in young children, especially in children who have not yet begun to think operationally, these two aspects remain uncoordinated;the children are not capable of certain elementary forms of reasoning because they focus too much on fixed states, without seeking to relate them operationally. For instance, the majority of four- to six-year-olds think that after a liquid is poured from a wide glass into a narrow one there is more of it, because they note only the fixed levels of the liquid and not the pouring action, which links the initial and terminal states.

PREOPERATIONAL THINKING (TWO TO SEVEN YEARS)

Operations are internalized, reversible actions, coordinated in total structures such as classifications, seriations, and multiplicative matrices. The psychological criterion for the existence of operational reversibility is the presence of the notion of conservation, a negative example of which is the children's reactions to the liquids, cited above.

Sensorimotor intelligence manifests the threshold of operativity, since the displacement group itself is a total structure characterized by reversibility, and there is an invariant, or a conservation schema, in the form of the schema of the permanent object. But internalization is missing here. These schemas consist merely of physical, successive actions and not yet of simultaneous representations.

One would be tempted to think that as soon as the symbolic function was formed, these sensorimotor structures would be internalized as operational structures. This is indeed what finally takes place but, because it is much more difficult to reproduce an action in thought than to execute it physically, it takes place much more slowly than one might suppose.

This internalization requires a total reconstruction on a new plane;and during the course of this construction, the child must go through the same difficulties he did on the sensori-motor level. For example, the four- to six-year-olds we studied knew perfectly well the route they took from home to school but could, nonetheless, not represent this route on a sand table.

Egocentrism and Decentering

The necessary condition for operational development at this age is a decentering from the child's own actions and own point of view. The phenomenon of the child's centering on his own point of view and on his own actions is what is called egocentrism (a term that has often been misunderstood because of confusion with affective egocentrism). By egocentrism, I mean nothing more than the absence of cognitive decentering. Already at the sensorimotor level the course of development is one of progressive decentering from an initial state of radical egocentrism. The newborn infant has no awareness at all of his own identity, precisely because of the fact that he does not distinguish his own point of view from other possible points of view.

As a result, he lives in a universe without objects, centered spatially, causally, and temporally on his own body. The construction of object permanence, the displacement group, and objective causality are characterized, in general, by progressive decentering, to the point where he becomes one element in a universe of objects and of spatial and causal coordinations. This Copernican revolution, as it were, must be effected all over again in the realm of representational thought and in social relations;another decentering is necessary to liberate the child from his own point of view.

One example, from the realm of spatial representation, involves a three-dimensional model containing three mountains;the child is given a series of drawings made from various positions and is asked to indicate the angle from which each of the drawings was made. Children at the preoperational stage cannot do this. A social example is the question of the number of brothers in a family. A child will say, for instance, that he has two brothers but that each of them has only one brother—because he doesn't count himself as a brother.

Absence of conservation in egocentrism. The main feature of egocentrism, however, is the absence of reversibility, and therefore of operations. None of the tests of conservation is successful at this level. We have already seen the cxamplc of thc pouring of liquids. We get the same results using small beads instead of a liquid. Similarly, if tcn bluc tokcns arc lincd up oppositc a row of ten red tokens, the child will think that the number or quantity changes if you spread out or push together one of the rows. Again, if you give him two similar balls of Plasticine and then reshape one as a sausage or as a pancake, he will think that the quantity has changed. By about 7 or 8 years of age, he will affirm that the quantity has not been changed;but he will continue to think, until 9 or 10, that the weight has been changed;and only at 11 or 12 will he believe that the volume, as measured by water displacement, remains unchanged. These experiments, which were first conducted in Switzerland, have been replicated in other countries with the same results.

In spatial conception at this age level, there is non-conservation of length. Two sticks of equal length will be judged equal by the child if they are placed side by side with their extremities aligned, but if one is moved so that it extends beyond the other, the child will now say that it is longer. Similarly, there is non-conservation of distance: the space between two points is considered smaller if an object is placed in the middle of it—empty space is not equated with filled space. Similarly, there is non-conservation of surfaces, volumes, etc.

THE CONCRETE OPERATIONS

At seven or eight years of age, the first operational structures take form. These first operations are limited, dealing with manipulations of objects themselves and not with verbal hypotheses. They are limited to classes, relations, and number, dealing either with discontinuous elements or with spatial and temporal continuums. They do not attain the general level of propositional logic. Moreover, these concrete operations do not cover the entire logic of classes and relations but only certain of the structures involved. These first operational structures, to which we have given the name of "groupings," relate to contiguous inclusions and relationships, without yet being generally combinatorial. They are only semilattices and incomplete groups, like seriations, classifications, multiplicative matrices, etc.

Seriation

Seriation, or succession of transitive asymmetrical relations, has its roots in early preoperational, even sensorimotor, schemas. Very young children can arrange a series of blocks in the order of their size. But at this level, it is done only by successive trial and error, with no use of deductive transitivity (knowing that $A > B$ and $B > C$ means that $A > C$). At seven or eight, there is a systematic method, consisting of finding the smallest of all, then the smallest of the remaining ones, etc., so that each element is understood as being bigger than all the preceding ones and smaller than all the following ones. This is the basis for an immediate deductive understanding of transitivity.

Classifications

Classifications, too, are present at the preoperational level, but in a form that remains elementary because it lacks operational reversibility. When small children, say four-year-olds, are asked to make classifications of objects, they make "figural collections," with them;that is, the spatial arrangement is made as if the class itself was dependent on a configuration in space. Slightly older children make non-figural collections. The collections no longer have a significant shape, but they are still only material collections and not logical classes, because the children do not understand the intensive quantification of class inclusions. Suppose, for example, that we present seven primroses (class A) and three other flowers (class A'), which together make up a collection of ten flowers (class B = A + A').

The child will agree that all the primroses are flowers and that all the flowers are not primroses, but he does not conclude that there are fewer primroses than there are total flowers (A > B). He will say there are more primroses because there are only three others. He cannot reason at the same time with both the whole class and a subclass. In trying to compare A with B, he must split B into A and A', and then since A is already one term of the comparison, the child uses A' as the other term. At an advanced operational level, however, he will understand that A B – A' and A' = B – A. Therefore A > (A + A'), or A > B. In other words, understanding class inclusion presupposes operational reversibility.

The same sort of analysis can be made of children's notions of correspondences, multiplicative matrices, etc. However, the operational mechanisms involved in the construction of the notion of whole numbers deserve special attention. We have already seen that even though children may use number names, it is not until the age of seven, on the average, that they are convinced of the conservation of number if the spatial arrangement is changed.

3The operational concept of number is a synthesis of class inclusion and ordering. On the one hand, there are the inclusionsI > (I + I) > (I+ I- I). On the other, since all the elements are equivalent, with all qualitative differences having been abstracted, the only way to distinguish one element, I, from another is by introducing order. This order may be a spatial array, a temporal array, or a logical enumerating order of the type I → I → I, where the sign → indicates any sort of transitive order. Bertrand Russell maintained that the cardinal number was based on one-to-one correspondence between classes of the same extension, without having to introduce order, whereas the ordinal number was based uniquely on ordering. But the one-to-one correspondence to which he referred is not the qualitative correspondence of the logic of classes, such as is found in multiplicative matrices, for example, where an element corresponds to another because of corresponding properties, but is rather a correspondence of one unity to another unity, with the qualities abstracted.

And this already presupposes an arithmetical unity, that is, number. Cardinal and ordinal numbers can be neither understood nor formalized independently of one another. Only by seeing number as a synthesis of inclusion and seriation can we avoid the vicious circle inherent in Russell's formalization. This interpretation of number, as a synthesis of inclusion and seriation, was discovered purely through psychology and has since then been formalized by the logician J. B. Grize. There is another whole area of operations at this level.

So far, we have been discussing discontinuous elements, where the operations deal with likenesses and differences. There is also the area of infralogical or spatiotemporal operations, which deal with proximity and separation in a continuum.

Representative Space

Representative space (as opposed to sensorimotor and perceptual space) is based on the following operations: partition and addition of parts (corresponding to addition of classes), placement and displacement (corresponding to seriation), and measuring as a synthesis of partition and displacement (as number is a synthesis of inclusion and seriation). There is a point of interest here from the point of view of philosophy of science. These spatial operations apply equally to Euclidean (metric) projective, and topo-logical space. In the historical development, Euclidean geometry is considered to have come first, followed much later by projective, and later still by topological, considerations. The psychological construction presented here is the contrary of this;topology is the most fundamental, with the other two being derived from it. We have found that in children, development follows this order. The first intuitions are topological, and from this come projective and Euclidean, or metric, representations.

TIME

The operations involved in the notion of time are again similar. There is the ordering of successive events;there is inclusion of time intervals;and the synthesis of these leads to time measurement. The notion of time is based on a primitive intuition of speed, which determines judgements of speed much before there is any metric notion of speed as a ratio of space to time. (Speed as a prerequisite to understanding time, rather than vice versa, is closer to relativity physics than to classical physics.) This primitive notion of speed is ordinal, based simply on the intuition that if one moving thing overtakes another on the same path, it is going faster. This judgement of speed is based on spatial order (behind and ahead) and temporal order (before and after) but does not require any evaluation of length of time or size of interval.

FORMAL, OR HYPOTHETICO-DEDUCTIVE, OPERATIONS

The period of formal, or hypothetico-deductive, operations begins at about 11 or 12 years of age. Children start to be able to reason not only about concrete objects but about verbal hypotheses. The operations of propositional logic, in a natural, non-axiomatized form, of course, are added to the operational structures.

There are at least three types of external evidence of this new development. (1) Children are able to reason with verbal material alone, that is, without concrete referents. (2) In experimental problems they are able to make hypotheses about the possible factors and vary them systematically to test the hypotheses. (3) In general terms, they are now capable of "reflection," that is, of thinking about thinking or of operations on operations. Propositional logic is a kind of system of operations raised to the second power, since the contents of the propositions are class or relational operations and since new operations are involved in the inter-propositional structure (implications, disjunction, etc.). This is why adolescents can construct theories, naive though they may be, whereas children cannot.

These operations have two main characteristics. First of all, they are combinatorial, giving rise, for example, to a more complex lattice structure in place of the simpler "groupings." Second, the two forms of reversibility found at the concrete operational level are united in a single system known as the group of four transformations. These two types of reversibility are inversion, or negation (N), which characterizes classification structures, and reciprocity (R), which characterizes relational structures. The operations involved in the groups of four transformations then are N, R, I (identity), and C (correlativity);so that NR = C, NC = R, NRC = N, and NRC = I. With these operations, 11-and 12-year-olds can develop new operational schemas, such as proportions, double reference systems, etc..

THE MECHANISM OF INTELLECTUAL DEVELOPMENT

The classical factors that usually are called upon to account for intellectual development are biological maturation, environmental influence (experience), and social transmission (education). Each of the three does play an important role, but they are insufficient to completely account for intellectual development. Thus a fourth is necessary. Biological maturation clearly needs to be supplemented when we see that the speed of development of operational structures is dependent upon cultural settings, individual experience, etc.

As for experience as a unique explanatory factor, it is indeed true that all notions need a basis in experience, even logical and mathematical notions. But there are two distinctly different types of experience, although they often go together. Physical experience consists of acting upon objects and drawing some knowledge about the objects themselves, for example, weighing things and finding out that weight is not always proportional to volume.

In logico-mathematical experience, on the other hand, the knowledge is drawn not from the objects that are acted upon but from the actions themselves. Arranging objects in various ways and finding out that the arrangement has no effect on the total number of objects is an example of this second type of experience. Physical experience certainly does not suffice to explain the development of intelligence. As for logico-mathematical experience, this is only a preparation for deductive thinking, which is based on the coordination of actions.

Finally, linguistic, educative, or social transmission, important though they are, can have an influence only to the extent that the child can assimilate what is offered to him into his own operational structures.

Progressive Equilibration

Another factor thus becomes necessary—the progressive equilibration of actions as they become coordinated. There are two reasons why equilibrium is a satisfactory explanatory model. First, intellectual equilibrium derives from the subject's activities as they compensate for external disturbances. Since compensation leads to reversibility, this progressive equilibration of the operational structures takes the form of progress towards ever-increasing reversibility.

Equilibration can thus be seen as a possible definition of intelligence, as well as an interpretation of its development. Second, an operational structure is equilibrated once it has achieved reversibility, but before then it passes through preoperational steps of successive equilibration. If we follow this progressive equilibration, we see that any given step, although not necessarily the most probable at the outset, becomes the most probable, once the preceding step has been reached. Equilibration thus includes a model of successive probabilities that is capable of dealing with factual detail, and which thus provides a learning theory based on internal reinforcement and not only on external or empirical reinforcement.

PERCEPTION AND MENTAL IMAGERY

The research on intellectual development is only a part of this line of developmental research. There is also work in the fields of perception and mental imagery.

Perceptual Development

In the area of perceptual development, two groups of phenomena have been identified: (1) effects that diminish in intensity but whose structure remains unchanged and (2) activities that become more articulated with age.

The effects that are not structurally modified but whose intensity decreases with age can be interpreted by a common probabilistic model. About 15 classic opticogeometric illusions have been studied developmentally. Examples of these are the Delboeuf illusion, the Müller–Lyer illusion, and illusions of angles, rectangles, parallelograms, etc. Each one was studied in a variety of different proportions;and at every age, positive and negative maxima were established for the proportions. The maxima proportions were found to be the same for every illusion, which permitted the effects of all of the illusions to be reduced to a general law, that of a "centration" effect: the areas focused on are overestimated, and the peripheral areas are underestimated. A study of ocular movement, by Piaget, Vinh-Bang, and Matalon (1958), was able to support this interpretation in some of the simpler situations. For instance, vertical lines are overestimated in comparison with horizontal lines, and subjects were in fact found to focus during much of the exposure on the summit of the vertical line.

This centration effect was itself reduced to a probabilistic explanation based in part on the distribution of the points of "encounters" between elements of the figure and elements of the receptor organs and in part on the series of correspondences, or "couplings," established among these points of encounter. Studies were carried out to establish temporal maxima for each of the illusions, in both children and adults, for exposures ranging from.01 second to 1.0 second. These studies confirmed the duality of these two factors.

The second group of phenomena—activities that become more articulate with age—stems from exploration activities, such as comparing parts of the figure, structuring the figure by introducing perceptual coordinates, anticipating parts of the figure, etc. These activities give rise to certain systematic secondary illusions by exaggerating the deformation resulting from systematic centration. Once again, eye movement studies have confirmed this interpretation, showing, among other things, how much more systematic adult perceptual exploration is than that of children. This explains why these illusions become more pronounced with age.

These perceptual activities, then, come more and more under the influence and direction of intelligence. Intelligence has no effect on the primary perceptual illusions, but it does have an effect on perceptual activity, guiding exploration and introducing its own structure. It is important to note to what extent a figurative function like perception lacks independent development and to what extent it is subordinated to operative functions. It has its beginnings in early motor behaviour, and its later development is directed by operational intelligence.

Mental Imagery

Another figurative function whose development has been systematically studied is mental imagery, which has been relatively neglected in recent years but, indeed, was never much studied in children. Once again there are two problems to study: (1) to establish whether the evolution of imagery is autonomous or whether it is influenced by operational development and (2) to establish whether imagery paves the way for operations or whether, on the contrary, it is modified and structured by the operations.

As far as the first problem is concerned, two principal types of imagery have been distinguished. Besides reproductive, or "copying," imagery there is anticipatory imagery (which may be as simple as imagining the rotation of a stick as it pivots about one of its extremities). In children who are too young to engage in operations, reproductive imagery is adequate, but anticipatory imagery is far from adequate. The errors made are, in fact, reminiscent of the errors in preoperational thought. Anticipatory imagery does not, then, derive directly from reproductive imagery but depends on the intervention of operations. At the operational level, this imagery becomes more flexible and can serve as a useful symbolic auxiliary for operational thought.

The second problem is examined by going back to the various operational tests (conservation, for example) and having the children anticipate how the situation will be, after telling them what transformation is about to be carried out. For instance, for the conservation of number, 12 blue tokens are placed in a row 15–20 centimeters long. About 30 centimeters away, 12 red tokens are spread out in a row 30–40 centimeters long. Each blue token is coupled with a red token by means of a channel with walls 1 centimeter high, so that the tokens can move towards each other only along the channel and must ultimately meet. The children are asked, with the tokens in their original positions, whether there are as many blue as red, whether there will be as many if the blues are all moved up to where the reds are, whether there will be as many if they are moved up only halfway, etc.

The findings are that small children are perfectly able to represent the displacement of the tokens, but before six and a half or seven years of age this does not lead them to assert that the number is the same. They report that the number increases as the row becomes longer, and decreases when the row is shorter. The anticipation remains transversal, focused on the length of the row. Later, at the operational level, it becomes longitudinal, focused on the paths traveled, and serves to verify the one-to-one correspondence. Other experiments support the same conclusion, namely, that adequate imagery in itself is not sufficient to bring about operational thinking but is structured and modified by the subject's operational level.

LEVINSON'S ADULT DEVELOPMENT THEORY

There's a saying that goes, 'The only thing constant is change.' I bet Daniel Levinson would have agreed with that. He was a psychologist who focused his time on investigating adult development, and the changes in life that create it. It was his belief that adults have a certain life structure, or pattern of life comprised of one's social dealings, relationships, and work life. This life structure is continuously affected by various seasons in life. The two reappearing seasons in life that Levinson stressed were the Stable Period, or a time of consistency when a person makes crucial life choices, and the Transitional Period, or the end of a certain life stage and beginning of a new one.

Levinson identified seven specific stages during adult development in his theory of the seasons of life. These stages include Early Adult Transition (age 17-22), Entering the Adult World (22-28), Age 30 Transition (28-33), Settling

Down (33-40), Mid-Life Transition (40-45), Entering Middle Adulthood (45-50), and Late Adulthood (60+).

BECOMING AN ADULT

Meet Doris. Doris is 70 years old and has a long awaited visit today from her granddaughter, Becky. Becky has just come home from college and has been sharing her new experiences with Doris. As Becky shares what it's like to be away from home for the first time, Doris starts thinking of her own memories from college. Even after Becky leaves, Doris continues day dreaming. She thinks about college more and then moves on to thinking about the other seasons of her life. According to Levinson, the time Doris left for college (17-22), was a key beginning stage in her adult development. It is the first time when Doris separated from her parents and began to decrease her emotional attachment to them. It was the first time she began planning out her adult life. Levinson called this time one's Early Adult Transition.

Doris continues to think about the next part of her young life. When she was in her twenties (22-28), she had her first set of years living and working in the adult world - working as a receptionist and later as an office manager. Levinson called this stage Entering the Adult World and believed this was the time for Doris to create her life structure. In that, he believed that young adults address four major tasks during this time: forming a dream and preparing for it, forming an occupation, forming mentor relationships, and forming love relationships, marriage, and family. Levinson considered the dream to be one's vision, desires, and core plan for his or herself in this world. This includes career and family. Doris recalls wondering often about when she would get married and start a family. Then, when she was 26, she met her husband.

ADULT DEVELOPMENT THEORIES AND THEIR IMPLICATIONS FOR PRACTICE

THE BEHAVIOURAL/ MECHANISTIC APPROACH

According to the mechanistic approach, people are machines whose response to external forces results in development. This approach asserts that past behaviour predicts future behaviour and that people's machine-like minds do not construct knowledge but instead absorb existing knowledge. Development can therefore be measured quantitatively.

Behaviourism exemplifies the mechanistic approach. It is a science interested in predicting and controlling human behaviour. People learn behaviours by responding to stimuli and by receiving positive or negative reinforcement or punishment. Positive reinforcement increases the likelihood that the immediately preceding behaviour will be repeated. For example, if a girl receives praise (an example of positive reinforcement) for helping her sister, she is likely to repeat the action. In contrast, negative reinforcement occurs when a desired action results in the cessation of an unpleasant stimulus. When a woman buckles her seatbelt to turn off the seatbelt alarm, she receives negative reinforcement. Punishment is a third kind of reinforcement. Instead of preceding the response as in the case of negative reinforcement, it follows the response and decreases the chance of the behaviour recurring. Scolding is an example of punishment.

Watson (1930), the father of behaviourism, believed that people were "an assembled organic machine ready to run" and that their personalities were a collection of complex habits. For example, he said that a deeply religious Christian develops a religious habit system of praying, attending church, and reading the Bible. Habits change, he believed, and develop most during the teen years and are set by age 30. Watson noted, "A gossiping, neighbour spying, disaster enjoying [person] of 30 will be, unless a miracle happens, the same at 40 and still the same at 60". Instructors who favour the behavioural/ mechanistic perspective provide students with plenty of opportunity for drills and practice. Using praise, grades, or some small prizes for their efforts positively reinforces learners. Students learn the appropriate response through reinforcement.

Programmed learning is one method of instruction used by teachers who champion the behavioural/mechanistic approach to development. This instructional technique, which was especially popular in the 1960s and 1970s, remains popular in the computer age. Programmed learning involves assessing a student's prior knowledge about a topic, then basing individual programmes of instruction on the student's level of expertise, and leading a student through a programme of instruction via a book, slides, or a computer programme. The material is divided into manageable portions called frames. After each frame, a question is asked and the student responds and receives immediate feedback. For example, learners in a research methods course may be presented with the explanation of a particular experimental research design. Next, they are asked a question about the information in the frame. After a correct response, the computer programme may respond "Great job!" An incorrect response may yield, "Nice try, but try again." This reinforcement results in retention of the information.

The teacher who embraces this paradigm sees development as correct behavioural responses. People's personalities are a series of habits and the teacher's job is to get the student to develop good habits. Learning is additive in nature. Each set of facts builds on previous knowledge and this addition of knowledge can be accomplished with various types of reinforcement.

THE PSYCHOLOGICAL/ COGNITIVE APPROACH

The psychological/ cognitive perspective focuses on an individual's "internal developmental processes" in interaction with the environment. Clark and Caffarella differentiate between sequential models of development and models based on life events or transitions. Sequential models, also called stage or phase models, assume that development is unidirectional in nature, that present development is build on past development, and that there is an endpoint. In this view, humans are active participants in their development, actively constructing knowledge rather than simply absorbing it. For example, a chronically ill woman changes medication and becomes increasingly lethargic.

She learns more about the new drug's side effects from friends, health professionals, and the Internet. She notices that when she eats certain foods in combination with the drug, it increases her fatigue. Her knowledge and personal experience help her realize she must change her diet to alleviate the lethargy.

Gould's (1978) model is an example of a stage/ phase model. In his theory of transformation, he discusses four major false assumptions that people must overcome in order to move successfully from childhood to adult consciousness and become more fully functioning adults. He maintains that identity formation occurs between the ages of 16 and 22, when people are challenging the false assumption "I will always belong to my parents and believe in their world". The false assumption to be overcome between 22 and 28 is: "Doing things my parents' way with willpower and perseverance will bring results. But if I become too frustrated, confused or tired or am simply unable to cope, they will step in and show me the right way". From the ages of 28 to 34, people confront the false assumption: "Life is simple and controllable. There are no significant co-existing contradictory forces within me," and from 35 to 45, people grapple with: "There is no evil or death in the world. The sinister has been destroyed".

The second psychological/ cognitive approach examines life events and transitions. Pearlin's (1982) model notes that anticipated life course role changes, such as getting married and having children, cause less psychological distress than unscheduled changes such as car accidents or the loss of employment. Pearlin maintains that social class, a person's coping skills, the social support networks available to a person, and the type of stress all have an impact on the individual route that a person's life course follows.

The psychological/ cognitive approach to development asserts that people reach more complex, integrated levels of development through active participation with their environment. Furthermore, individuals construct knowledge as opposed to responding to existing knowledge. In essence, adult development is a continuous journey towards increasingly complex levels of development. Hence, teachers taking this perspective favour ideas found in the transformational learning literature, such as critical reflection and discussion.

Mezirow (1990) asserts that through reflection, individuals often arrive at an "a more inclusive, differentiated, permeable and integrated perspective".

To encourage critical reflection, instructors may have people engage in role plays. Role reversal activities help learners to explore and express views other than their own, which could encourage them to broaden their perspectives. Another technique involves a method of journal writing, in which learners use one side of the page for observation and descriptions and the other side for thoughts, feelings, related experiences, or images provoked by the description.

Mezirow (1991) maintains that discussion with others is integral to adult learning and development. Instructors who champion the psychological/ cognitive view provide discussion guidelines that ensure an atmosphere of trust, safety, and respect in which learners felt comfortable expressing their ideas. Instructors also allow for quiet time in the discussion groups.

Lastly, teachers recognize that learners' receptiveness to information may be based on their life stage or time of transition. People often return to the classroom during a time of transition. Instructors holding the psychological/ cognitive view watch for what Havinghurst (1972) has termed "teachable moments," in which people are ready to learn and apply a concept because of their life situation.

Teachers who champion the psychological/ cognitive framework believe that knowledge is constructed and that adults are active participants in their development. Instructors encourage critical reflection and discussion through a variety of activities. They realize that learners often return to school during a time of transition and look for "teachable moments" in which learners are receptive to new ideas.

CONTEXTUAL/ SOCIOCULTURAL

The contextual/ sociocultural perspective on development works from the point of view that adult development cannot be understood apart from the sociohistorical context in which it occurs. Vygotsky (1978), a well-known proponent of the contextual approach, believed that people are not separated from the contexts in which they live, but are part of them. Vygotsky (1978) called this the child-in-activity-in-context. This developmental stance also asserts that culture influences what people think about, what skills they obtain, when they can participate in certain activities, and who is allowed to do which activities. Miller (1993) writes, "Different cultures emphasize different kinds of tools (for example verbal or non-verbal), skills (reading, mathematics, or spatial memory), and social interaction (formal schooling or informal apprenticeships) because of different cultural needs and values". This, in turn, influences whom people become.

Sociocultural elements such as race, class, gender, ethnicity, and sexual orientation influence adult development. These factors position people in relation to each other and in relation to a society that rewards those who fit the US "mythical norm," which Audre Lorde (1984/1995) defines as "white, thin, male, young, heterosexual, Christian, and financially secure" (italics in the original). US society devalues those outside this mythical norm.

It is the intersection of these factors rather than a single factor that affects adult development and learning. For example, Johnson-Bailey (2001) examined the common experiences shaping the persistence in higher education of African-American women who enrolled at a non-traditional age. Through these women's stories, she poignantly demonstrates how discrimination based on race, class, and gender affects their educational journeys. Speaking about the influence of racism and sexism in their lives, Johnson-Bailey notes, "Racism and sexism impact the educational experiences of Black women in many ways. As Blacks, they are thought to be intellectually and morally inferior. As women, they are held to task for the alleged inadequacy of their gender's intellect". The contextual/ sociocultural approach views individuals as inextricable from the society in which they live;they develop in ways intrinsic to themselves but molded by the discriminatory forces of society within which they function.

Instructors utilizing this framework may use Vygotsky's (1978) idea of guided learning. The teacher and learner are active participants in the learning process. Learning involves observation, collaboration, and "scaffolding". Scaffolding requires that the teacher adjust the instructional level based on the learner's response. The learner is an apprentice who develops culturally relevant skills through thought and action.

Teachers who adopt a contextual/ sociocultural approach to adult development also focus on how social inequities based on various attributes including race, class, and gender affect adult development and learning. Like their colleagues who work within the psychological/ cognitive paradigm, the instructors who believe in the sociocultural context are interested in having their students gain increasingly integrated and higher levels of understanding through critical reflection and discussion.

However, they may take an approach that focuses on social justice, encouraging students to question critically why social inequities exist and how these inequalities remain part of the educational experience. For example, they may ask students to reflect on how school policies, procedures, and curriculum continue to privilege some while discriminating against others.

Educators who ascribe to the contextual/ sociocultural view of adult development also recognize the importance of increasing students' cultural awareness. Sleeter and Grant (1988) write, "The ideology of multicultural education is one of social change - not simplyintegrating those who have been left out of society but changing that very fabric of society".

Furthermore, these educators strive to introduce the idea of cultural pluralism, defined as "maintenance of diversity, respect for differences, and the right to participate actively in all aspects of society without having to give up one's unique identity".

These instructors infuse materials from different cultures into their curricula, perhaps gathering stories to demonstrate a particular concept through a variety of cultural lenses. For example, a teacher of General Educational Development (GED) students may provide reading materials that examine the institution of marriage through different cultural lenses. She might help her students analyze how various aspects of a person's identity affect marriage.

Teachers who choose this paradigm realize how race, class, gender, and sexual orientation influence adult development. They encourage students to question critically how societal inequities are reproduced in the classroom. Instructors who see adult development through this lens also work to increase people's cultural awareness.

INTEGRATED APPROACH

The integrated approach to adult development takes a holistic view of adult development. This perspective is focused on how the intersections of mind, body, and sociocultural influences affect development. Spirituality is also sometimes included in the integrated approach.

Perun and Bielby's (1980) proposed integrated model of development suggests that the life course is composed of changes on several levels across time. Changes in each area follow their own timetables. Different types of changes include physical changes, changes in the family life cycle such as being married and having children, changes in work roles, and in emotional tasks. Stress results when the timetables are asynchronous.

While others do not present a model, they draw attention to aspects of adult development that are not widely discussed, including spirituality. For Tisdell (1999), spirituality is connection to history, to others, and to moral responsibility. Moreover, Tisdell notes the inextricable tie between culture and spirituality. All are interconnected and, maintains Tisdell, all are important for adult learning. Recognizing spirituality as an aspect of the adult learner's experience, realizing its importance in meaning-making, and understanding "spirituality as the grounding place for the work of many emancipatory adult educators" are important concepts for adult educators to grasp.

Dirkx (1997) discusses "nurturing the soul" in adult learning. Instead of relying exclusively on logic, he invites educators to explore "ways of knowing grounded in a more intuitive and emotional sense of our experiences". In this type of transformative learning, students move beyond the rational to the extrarational. Images and symbols are important in this type of learning. Learning through the soul "has to do with authenticity, connection between heart and mind, mind and emotion, the dark as well as the light".

Teachers who espouse the integrated approach to adult development believe in the interconnection between mind, body, spirit, and sociocultural factors. They are interested in promoting students' growth intellectually, physically, emotionally, aesthetically, and spiritually. Encouraging students to connect to course content in a variety of ways requires myriad techniques. Instead of relying solely on class discussion and written work, teachers may encourage students to construct a learner's portfolio in which course content is addressed in a variety of ways including, for example, art music, poetry and fiction, or dance. Other techniques may include visualization and meditation.

Instructors who see adult development as an integrated process may be more sensitive to the idea of multiple intelligences. This theory notes that there are seven kinds of intelligence: linguistic, logical-mathematical, musical, bodily-kinesthetic, spatial, interpersonal, and intrapersonal. These teachers incorporate activities that address different types of intelligences into their teaching. Promoting spiritual development in learners' lives is of interest to those who adopt an integrated approach to development. Spirituality is often equated with connection to others and to something larger than oneself. Connecting subjective feeling with objective fact by journaling, by promoting discussion that "generates a sense of unified consciousness", or by creating sensory experiences such as viewing a beautiful painting or engaging in a walk outdoors is a way to achieve this connection and begin to discuss larger life questions.

Those who adopt the integrative framework of adult development may also be acutely aware of the teacher student interaction. They may simultaneously observe themselves and their students in interaction with each other. They may encourage themselves and their students to engage in an activity and then journal the physical feelings, emotional issues, and analyze the situation.

Those believing in the integrative approach recognize the intersection between mind, body, spirit, and sociocultural factors. They recognize the importance of connecting students to course content in a variety of ways to promote growth on several levels. Writing stories, discussion, drawing, other artwork, and engaging in visualization and meditation may be techniques used to encourage this development.

ADULT LEARNING THEORIES

OVERVIEW

Typical adult learning theories encompass the basic concepts of behavioural change and experience. From there, complexities begin to diverge specific theories and concepts in an eclectic barrage of inferences. Up until the 1950s basic definitions of learning were built around the idea of change in behaviour. After this point more complexities were introduced "such as whether one needs to perform in order for learning to have occurred or whether all human behaviour is learned ".

Jean Piaget states that there are "four invariant stages of cognitive development that are age related". According to the authors, Piaget contends that normal children will reach the final stage of development, which is the stage of formal operations, between the age of twelve and fifteen. As cited by Merriam and Caffarella (1999), Arlin (1975, 1984), established from the work of Gruber (1973)on the development of creative thought in adults, has attempted to identify a fifth stage of development, in addition to Piaget's formal operations. "She [Arlin] contends that formal thought actually consists of two distinct stages, not one, as Piaget proposed".

Arlin (1975) proposes that Piaget's fourth stage, formal operations, be renamed the problem-solving stage. According to Merriam and Caffarella (1999), Arlin's hypothesized fifth stage was the problem-finding stage. This stage focuses on problem discovery.

Though Arlin's proposed fifth stage produced more questions than answers, it opens the door to understanding the learning needs of adults;to be approached as thinkers. According to a literature review by Ross (2002), humanism, personal responsibility orientation, behaviourism, neo-behaviourism, critical perspectives, and constructivism are all important facets of, and perspectives on, adult learning theory. The most common treatments of the research of these areas of self-directed adult learning are learning projects, qualitative studies, and quantitative measures. Collins (1991) explores adult learning as the interactive relationship of theory and practice. In basic terms, the adult learner studies a particular theory and then puts it into practice when presented with the opportunity to do so. Thus, the understanding of an adult learning theory can prompt practice and practice can prompt adult learning theory revision.

Adult learning theories in and of themselves have very little consensus amongst them. There is great debate on an actual determined amount of theories that are even possible, as well as labeling those theories into groups like Hilgard and Bower's (1966) stimulus-response and cognitive theories as large categories of their eleven theories. Another groups dynamic labels theories as mechanistic and or organismic. Overall it seems that the theory of adult learning is broken down into two elements;1) a process that creates change within the individual, and 2) a process to infuse change into the organization.

Malcolm Knowles might well be considered the founding father of adult learning. He contrasted the "concept of andragogy, meaning "the art and science of helping adults learn,"...with pedagogy, the art and science of helping children learn".

Knowles' original studies and writings arose from the assumption that there are significant, identifiable differences between adult learners and learners under the age of eighteen. Primarily, the differences, according to Knowles, relate to an adult learner being more self-directing, having a repertoire of experience, and being internally motivated to learn subject matter that can be applied immediately – learning that is especially "closely related to the developmental tasks of his or her social role".

ANDRAGOGY

Knowles (1968) popularized this European concept over thirty years ago. Andragogy, (andr - 'man'), contrasted with pedagogy, means "the art and science of helping adults learn". Knowles labeled andragogy as an emerging technology which facilitates the development and implementation of learning activities for adults.

This emerging technology is based on six andragogical assumptions of the adult learner:

1. *Need to Know:* Adults need to know the reason for learning.
2. *Experience:* Adults draw upon their experiences to aid their learning.
3. *Self Concept:* Adult needs to be responsible for their decisions on education, involvement in planning and evaluation of their instruction.
4. *Readiness:* The learning readiness of adults is closely related to the assumption of new social roles.
5. *Orientation:* As a person learns new knowledge, he or she wants to apply it immediately in problem solving.
6. *Motivation (Later added):* As a person matures, he or she receives their motivation to learn from internal factors.

These six assumptions dovetail with the thoughts and theories of others. Merriam and Caffarella (1999) point to three keys to transformational learning: experience, critical reflection and development. The aspect of experience (the second assumption to andragogy) seems like an important consideration in creating an effective learning opportunity for adults. The learning opportunity needs to be relevant and applicable to a person's set of experiences. Argote, McEvily, and Reagans (2003) point to experience as an important factor in one's ability to create, retain and transfer knowledge. Critical reflection is the second key to transformational learning and part of andragogy's self-directed learning. Reflection/think time is yet another essential principle to creating an effective learning experience for adults. Garvin (1993) shares the importance of fostering an environment that is conducive to learning including time for reflection and analysis. Adult learners need time to contemplate the ramifications of the learning experience to their experience and responsibilities.

The third key to transformational learning is development (corresponding to the third assumption of andragogy). Merriam and Caffarella state that "the ability to think critically, which is mandatory to effecting a transformation, is itself developmental". If development is the outcome of transformational learning, then an effective adult learning opportunity needs to be created that will take personal development into consideration

Andragogy assumes the following about the design of learning:

1. Adults have the need to know why they are learning something.
2. Adults learn through doing.
3. Adults are problem-solvers.
4. Adults learn best when the subject is of immediate use.

According to Knowles an example used to apply the principles to personal computer training:

1. Explain why certain skills are taught (functions, commands).
2. Task oriented instead of memorizing. Tasks should be common tasks.
3. Take diversity into play. Acknowledge different learning levels and experience.
4. Allow adults to learn on their own and from their mistakes. (M.Knowles)

Some would contend that Knowles only introduced a theory of teaching rather than a theory of adult learning. In commenting on this thought, Merriam and Caffarella (1999) referring to Hartree suggest, "that it is not clear whether Knowles had presented a theory of learning or a theory of teaching, whether adult learning was different from child learning, and whether there was a theory at all-perhaps these were just principles of good practice". It is further contended that Knowles did not establish a proven theory, rather he introduced a "set of well-grounded principles of good practice".

"Within companies, instructional methods are designed for improving adult learners' knowledge and skills. It is important to distinguish the unique attributes of adult learners so as to be better able to incorporate the principles of adult learning in the design of instruction".

Within this context, adult learning is aimed at not only improving individual knowledge and skill, but ultimately it is the goal to improve the organizational performance by transfer of learning directly to work applications. Yi suggest three methods to foster learning in adult organizations: Problem-Based Learning which seeks to increase problem-solving and critical thinking skills;Cooperative Learning, which builds communication and interpersonal skills;and Situated Learning, which targets specific technical skills that can be directly related to the field of work. Each of these methods support the assumptions about how adults learn;specifically they are more self-directed, have a need for direct application to their work, and are able to contribute more to collaborative learning through their experience.

MULTIPLE INTELLIGENCES

Howard Gardner represents those theorists who have dismissed the idea of one type of intelligence as typically measured by today's psychometric instruments. He posited that there were seven (later eight) types of intelligences:

1. Linguistic intelligence
2. Logical-mathematical intelligence

3. Spatial intelligence or the ability to form a mental model of the spatial world and to maneuver within it using this model.
4. Musical intelligence.
5. Bodily-kinesthetic intelligence, or the ability to solve problems using one's body as performed by athletes, dancers and other craftspeople.
6. Interpersonal intelligence which is the ability to understand other people.
7. Intrapersonal intelligence which is the ability to understand one's self.

Gardner (1993) maintains that the first two are the types of intelligence commonly measured by IQ tests, and which are commonly accepted as "intelligence."

Gardner later added an eighth intelligence to his taxonomy, Naturalist Intelligence, which he defined as "expertise in the recognition and classification of the numerous species — the flora and fauna — of his or her environment" Sternberg's Triarchic Theory can be viewed as an interpretation of intelligence as information processing. Li (1996) provides us with a useful summary of Sternberg's theory. He tells us that: "In Sternberg's general theory, there are three subtheories: the componential subtheory, the experiential subtheory and the contextual subtheory, each divided into subdomains of concern.

The contextual subtheory deals with the context of intelligence. Intelligence in the real world requiring adaptation, selection, and/or shaping the environment. Measurement of contextual intelligence would relate to the issue of social perception, culture fairness, and cultural relativeness. The experiential subtheory deals with the issue of novelty and automatizing of processing. It is related to the notion of learning and the dynamic interplay between controlled and automated processing in the competition for cognitive resources. Finally, there is the componential subtheory, which is subdivided into (a) metacomponents, (b) performance components, and (c) knowledge acquisition components, which are directly related to learning".

CONDITIONS/ENVIRONMENT

Some research suggests that situational circumstances constitute an environment that promotes or discourages learning. Those circumstances may be created by organizational structure, positive or negative environmental situations, or time constraints. Child and Heavens (2003) suggest, "The learning capabilities of organizational members are, at least in part, socially constructed by national, occupational, or other institutions". They further suggest that internal boundaries are established by specialities or departments within the framework of organizations that hinder cross-boundary learning.

In following the thread of environmental issues within organizations supporting or hindering learning, Starbuck and Hedberg (2003) suggest that positive outcomes are much more apt to result in a positive and successful learning experience. They contend, "Pleasant outcomes (successes) reinforce Stimulus-Response links whereas unpleasant outcomes (failures) break Stimulus-Response links.

As a result, pleasant outcomes are much more effective at teaching new behaviours". This concept follows the transformational leadership theory providing positive opportunities for individuals to grow within the framework of organizational life. However, it may be contended that learning through failure (*i.e.* experiments which do not result in the anticipated outcomes) may provide a more thorough and circumspect understanding of the given topic or issue under examination, although this method will generally involve a longer learning curve. —The license to fail is often the surest key towards successful learning which an organization may provide.

Weber and Berthoin Antal (2003) suggest, "A key question is how long organizational learning processes take and whether the duration can be externally influenced". They further contend that learning processes that require practice are much slower than those that do not require practice. Time consideration is an important element in considering the process of learning within an organization that must meet specific deadlines or has a client base that needs to be managed continuously.

The conditions may not be suitable for an elaborate training or educational programme. Organizations must consider time pressure as a tool that can encourage learning and speed up processes. However, Weber and Berthoin (2003) contend, "Time pressure can both accelerate and slow down learning processes...is experienced as motivating or threatening...if the sense of threat becomes too excessive, however, learning can be slowed or made impossible altogether".

In 1998, the American Psychological Associations Media Psychology Division 46 Task Force Report on Psychology and New Technologies broadened the definition of media psychology and included eLearning and distance learning in among array of theories of learning to be included in research on adult learning.

Learning psychologist and media psychology pioneer, Bernard Luskin expanded the understanding of "e" learning beyond electronic to included sensory response in this type of learning when he interpreted the "e" to mean education, excitement, enthusiasm, enjoyment and energetic, among other perceptions attached to media in the adult learning environment. This expansion added twenty-first century thinking into the theoretical framework comprising theories in adult learning.

EXPERIENTIAL LEARNING

Experiential Learning Theory emphasizes the role that true experiences play in the learning process. It is this emphasis that distinguishes itself from other learning theories. Cognitive learning theories emphasize cognition over affect and behavioural learning theories deny any role for subjective experience in the learning process.

Scholars in the field of education have two contrasting views when it comes to the concept of experiential learning. The first view defines experiential learning as a sort of learning which enables students to apply newly acquired knowledge in a relevant setting. The relevant setting can be a sponsored institution of learning with trainers, instructors, teachers, or professors to guide the lesson. The other school of thought defines experiential learning as "education that occurs as a direct participation in the events of life". Thus, learning is not achieved in a formal setting, but in the practice of reflection of daily experiences. Kolb furthers the second definition of experiential learning by developing a model which details learning process through experiences. Kolb and Fry's (1975) experiential learning model is a continuous spiral process which consists of four basic elements:

1. Concrete experience
2. Observation and reflection
3. Forming abstract concepts
4. Testing in new situations

Immediate or concrete experiences are the basis for observation and reflections. These reflections are assimilated and distilled into abstract concepts from which new implications for action can be drawn.

According to Kolb and Fry (1975), the adult learner can enter the process at any one of the elements. The adult learner moves to the next step once he or she processes their experience in the previous step.

ANXIETY AND THE ADULT LEARNER

An interview with psychologist Edgar Schein, Coutu suggests that more often than not, organizations fail at transformational learning. They rarely fundamentally change the behaviours within the organization. Schein dismisses the notion that learning is fun, especially for adults. He equates adult learning within organizations with that of the brainwashing techniques he observed while studying prisoners of the Korean War. Organizations must find a method to deal with the anxiety adults experience when they are forced to "unlearn" what they know and learn something new. Schein discusses two kinds of anxiety: learning anxiety and survival anxiety. It is in this manner that he draws the parallel to brainwashing;that is "learning will only happen when survival anxiety is greater than learning anxiety". Each of these anxieties could be managed, for example learning can be constructed in a "safe" environment where the consequences of failure are minimal. Survival anxiety can obviously be increased by threatening job loss, a lack of security, or recognizing competitive elements of the market.

JARVIS'S LEARNING PROCESS AND ADULT LEARNING THEORY

One of the most significant qualities unique to adult learning as compared to that of children, teens, and traditional college students is life experience. That experience offers adult learners a meaningful advantage in the learning process. The sum of those experiences provides many reference points for exploration, new application, and new learning.

Merriam and Caffarella (1999) review Jarvis's Learning Process in a wider discussion of adult learning. These authors quote Jarvis who suggests, "All learning begins with experience." Real learning begins when a response is called for in relation to an experience. If an individual is unchanged by a situation, Jarvis questions whether real learning has taken place. He proposes that new experiences need to be experimented with, evaluated, reflected upon and reasoned about for the most effective change and therefore learning to take place. Jarvis continues, suggesting that these post experience behaviours culminate in the best and highest form of learning where change and increased experience have happened. Jarvis's model offers an excellent learning model that can assist both facilitators and learners in advancing education and learning situations.

A few questions come to mind in light of Jarvis's theory. Does Jarvis's model reflect a deeply postmodern worldview where experience is either ultimate or paramount? How might this worldview expand or narrow learning theory? Does Jarvis's model seem to accept the maxim that 'experience is the best teacher'? We can of course qualify this statement by asking whether there is any learning which does not consist of experience in some form, whether in the classroom, on the playground or on the battlefield.

Is it possible that some hurtful and negative life experiences could be avoided if a person learned from another person who has already encountered and experienced a significantly negative life situation? Learning from an older or more experienced mentor provides an incredibly valuable learning forum and support network. Listening, and learning from a mentor's successes, failures, or mistakes can help expand one's knowledge base and shorten learning cycles experience alone would require. It seems that living largely out of one's personal experiences also short-circuits meaningful, relational connections that expand one's horizons and better equip one to succeed in this world and avoid so many of its pitfalls. Yet, it may be reasonably argued, that personal experience provides the most integral and visceral form of learning.

CASE STUDIES AND WORKPLACE EXAMPLES

The adult learning experience presented itself in all of its glory and contradictions through a curriculum review taking place in a school setting. The objective was to examine the current school curriculum and evaluate it for strengths and weaknesses. The purpose for this review was to both align the curriculum with current practice and augment the curriculum to enhance student learning. Interestingly, the teachers involved in this process seemed to exhibit all the qualities of adult learners mentioned previously: learning through projects, applying self-direction to the process, challenging the process for purpose, and some approached the process with much anxiety. Engaging in the process illustrated that adult learning is individual and there were as many approaches to adult learning as there were people involved in the process.

At GM, there are several examples of learning opportunities in manufacturing operations that fulfill the key criteria of adult learning. That is, they provide adults with the need to know why they are learning something, usually via a review of competitive analysis and the importance of the topic to our improved competitive position. Secondly, they are often done in a workshop-type format, where adults can learn through doing. Next, the format typically will cover an application that will have immediate use and will require the students to bring their experiences to the class to assist and involve themselves with problem solving.

Typical courses or learning opportunities cover safety issues, quality improvements, and productivity improvements as they apply to specific departments in the plant. In these workshop-style classes, actual problems are brought to the class for the students to learn and practice problem-solving skills. The outcomes and recommendations are then immediately applied in the regular operations.

At Medical Protective, adult learning has been promoted and encouraged among the entire community. Some learning is required for work-related functions, but other types of courses are intended to benefit professional development. Motivational factors, such as monetary incentives, courses being paid for, recognition, and the hope of advancement have encouraged all employees to participate in a learning course. By utilizing various information technologies, knowledge programmes can be accessed online, downloaded to a PC, or printed off for manual review, depending on the need of the individual learner. Medical Protective employees are constantly adapting to the changing IT environment in the market around them, and are using these systems to become more efficient, knowledgeable workers.

BEHAVIOURALIST THEORIES

Behaviourism, as a learning theory, can be traced back to Aristotle, whose essay "Memory" focused on associations being made between events such as lightning and thunder. Other philosophers that followed Aristotle's thoughts are Hobbes (1650), Hume (1740), Brown (1820), Bain (1855) and Ebbinghause (1885). Ivan Pavlov, John B. Watson, Edward Thorndike and B.F. Skinner later developed the theory in more detail. Watson is the theorist credited with coining the term "behaviourism".

A key difference in these various forms of associationism is that until Skinner, they were considered to be associations of mental or cognitive events. Skinner departed from this mental associationism and claimed that what associates two things is the environment itself, not the mind of the spectator. This departure has been noted as being part of a substantial number of changes in what was, until then, called Behaviourism - and which Skinner called Radical Behaviourism - that it may be a historical accident that it was called Behaviourism at all.

BEHAVIOURISM AS A LEARNING THEORY

The school of adult learning theory that adopted these principles has become known as the school of Behaviourism, which saw learning as a complex process of responses to several kinds of distinct stimuli. Skinner always referred to it as a three-term contingency comprised of a discriminative stimuli, or S, a response, or R, and a reinforcing stimulus, or S. Conditions of deprivation and satiation, and other changes in the environment, have come to be generally acknowledged p[' as a kind of fourth term, and are denoted as Motivating Operations (MO) generally, Abolishing Operations (AO), or Establishing Operations (EO) depending on whether they make a reinforcer less effective (abolishing), more effective (establishing) and so on. Jack Michael has been instrumental in refining and exploring these elements

A reinforcement is defined as a stimulus that strengthen the response, which is to say that it makes it more probable, or alters its frequency. Spillane (2002) states, "the behaviourist perspective, associated with B. F. Skinner, holds that the mind at work cannot be observed, tested, or understood;thus, behaviourists are concerned with actions (behaviour) as the sites of knowing, teaching, and learning".

THE TECHNOLOGY OF TEACHING

There have been several major Behaviourist innovations for improving learning. A few were B.F. Skinner's Programmed Instruction, Fred Keller's Personalized System of Instruction (PSI), Ogden Lindsley's Precision Teaching, and others. Technology of teaching must go hand in hand with that of learning.First the teacher must SURVEY the content of teaching.Then,QUESTION the topic to be teached.Followed by READING the topic and RECALL them.REVIEW in subsequent lesson-chapters. B.F. Skinner also wrote a book on major problems in popular teaching theories called The Technology of Teaching which attacked educational problems which were then current. The descriptions of educational problems, not surprisingly, seems like it was written today: truancy, vandalism, violence in the classroom and more.

One of the keys to effective teaching is discovering the best consequence to shape the behaviour. Consequences can be positive or negative – rewarding or punishing. Consequences transpire after the desired behaviour occurs and can involve either positive or negative reinforcement. Positive reinforcement involves a stimulus that increases the likelihood of a particular response, such as a child receiving a gold star for doing a chore. Negative reinforcement also increases the probability of the desired response and involves removing an undesirable stimulus upon completion of the desired response. An example might be entering the correct password to turn off a loud alarm.Punishment is often confused with negative reinforcement;however, punishment is used to erase undesirable behaviours by presenting a distressing stimulus when the behaviour occurs. Paying a fine for bouncing a check is a form of punishment. "Extinction" occurs when there is no consequence at all – for example if you knock at the door and no one answers, pretty soon you simply stop knocking.

VERBAL BEHAVIOUR

The seminal work of Pavlov demonstrated that the application of neutral stimuli could be used to elicit a response from animals in the same way that an unconditioned stimulus could From these initial studies other psychologists such as John Watson demonstrated that these principles could be applied to humans. Skinner invented the term operant to describe his attempt to better account for volitional behaviour we usually call free.

In Skinner's original work it was confined solely to animals, particularly the white rat. However, it wasn't long before operant behaviour was observed in humans. Skinner's attempt to account for the operant behaviour of humans, including complex language functions, resulted in his seminal work, Verbal Behaviour (1951) which accounted for ways in which human operants differed for non-human ones. This was extended with the conception of rule governed behaviour

THE ILLUSION OF FREE WILL

One of the assumptions of many behaviourists is that free will is illusory, and that all behaviour is determined by a combination of forces. These forces comprise genetic factors as well as the environment either through association or reinforcement. The "illusion of free will" concept is deeply embroiled in the nature vs. nurture controversy. Asking the question, "Are individuals shaped by genetics or by existentialism?" is the essence of this debate. Behaviourists believe that the environment is the primary influence that determines who individuals will be and the behaviour they will develop. Hence, the reason why free will is only an illusion or imaginary deduction.

Skinner argued that the assumption of lawfulness in human behaviour was an unprovable prerequisite to the scientific investigation of human behaviour.

Without the assumption of lawfulness, that is the lack of freewill, such a science could not exist.

Skinner has continued this argument by noting in his controversial book Beyond Freedom and Dignity that the historically beneficial forces that have arisen to defend Freedom and Dignity may be violently opposing the scientific conception of man.

CRITICISM

This theory has latterly been criticized as overly simplistic. Nevertheless, its influence can be seen in educators' insistence that feedback is critical to learning. The stimulus-response method is used frequently in adult learning situations in which the students must learn a time sensitive response to a stimulus. Aircraft emergency procedures, for example, are divided into two parts.

The first, the time sensitive portion, must be immediately performed by rote memory upon recognition of a stimulus – a warning light, horn, buzzer, bell, or the like. These procedures are taught and reinforced with rote drills and successfully passing the tests is the reinforcement. The second portion of the procedure, which may be viewed as diagnostic action is performed with mandatory reference to checklists and other reference material and depends on what may be viewed as higher level learning and understanding of aircraft systems and performance characteristics.

Behaviourist Theory maintains a focus on the change in observable behaviours as the manifestations of learning. The theory emphasizes changes in behaviours due to the influence and control of the external environment, rather than the internal thought process of the subject. Simply put, people will learn desired behaviours due to stimuli from their external environment that recognize and reinforce the behaviour in a positive manner. Undesired behaviours can be controlled or eliminated by an absence of attention to or recognition of such.

Behaviourism is comprised of several individual theories that have a common theme functioning within them. This common theme is found in the ways the theorists define what learning is, and how it is accomplished. The common assumptions of these theorists are threefold, as explained by Merriam and Caffarella (1999). The first common assumption is the emphasis on observable behaviour rather than internal thought processes create learning. Second, ultimately it is the environment that creates learning and it determines what is learned, not the individual learner. Lastly it is the ability to understand the overall process, and the ability to repeat or reinforce that process that is a common thread. This theory is most commonly seen in adult learning when organizations take repeatable training steps and systematize them into manageable tasks.

The hypothesis behind behaviouralist learning theories is that all learning occurs when behaviour is influenced and changed by external factors. Behaviouralism disregards any notion that there may be an internal component to man's learning. Grippin and Peters (1984) emphasize that "contiguity...and reinforcement are central to explaining the learning process" in regard to an individual's subjugation to external stimulus as a determinant of response (*i.e.*, behaviour). Contiguity is understood as the timing of events that is necessary to bring about behavioural change, while reinforcement refers to the probability that repeated positive or negative events will produce an anticipated change in behaviour.

Behavioural theory is a key component of animal training and skill training in humans. Teaching animals to sit for a kibble is very similar to clapping and hugging your child for their first steps or bike ride. Slot machines are based on intermittent reinforcement, which in turn leads gamblers to put more quarters in the machine to be reinforced by the ching ching of winning.

Behavioural theories have also been studied and applied in organizational leadership. Dating back to the 1940's, studies were conducted at Ohio State University (OSU) and the University of Michigan (UM). What the researchers found in the OSU and UM studies can be classified into two categories: relationships and results. In the OSU studies, researchers compiled behaviours into two dimensions: initiating structure (results) and consideration (relationships). UM researchers compiled their leader behaviour under two similar dimensions: employee oriented and production oriented. From this research, Blake and Mouton developed the Managerial Grid, later to be called the Leadership Grid.

This grid assists leaders in assessing possible outcomes to their behaviour within an organization. Robbins states, "The grid does not show results produced but, rather, the dominating factors in a leader's thinking in regard to getting results". Behavioural leading and learning is based on organizational and cultural conditioning. This can be observed in the tough-handed, "hatchet wielding" approach of Jack Welch and in the benevolent "lend-a-hand" approach of Herb Kelleher. Behavioural theories within leadership have had "modest success in identifying consistent relationships between patterns of leadership behaviour and group performance. What seems to be missing is consideration of the situational factors that influence success or failure".

SIMPLISTIC OR FUNDAMENTAL?

Some might view this theory as being a very elementary learning process. It suggests, by and large, that any learning is result oriented, and, therefore, learned by repetitive actions based on punishments or rewards. Merriam and Caffarella (1999) refer to Thorndike's work which used animals in controlled experiments to determine learning behaviour based on the stimulus presented.

This process, while presenting a possible outcome for comparison, is unrealistic when compared to the intelligence capabilities of humans. It could be argued that this theory tends to diminish the possibilities in human learning. In some circumstances, however, this method of learning is necessary;particularly when dealing with individuals with lower reasoning abilities or lower intelligence.

Pattison (1999) suggested that American adult education's roots in liberal arts education and then progressive education quoting. This progressive education focused upon the broad populace, not just social elites which liberal education intended to do according to Pattison. This progressive education began taking hold in the 1920's in public education settings. Into this social setting Behaviourism came. Pattison suggests that early behaviourists like John Watson focused on job skills and behaviour adaptation that would "secure the survival of humans, societies, and individuals." Behaviourism coupled with progressive education would help "control human behaviour and viewed education as a tool for bringing about societal change".

Behaviourist theory presents learning in short manageable blocks that build on previously learned behaviours. Kearsley (1994) identified three fundamental principles common in behaviourist learning:

1. Positive reinforcement of the desired behaviour will most likely prompt the same behaviour.
2. Learning should be presented in small manageable blocks.
3. Stimulus generalization of learning can produce secondary conditioning.

The goal of this learning method is to transform the learner's behaviour to a "desired" behaviour. The learner is rewarded often for exhibiting the desired behaviour when they accomplish a learning block. This method is heavily used in the federal government to quickly train employees on the latest policies and procedures (*i.e.* government credit card use, anti-terrorism, and sexual harassment). In addition, this method is ideal for short lessons (no more than 20 minutes) which can be accomplished over the internet from the employee's desktop computer. Within the 20 minute timeframe, the employee will normally retain key points of the lesson. However, when the lesson goes beyond the 20 minute window, there is a potential for the employee to lose focus and hurry through it in order to fulfill the requirement and get back to work. As a result, the employee retains very little and the organization has very little success in achieving the desired behaviour.

While it is true behaviourist theories can be simplistic in their concept, their application to the human has allowed for much to be discovered about learning, memory and even neuroscience. Since the late 1800s, psychologists using behavioural principles have established hundreds of tests to identify both how learning and memory occur in varying complexities of brain structures. Across many species, for example, it has been shown that when the reinforcing agent is "painless" then learning occurs in the cerebellum. However if there is an emotional connection (particularly negative such as fear) to the reinforcer then learning and memory occur in the amygdala

Training of individuals centers on the concept that all learning is the result of the environment acting upon behaviours. The environment of an individual reinforces behaviours either positively or negatively and all of learning takes place through environmental influences. Adult learning can be seen strictly through this focus, but a more centrist approach is neo-behaviourism. Neo-behaviourism suggests that not only does the environment reinforce behaviour, but there is an interaction between the individual and the environment. This is an important concept as it relates to adult learning because of the relative importance of choices to motivation in the learning process.

While Behaviourist Theory was founded in the early decades of the twentieth century, there still exist many examples of support for the theory. It is not uncommon for organizations to articulate the desired behaviours they expect will lead to positive business results. Organizations then reinforce those behaviours through performance management and by adjusting the environment to reward or recognize the desired behaviours. For example, many companies measure employee performance on two dimensions: business results and desired behaviours.

As well, organizations encourage, through recognition, such positive behaviours as perfect attendance, employee suggestions for improvements, raising quality issues that would adversely impact a customer, and good safety behaviours. Various approaches to promote behaviouralist theory in Organizational Learning are many times predicated on the belief that organizational members prefer, if not altogether require, specific standard operational procedures (SOP). In other words, creative problem solving does not come naturally with most group members. Following such rationale, Foil and Lyle (1985) note that this theory is counter to cognitive reasoning which would look at what is happening environmentally and determine whether SOP is the most appropriate response to each various event.

CASE STUDIES AND WORKPLACE EXAMPLES

ATTENDANCE POINT SYSTEM

One example of behavioural learning in the workplace is through an attendance point system. Often times, this type of system offers both positive and negative reinforcement. For example, most companies using a point system have a written policy stating that employees may accrue a maximum amount of points during a 12-month revolving period. An employee is then given a partial point, or more, towards an accrual of the maximum allowable any time there is an infraction of the policy – especially an attendance infraction.

The negative reinforcement is the notification of accrued points and disciplinary action taken per level of point accrual – sometimes culminating in termination of the employee. Positive reinforcement can occur when there is periodic recognition of employees with "perfect" attendance or zero points. There is one possible fallacy in the system, however. It occurs when an employee appears to be no longer controlled by the point system, but rather controls the system by knowing just how many points can be accrued without soliciting discipline. It is in this last scenario that one understands why most theorists have come to believe that learning is not solely comprised of external influence but that it also includes an internal component as well.

CONTINENTAL AIRLINES

Continental Airlines applied this behavioural learning approach in a very successful effort to reduce absenteeism and increase performance during the turnaround engineered by Gordon Bethune. Taking over after the disastrous reign of Frank Lorenzo when employee morale and commitment declined to the point that Continental employees would frequently remove the company logos from their uniforms, Bethune realized that rewarding employees for what was really important would drive important behavioural changes. Bethune realized that what was important was rebuilding passenger confidence and preference by providing service that met customer needs. To this end, the company implemented quarterly bonuses for all employees based on achieving targeted levels of performance in the FAA quarterly ratings of airlines based on lost baggage claims, on time departures, and customer complaints. In addition, employees with perfect attendance each quarter were entered into drawings for Ford Explorers. Both programmes resulted in marked changes in behaviour and contributed to the turnaround from the edge of bankruptcy.

TIME CLOCK

Another example that is elementary yet worth mentioning is The Salvation Army, Canton Corps' use of a time clock. The initial purpose of the clock in that environment was uncertain. We found that most people who use the time clock were not using it as intended. Many did not remember to clock in or out, or they would not use the clock at all. Not until pressure was exerted on each employee by ruling that they would not get paid if their cards were not adequately punched, did employees begin to use the time clock appropriately. In a few short weeks of reminders and a few short paychecks, the time clock was being used properly.

CONSTRUCTIVIST THEORIES

Constructivism is a learning theory that attempts to explain how good learners learn by constructing understanding for everyone. This chapter will explore the constructivist learning theory by defining constructivism, providing varying views of constructivism, and illustrating how constructivism relates to independent learning and higher education. Constructivism really got its start in the late 1980s. But many people did not know how to label what they were doing. In the 1990s, constructivist books abounded. Many people became interested in it.

The principles of Constructivism are broadly adopted in many areas of education today. The notions of authentic activities, social negotiation, juxtaposition of instructional content, nurturance of reflexivity, and student-centered instruction inspired many instructors to examine and think about the importance of interactions between teachers and students, students and students, and students and learning materials as well. Therefore, both instructors and students may have opportunities to enhance the effectiveness of their teaching and learning.

Constructivism gives teachers another perspective to rethink how students learn and to focus on process and provide ways of documenting change and transformation. It also reminds teachers to look for different ways to engage individual student, develop rich environments for exploration, prepare coherent problem sets and challenges that focus the model building effort, elicit and communicate student perceptions and interpretations.

Principles of Constructivism:

1. Constructivist learning environments provide multiple representations of reality.
2. These representations represent that complexity of the real world.
3. Knowledge construction is emphasized over knowledge reproduction.
4. Authentic tasks are emphasized in meaningful context.
5. Real world settings or case-based learning is provided.
6. Thoughtful reflection on experience is encouraged.
7. Enable context- and content- dependent knowledge construction.
8. Supports collaboration and social negotiation among learners.
9. Discovery learning
10. Collaborative activity
11. Integration and activation of prior knowledge
12. Opportunities for hands-on activities.

CONSTRUCTIVISM DEFINED

Constructivism is a synthesis of multiple theories diffused into one form. It is the assimilation of both behaviourialist and cognitive ideals. The "constructivist stance maintains that learning is a process of constructing meaning;it is how people make sense of their experience".

This is a combination effect of using a person's cognitive abilities and insight to understand their environment. This coincides especially well with current adult learning theory. This concept is easily translated into a self-directed learning style, where the individual has the ability to take in all the information and the environment of a problem and learn.

Constructivism reflects the organismic world view.Compared with behaviourism which is originated from the mechanistic world view, constructivism concerns how change occurs in development. For behaviourists, change comes about when an external force acts upon an object that is inherently at rest. For organismic theorists, behavioural change is inherent in the living organism itself rather than extremely driven.

Contrary to criticisms by some (conservative/traditional) educators, constructivism does not dismiss the active role of the teacher or the value of expert knowledge. Constructivism modifies that role, so that teachers help students to construct knowledge, rather than to reproduce a series of facts.

Constructivism is also often misconstrued as a learning theory that compels students to "reinvent the wheel." In fact, constructivism taps into and triggers the student's innate curiosity about the world and how things work. And then, students create organizing principles that they can take with them to other learning settings.

VIEW POINTS

Although varying constructivist theories exist, there is agreement between the theories "that learning is a process of constructing meaning;it is how people make sense of their experience". Two viewpoints of constructivist theories exist. They include the individual constructivist view and the social constructivist view. The individualist constructivist view understands learning to be an intrinsically personal process whereby "meaning is made by the individual and is dependent upon the individual's previous and current knowledge structure" and as a result can be considered an "internal cognitive activity". The social constructivist view, however, premises that learning is constructed through social interaction and discourse and is considered, according to Drivers and others (1994), to be a process in which meaning is made dialogically.

CONSTRUCTIVIST THEORY AND INDEPENDENT LEARNING

When applying this theory to independent learning, it is essential to understand that we need to consider the cultural environment in which this learning takes place. Isolated learning is an oxymoron. Merriam and Caffarella (1999) suggest that adult learning, while self-directed, must have input from outside influences. That may take the form of investigation, social interaction, or more formal learning environments.

The constructivistic learning approach involves educators building school curriculum around the experience of their students. Constructivists believe learner-centric instructional classroom methods will strengthen the commitment and involvement of self-motivated learners because of their high level of interaction. Today, there is a trend for incorporating technology into the classrooms to support instructional learning methods. Yet, recent studies have revealed technology is not effectively integrated with the concepts of constructivism.

Nevertheless, constructivistic methods of instruction with using computer technology have developed to meet the instructional goals and conditions. One of the most powerful and versatile tools is the web-based learning. The web-based learning provides learners with optimal learning environment. They can be exposed to the multiple perspectives through collaborative social negotiation within peers or teachers. Additionally, in spite of PC games which originally have not been developed for instructional purposes, even in games such as games for virtual flight simulation or city planning simulation, learners can be exposed to the complex or probable environments. In order to improve the problem-solving skills, it is important for learners to be exposed to complex environments. Constructivism might be broad learning theory because it is synthesized with multiple theories into a single form. Thus it is evident that the method of instruction using technology can be applied with various approaches.

Constructivist theory's (J. Bruner) main theme is that learning is a process in which the learner is able to build on present and previous information. The student is able to take information, create ideas and make choices by utilizing a thought process. The trainer should encourage the student to develop the skills to find out principles on their own. There should be on-going dialog between the student and the trainer. The trainer is responsible for making sure the information is in a format the student can comprehend. The key is to assure the course builds on what has already been learned.

Constructivists think that learners build knowledge actively through the interactions with environmental stimuli. In other words, learning focuses on the learners' questions and exposure. Assessment should avoid standardized tests and grades such as achievement tests designed with multiple choices to test subject-specific knowledge. Assessment appears in the learning process, so students play an important role in examining their own progress.

POST-MODERN THEORIES

Postmodernism, by the nature of the movement itself, is not easy to define. To understand postmodernism in the context of adult learning, it may be beneficial to first understand that the postmodern movement is much larger than adult learning. It is inclusive of a wide variety of disciplines and areas of study including art, architecture, music, film, literature, sociology, communications, fashion, technology, and education. Because postmodernism is as much a philosophical movement as it is a learning theory, it is impossible to discuss the movement without also discussing the underlying philosophy and ubiquity of the postmodern movement.

Post-modernism differs from most approaches to learning in two fundamental ways. The first is that rationality and logic are not important to attaining knowledge. The second is that knowledge can be contradictory. Because of the contextual nature of knowledge, individuals can hold two completely incongruent views of one subject at the same time.

Post-modernism relates to post-industrialism. The industrial era came about as a result of Newtonian thinking – an era wherein thought and processes were considered in mechanistic terms of efficiency and effectiveness and understood scientifically through the processes of reductionism (the simplification of the complex into understandable, and at times oversimplistic terms). The learning gleaned from the industrial (modern) era laid a foundation for the world to add new knowledge through a new era - what is now termed as the "post-modern" era. Presently, several post-modern theories exist, but at the core of each of these theories is the basic concept that what was once only understood within the context of reductionism is now beginning to be understood within the context of interrelatedness - an understanding that "things are much more diverse, fluid, illusionary, and contested, including the reality of the world itself" than originally thought.

Though truth is central to postmodern thinking, it is not the search for truth that is valued. In contrast, the postmodern mind challenges what is accepted truth. According to Astley (1985) and Gergen (1992), as cited in Dierkes et. al. (2003), postmodernists challenge "the conventional wisdom, routines, static meanings, and axioms of 'normal' science, thereby exposing knowledge to non-dogmatic forms of thought". One can see how this philosophy has become embraced in academia and one could argue that it is the primary modus operandi in many institutions of higher learning, especially in philosophy and the humanities.

The postmodern approach to learning is founded upon the assertion that there is not one kind of learner, not one particular goal for learning, not one way in which learning takes place, nor one particular environment where learning occurs.

Kilgore (2001) makes several assertions about the postmodern view of knowledge:

1. Knowledge is tentative, fragmented, multifaceted and not necessarily rational.
2. Knowledge is socially constructed and takes form in the eyes of the knower.
3. Knowledge is contextual rather than "out there" waiting to be discovered.

Hence, knowledge can shift as quickly as the context shifts, the perspective of the knower shifts, or as events overtake us.

The label of postmodernism defines a shift in culture that occurs over time. This can be understood best through defining causality, an understanding of cultural shifts, and collecting the basic overall concept of postmodernism.

DEFINING CAUSALITY (WHAT CAUSES SHIFTS)

Ultimately, shifts occur through modes of communication. The largest shift in the past century is the development of a global community through the use of internet. Past shifts in society have also connected to modes of communication. Technology shifts like Guttenberg and his creation of the printing press gave the power of books into the hands of the common people. This empowerment of information started a shift in society that affected the world.

CULTURAL SHIFTS (HOW IT OCCURS)

Cultural shifts happen in waves. Postmodernism as a cultural shift began its shift as early as the 1930s and 1940s in conversations about postmodernism and architecture. Over time the concepts and ideas that are on the fringe of society will affect conversations, artistic pieces, and eventually become pervasive on a large enough scale to affect the whole of a society.

THE CURRENT DEBATE (THE BASIC DEFINITIONS OF POMO)

In postmodernism everything is relative and is deconstructive. The division of the term "postmodernism" breaks down into two major parts, post and modernism. Post is built philosophically on thoughts from multiple arenas, and varied sources, who use deconstructionism as a modus-operandi. The idea of postmodernism is not to know what you are not, but to not really know what you are. What postmodernism is not is modernism. It is an after effect of the modernistic era that capitalized on individuality, built on absolutes, and the scientific method as its structure. Postmodernism in its current form is still developing and is not completed. Leonard Sweet and other futurists say this wave will be complete somewhere in the range of 2020, shifting the society from modernism into what it will become. All that may be understood at this stage is what the society on the fringes is saying we are not, which is modernism.

Deconstruction is a powerful postmodern tool for questioning prevailing representations of learners and learning. According to Kilgore (2001), the purpose of deconstruction is to identify and discredit the false binaries that structure a communication or "discourse";that is, to challenge the assertions of what is to be included or excluded as normal, right, or good. In postmodernism there are no universal norms or "truth" on which to judge the validity of any message of knowledge;rather the postmodernist works towards a continuous construction of truth as multiple alternatives are included in the body of known information.

Sometimes it is easier to understand what a concept is by comparing it with what it is not. For example, according to Boje and Prieto (2000), when comparing modern to postmodern principles in the area of leading, Theory X or Y is modern while servant leadership is postmodern. Centralized leading is to modern as decentralized, wide spans, and few layers is to postmodern. Modernism is boss centered while postmodern is people centered. White male career track reflects modernism and tracks for women and minorities looks like postmodernism. Comparison of the theories indicates that servant leadership can indeed be considered a postmodern theory.

Merriam and Caffarella (1999) contend that "The self in post modern thought is not the unified, integrated, authentic self of modern times. Rather, the self is multiple, ever changing, and some say fragmented". Postmodern thinking has moved individuals to consider a new reference for self-identification.

A life that was once in order based on societal norms is now in a state of constant flux as societal norms have shifted dramatically in recent decades. The "Leave it to Beaver" lifestyle is a faded memory. This causes educational institutions and adult learners to shift education and teaching towards a more non-traditional forms.

Postmodernism accepts a worldview that what is real is what one observes, believes, or experiences. For example, anthropologists see that ... "the relation between part and whole has been made problematic"... because "the conception of the whole is a construct of the observer .... Hence, what is real is what one observes occurring around them and gives definition and reality to a situation.

Postmodernism calls into question many of the assumptions once accepted by modernists. "From the postmodern point-of-view, modernism is defined by its belief in objective knowledge". "Postmodernism ... argues that what we call knowledge is a special kind of story, a text or discourse that puts together words and images in ways that seem pleasing or useful to a particular culture. ... It denies that we can have objective knowledge, because what we call knowledge has to be made with the linguistic and other meaning-making resources of a particular culture, and different cultures can see the world in very different ways, all of which "work" in their own terms. It argues that the belief that one particular culture's view of the world is also universally "true" was a politically convenient assumption for Europe's imperial ambitions of the past, but has no firm intellectual basis" (Lemke).

So what about the age-old questions about truth and knowledge? Postmodernists might say, "Truth is what people agree on," or "Truth is what works," or "Hey, there is no Truth, only lots of little 'truths' running around out there!" Postmodernists tend to reject the idealized view of Truth inherited from the ancients and replace it with a dynamic, changing truth bounded by time, space, and perspective. Rather than seeking for the unchanging ideal, postmodernists tend to celebrate the dynamic diversity of life.

One can see that even once firm historical events, verified through empirical verification, are no longer viewed as an objective truth, but became the object of one's understanding of the historical perspective out of their interpretation and story. Lemke quotes Foucault who "said, in effect, that it was chimerical to imagine that historians could reconstruct a real past;historical discourse is a discourse of the present, serving present ends, making sense for us today out of the archeological traces of past human activity".

One of the significant difficulties organizations and individual relationships encounter is communication breakdowns when widely varied world views exist in the same discussion or dialogue. Lemke suggests that: "The phenomenological perspective does not need to be limited to conceptualizing how the world looks different to men and women;it can be used to examine how it looks different to the young and the middle-aged, to the novice and the expert, the student and the teacher, the ghetto child and the comfortable academic.

We each construct our own lifeworlds, and even when we are in the same room, trying to talk to one another, we may still be worlds apart". Kilgore (2001) points to the difficulties in communication that often misrepresent a message. The communication process is so convoluted that a message can be distorted in many ways. The construction of the message in the language used can be misinterpreted and misapplied by the learner. The cultural context of the communication can cause a lack of clarity or bias. The recipients of the knowledge are affected by other messages and experiences that result in many interpretations of the same information.

Postmodernism, in the context of an adult learning theory, invites contention in the attempt to discover the truth. Once considered a passing fad, postmodernism earned a strong following because of its motivation to draw upon multiple theories. In higher education, postmodernism encourages its followers to question every facet of the institution's structure and learning methods.

CASE STUDIES AND WORKPLACE EXAMPLES

The postmodern approach to learning offers the freedom from absolutes. There is no one good way to learn. In fact, there is not one good thing to learn. Learning takes place in the experience between the learner and the knowledge presented. Our current experience with all the do-it-yourself and information presenting, learning-based television shows illustrates this point. So many of us find ourselves watching a television show that informs us of a process or experience in which we will never participate or apply that knowledge. We will never overhaul a car, build a fountain in our backyard, travel to Peru to examine ancient ruins, or remodel our neighbour's house. The experience of interacting with the knowledge brings satisfaction in and of itself. What each of the viewers takes from the same show is inconsequential to most of the producers, the importance lies in interacting with and enjoying the content.

4

Physical Change in Adult Development

The life stage called early adulthooddefines individuals between the ages of 20 and 35, who are typically vibrant, active and healthy, and are focused on friendships, romance, child bearing and careers. Yet serious conditions, such as violent events, depression and eating disorders, can negatively impact young adults.

PHYSICAL CHANGES

Females reach their adult heights by age 18, and, except for some males who continue to grow in their early 20s, most have reached their adult heights by the age of 21. However, muscles continue to gain mass - especially among males, and both genders continue to add body fat. Average weight gain for both women and men is about 15 pounds.

Death rates due to disease are low in this life stage, but the rate of violence-related deaths is high. A 2005 report by the Centers for Disease Control and Prevention (CDC) National Violent Death Reporting System states that violent death is highest for people ages 20 to 24, and overall, men are more likely than women to die violently. Violent death includes homicide, suicide and motor-vehicle deaths. The CDC reports that of approximately 50,000 violent deaths in the United States each year, more than 56 per cent of those deaths are suicide, and 30 per cent are homicides.

Another area of concern for people in this age group is eating disorders, which include anorexia nervosa, bulimia nervosa, and binge-eating disorder. A study by the National Association of Anorexia Nervosa and Associated Disorders reported that 5 per cent to 10 per cent of individuals with anorexia die within 10 years after contracting the disease, and 18 per cent to 20 per cent die after 20 years.

COGNITIVE CHANGES

Debate among developmentalists center on whether or not to assign a formal cognitive stage to early adulthood. Earlier life stages result in dramatic and critical changes, whereas in early adulthood essential brain growth already has taken place, and individuals are now applying and using their knowledge, and analytical capabilities.

However many researchers point to continued changes, such as those taking place in the frontal lobes of the cerebral cortex of the brain, which are areas where judgement, planning, speaking, and moving muscles are localized. Brain growth in this area only reaches final development in the early 20s.

Additionally, many theorists, such as Jean Piaget (1896-1980) noted a significant difference between adult and adolescent thinking. Adults have more flexibility in their thought patterns, understanding that there are multiple opinions on issues, and that there is more than one way to approach a problem.

Young adults are able to assimilate and synthesize complex and contradictory situations and arguments, and unlike adolescents, aren't set on finding absolute truths. They are focused on developing their careers and achieving independence from their families - a crucial requirement for balanced, well functioning adults.

EMOTIONAL CHANGES

Theorist Erik Erikson (1902-1994) maintained that individuals develop in psychosocial stages, and that early adulthood marks the time when individuals seek to form intimate relationships. And Sigmund Freud (1856-1939) argued that a healthy adult is one who can "love and work." Simply stated, this developmental stage is characterized by relationships and work.

Intimacy can be actualized through close friendships, romantic relationships, starting a family, or all three. Erickson argued that a firm sense of identity, gained in earlier developmental stages, was integral to entering intimate relationships, and research has supported this argument. Studies repeatedly find that those lacking a strong sense of identity have less satisfactory relationships, and they tend to be more emotionally isolated, lonely and depressed.

And depression is a major concern for individuals in their 20s to mid-thirties: most people diagnosed with major depression receive a diagnosis in this life stage. Depression is linked to violence, especially suicide, and eating disorders.

The Eating Disorder Foundation asserts that "eating disorders are not just about food and weight. They are an attempt to use food intake and weight control to manage emotional conflicts that actually have little or nothing to do with food or weight." The Foundation reports that eating disorders affect more women than men, about 10 million U.S. women, but the rates in men are rising. Approximately 1 million U.S. men suffer from an eating disorder, a number that has doubled in the last ten years.

And episodes of mild or severe depression in earlier developmental stages should not be minimized.

Developmental psychology professionals are often involved in designing programmes that enhance social problem-solving and coping skills, and skills dealing with stressful life events. They work to develop programmes designed to help adults with a host of issues, including eating disorders, depression, and other conditions that affect daily living. They also research and study intimacy issues, and develop programmes that help individuals find rewarding and suitable careers.

PHYSICAL DEVELOPMENT DURING ADULTHOOD

Fig. Physical activity is important to stay healthy in adulthood.

Much of your body is already fully developed even before you reach adulthood. According to Medline Plus, men's genitals are fully developed by 16 to 17 years old. Although you might reach maturity in many areas before adulthood, there are still changes and declines that take place, especially between 35 to 60 years old during middle adulthood.

APPEARANCE

You will reach your full height by the time you are in your mid-20s. As you progress through adulthood, you might notice that your skin becomes thinner and loses elasticity;wounds take longer to heal, and you start to get wrinkles. To protect your skin and its appearance, wear sunscreen that is at least 30 SPF, even in winter. Your hair might start to turn gray. You are most likely to get gray hair around the same time that your parents did.

HEALTH

As you age, substances such as alcohol will stay in your system longer. You are also at an increased risk for heart disease and high blood pressure. To stay healthy, the World Health Organization recommends doing 30 minutes of moderate activity at least five days a week. This helps prevent heart disease, osteoarthritis and hypertension as well as improving balance and coordination.

HEARING AND VISION

Your vision and hearing might start to decline during middle adulthood. According to Minnesota State University, you might experience a small decline in hearing during early to middle adulthood. Hearing decline is most noticeable in your mid-40s. You also might have less focus and lose near vision, causing you to need more light for tasks such as reading.

FERTILITY

Somewhere in middle adulthood, women will experience menopause. In menopause, hormonal changes cause a stop in menstruation and ovulation, completely reducing fertility and making it impossible to bear children. Men have reduced fertility because of a lower sperm count and a decline in testosterone levels, but they still can produce children until the mid-70s.

ABILITIES

Minnesota State University says you might experience a decline in physical performance around 30. Inactivity can cause you to lose muscle mass and flexibility. You can increase your physical performance and muscle mass by exercising regularly, especially with weight-bearing exercises such as lifting.

SEXUALITY AND PHYSICAL CHANGES WITH AGING

Sex and sexuality communicate a great deal: affection, love, esteem, warmth, sharing, and bonding. These gifts are as much the right of older adults as they are of those who are much younger. Three aspects of sexuality are covered in this topic: the changes that come with aging, suggestions on how to adjust to these changes, and information about sexually transmitted infections.

In most healthy adults, pleasure and interest in sex do not diminish with age. Age alone is no reason to change the sexual practices that you have enjoyed throughout your life. But you may have to make a few minor adjustments to accommodate any physical limitations you may have or the effects of certain illnesses or medicines.

SEXUALITY AND PHYSICAL CHANGES WITH AGING

Common Physical Changes in Men

Most physical changes are the result of gradually decreasing testosterone levels. These changes affect energy, strength, muscle and fat mass, bone density, and sexual function.

- A man's sexual response begins to slow down after age 50. But a man's sexual drive is more likely to be affected by his health and his attitude about sex and intimacy than by his age.
- It may take longer for a man to get an erection, and more time needs to pass between erections.
- Erections will be less firm. But a man who has good blood flow to his penis will be able to have erections that are firm enough for sexual intercourse throughout his entire life.
- Older men are able to delay ejaculation for a longer time.

COMMON PHYSICAL CHANGES IN WOMEN

Most physical changes take place after menopause and are the result of decreased estrogen levels. These changes can be altered if a woman is takinghormone therapy.

- It may take longer for a woman to become sexually excited.
- The walls of the vagina become thinner and drier and are more easily irritated during sexual intercourse.
- Orgasms may be somewhat shorter than they used to be, and the contractions experienced during orgasm can be less intense.

Not all women experience these problems. Those who do can experiment to find ways to enjoy sex despite these physical changes.

CULTURAL AND PSYCHOLOGICAL FACTORS

In addition to physical changes, there are cultural and psychological factors that affect sexuality in later years. For example, in our culture, sexuality is equated with youthful looks and youthful vigour.

Too many people seem to think that as a person ages, he or she becomes less desirable and less of a sexual being. Older adults may accept this stereotype and buy into the notion that they are not permitted or expected to be sexual.

Joy in sex and loving knows no age barriers. Almost everyone has the capacity to find lifelong pleasure in sex. To believe in the myth that older people have no interest in sex is to miss out on wonderful possibilities.

Being single through choice, divorce, or widowhood can present a problem also. As you get older, you may not have as many people in your age group to choose from for partners. Women and men who are single may not know how to deal with their sexual feelings. Generally speaking, it is better to express your desires than to suppress them until you are no longer aware that they exist.

Physical and emotional needs change with time and circumstance. Intimacy and sexuality may or may not be important to you. The issue here is one of choice. If you freely decide that sex is no longer right for you, then that is the correct decision. It is possible to live a fulfilling life without sex. But if you choose to continue enjoying your sexuality, you deserve support and encouragement. You may still find uncharted sensual territories to explore.

STAYING SEXUAL

Just as exercise is the key to maintaining fitness and health, having sex on a regular basis is the best way to maintain sexual capacity.

And just as it's never too late to start an exercise programme, it's never too late to start having sex. Many older people who have been celibate for years develop satisfying sexual practices within new loving relationships. For others, self-stimulation (masturbation) is common and poses no health risks or side effects.

You may have sexual changes as you get older. But some changes may be the first sign of a medical problem. So talk with your doctor about any changes that concern you. He or she may be able to recommend treatments that will help you.

Here are some other considerations:

- To enhance sexual response, use more foreplay and direct contact with sexual organs.
- The mind is an erogenous zone. Fantasy and imagination help arouse some people. Try setting the mood with candlelight and soft music, or whatever else "turns you on."
- Many medicines, especially high blood pressure medicines, tranquilizers, and some heart medicines, inhibit sexual response. Ask your doctor about these side effects. Your doctor may be able to reduce your dosage or prescribe different medicines. Do not stop taking prescription medicines without talking with your doctor first.
- Colostomies, mastectomies, and other procedures that involve changes in physical appearance need not put an end to sexual pleasure. Communicating openly about your fears and expectations can bring you and your partner closer together and help you overcome barriers. If needed, a little counselling for both of you can help you adjust.
- People who have heart conditions can enjoy full, satisfying sex lives.

Most doctors recommend that you abstain from sex for only a brief time following a heart attack. If you have angina, ask your doctor about taking nitroglycerin before you have sex. Do not take Viagra if you are using nitroglycerin.

- If arthritis keeps you from enjoying sex, experiment with different positions. Try placing cushions under your hips. Also try home treatment for arthritis pain.
- Use a water-based vaginal lubricant, such as Astroglide or K-Y Jelly, to reduce vaginal dryness or irritation. Do not use petroleum jelly. A doctor can also prescribe a vaginal cream containing estrogen, which will help reverse the changes in the vaginal tissues.
- Drink alcohol only in moderation. Small amounts of alcohol may heighten your sexual responsiveness by squelching your inhibitions. Larger amounts of alcohol may actually decrease your sexual performance.
- Prescription medicines that can enhance the sexual response are available. Some people find that herbs such as ginkgo biloba and ginseng enhance their sexual function. Both prescription drugs and herbal remedies carry the risk of side effects. Always talk to your doctor before you use any new medicines or natural health products.

OTHER ASPECTS OF SEXUALITY

Sexuality goes far beyond the physical act itself. It is part of who we are. It involves our needs for touch, affection, and intimacy.

Touch

Touch is a wonderful and needed sensation. Babies who are not touched do not thrive. Children who are not touched develop emotional problems. Touch is important to older adults as well. Touch helps us feel connected with others and enhances our sexuality.

- Get a massage. Professional massages are wonderful, but simple shoulder and neck rubs feel great, too. Find a friend who will trade shoulder rubs with you.
- Look for hugs. Everybody needs them. Some people are a little shy about hugs, but it's okay to ask, "Would you like a hug?"
- Consider getting a pet. Caring for a pet can help meet your needs for touch. Some studies have shown that older people who have pets to care for live longer.

Affection

To give and receive affection is a wonderful feeling. If you like someone, be sure to let them know. If someone seems to like you, appreciate it. It is never too late to make new friends and strengthen bonds with longtime companions.

Intimacy

Intimacy is the capacity for a close physical or emotional connection with another person. Intimacy is a great protector against depression.

Talking with a confidant can help ease life's problems. When you lose a loved one, intimacy may be what you miss most. You may not find someone to fully replace a loved one who died, but you can begin to rebuild intimacy in your life in the following ways:

- Turn to your children, siblings, or old and new friends.
- Look for another person who is in the same situation as you are. One of the richest benefits of support groups is that members often find intimacy with one another.
- Be available to others. Just as you need people, there are people who need you, too.

SEXUALLY TRANSMITTED INFECTIONS

Sexually transmitted infections—also known as STIs or venereal diseases—are infections passed from person to person through sexual intercourse, genital contact, or contact with semen, vaginal fluids, or blood. Older people may think of STIs as a problem that affects only young people. But because of physical changes related to age, older adults who are exposed to STIs may be more likely than young people to get STIs.

As you age, your immune system is not as strong, so it's harder to fight off disease. And women who are past menopause have thinner vaginal walls and less vaginal moisture than they did before menopause. Using a lubricant, such as K-Y Jelly, may keep you from getting a sore or a tiny cut on your penis or inside your vagina. This can reduce your risk of getting STIs or HIV. Practice safer sex. For older adults, this means always using condoms and lubricants until you are in a monogamous relationship and know your partner's sexual history and HIV status.

AGING AND PHYSICAL ACTIVITY

Sedentary lifestyles are becoming increasingly common at any age. Aging leads to lower activity levels and a further narrowing of physical activity options. Data from the Behavioural Risk Factor Survey showed that more than 40per cent of U.S. women aged 65 and older reported no leisure time activity in 1992. Recent cross-sectional data from the Aerobics Center Longitudinal Study showed that older adults expended significantly less energy on exercise than did younger adults. In the Zutphen Elderly Study of elderly men, mean time spent on physical activity other than walking decreased by 28 minutes/day during 10 years of follow-up. Walking was the most common physical activity reported by adults . Older adults in the United States were more likely to report lower-intensity activities such as walking, gardening, or golf, rather than running, aerobics, or team sports. Although the time spent on bicycling and gardening showed a significant drop with age in the Zutphen cohort, the time spent on walking was not affected.

Significant disparities in activity levels by sex and ethnicity were also noted. Reported levels of leisure-time physical activity were lowest for minority respondents and for older women. Data from the Coronary Artery Risk Development in Young Adults study showed that important ethnic differences in physical activity patterns remained even after adjustments were made for important demographic factors such as education or income. Significantly, unfavorable perceptions of one's own health were associated with lower participation in a cardiac rehabilitation programme. In contrast, perceived enjoyment and satisfaction were positive predictors of physical activity in men and women of all ages. These data suggest that psychosocial rather than biomedical variables may influence continued participation in exercise programmes.

The recommendation that every American accumulate at least 30 minutes of exercise on most—and preferably all—days is based on evidence that even moderate physical activity is associated with a substantial drop in all-cause mortality. Although there is evidence that current activity is more protective than past activity, cumulative lifetime activity pattern may be the most influential factor of all.

The question remains as to whether a sustained active lifestyle can delay the age-associated changes in body composition and decline in lean body mass. Studies of physical activity and aging, including some outlined in this volume, suggest that fat-free mass and body composition of active elderly subjects are not very different from those of inactive elderly subjects. In contrast to younger subjects, the effect of exercise programmes on total activity of elderly subjects was minimal because elderly subjects compensated for exercise training by reducing their spontaneous physical activity. However, exercise training did have a positive effect on muscle function and may have contributed to the activities of daily living.

Continuing to function without assistance may be the most salient outcome variable. Some 7 million Americans over age 65 depend on others for help with some basic task of daily living. According to NHANES III data, 23per cent of people 80 years and older were unable to prepare their own meals and 17per cent were unable to walk. The Activities of Daily Living score includes capacity for daily self-care as well as other functions related to cooking, eating, and access to food. Such activities are essential for ensuring independent living and contribute importantly to overall quality of life.

Physical activities that improve muscular strength, endurance, and flexibility also improve ability to perform the tasks of daily living. For example, strength training can result in substantial improvements in muscle size and strength in elderly men and women and can also increase resting metabolic rate, resulting in increased energy requirements. In addition, strength training improves balance and gait speed in very old and frail nursing home residents, improves bone health, and decreases many of the risk factors for an osteoporotic fracture. Exercise programmes for elderly adults can delay the age-induced impairment in personal mobility necessary for the performance of routine activities.

PHYSICAL AND COGNITIVE DEVELOPMENT IN EARLY ADULTHOOD

Physical development changes as the growth period of youth is over.

BIOLOGICAL AGING BEGINS IN EARLY ADULTHOOD

- Biological aging (senescence) is genetically influenced declines in the functioning of organs and systems that are universal in all people. Aging is asynchronous, in that some organ systems age faster than others. Individual differences are great at this point, cue to genetics, lifestyle, stress, and cultural period. Life expectancy has grown over that past 100 years, adding 30 years overall in industrialized countries. It was thought that the body wore out from hard use: the "wear-and-tear" theory of aging. It's not so simple.
- Aging at the level of DNA and body cells
  - Two types of aging
  - Those that emphasize the programmed effects of specific genes: this is seen in kinship studies, indicating that rates of aging are specific to families. Telomeres are a special type of DNA located at the ends of chromosomes. They shorten with each replication of cells. We have a lifespan of 50 divisions + 10. Once the telomeres are shortened too much, there is no more ability to reproduce.
  - Those that emphasize the cumulative effects of random events: suggest that DNA is gradually damaged due to changes in DNA- they can be caused by internal or external events. Random mutations accumulate and cell repair becomes less efficient, or cancerous cells develop.
- Free radicals are one cause of cellular abnormalities. These are naturally occurring, highly reactive chemicals that form in the presence of oxygen. When oxygen molecules break down within the cell, the reaction takes away an electron and creates a free radical. It

destroys nearby cellular material to replace that electron. Free radicals are related to 60 disorders of aging: heart disease, cancer, cataracts, arthritis. This damage builds up over time. Anti-oxidants, Vitamin C, E, and beta carotene can limit this damage.

- Radiation and pollutants also trigger cellular breakdowns.
- Aging at the level of organs and tissues
  - Cross-linkage theory of aging says that over time, protein fibres that make up the body's connective tissue form bonds, or links, with one another. When these normally separate fibres cross-link, tissue becomes less elastic, leading to negative outcomes such as loss of flexibility, clouding the lens of the eye, clogging arteries, kidney damage.
  - Loss of hormones, as the endocrine system gradually fails also contributes to aging. Menopause affects many bodily functions. A drop in growth hormone leads to loss of muscle and bone mass, additional fat, thinning of the skin, and decline in cardiovascular function. Hormone therapy can reduce this loss, but side effects include risk of cancer. Diet and physical exercise can slow some of these losses.
  - Declines in immune system function lead to susceptibility to infections, risks of cancer, changes in blood vessel walls.

Physical Changes

Cardiovascular and respiratory systems:

- Hypertension is high blood pressure, and it occurs 12per cent more often in African Americans than in white population. Death rate due to heart disease is 25per cent higher in African Americans. The heart muscle becomes more rigid and there is a decrease in maximum heart rate. Symptoms show up during strenuous exercise, as the heart doesn't bounce back from strain.
- Atherosclerosis is the CVD in which heavy deposits of plaque with cholesterol and fats collect on the walls of main arteries. The process begins early in life, progresses in middle adulthood, and leads to serious heart disease and disability. Sex hormones seem to intensify the effects of a high-fat diet, so we aren't at much risk before puberty. Heart disease has declined as people are smoking less and becoming aware of their diet. There is better medical detection and treatment now, too. Young and middle aged people with low risk factors (don't smoke, low cholesterol, normal blood pressure) have 40 60per cent lower death rates.
- Lung performance declines 10per cent per decade after age 25, due to stiffening of the tissue.

Motor performance is affected by declines in heart and lung function as well as gradual muscle loss. Athletic skill with training peaks between 20 and 30 and then declines. Endurance sports peak a bit later- late 20s and 30s. With continued practice, running performance maintains into the 60s.

Immune system mobilizes when the body is attacked by antigens, foreign substances in the body. T cells come from the bone marrow and mature in the thymus (gland in upper chest) and attack antigens directly. They come in a large variety, since the receptors on their surfaces only recognize a single antigen. B cells come from the bone marrow, to secrete antibodies into the bloodstream that multiply, capture antigens, and allow the blood system to destroy them. The capacity of the immune system declines after age 20. The thymus shrinks steadily as we age. So it is less able to differentiate T cells. B cells depend on T cells, so the immune response is multiply compromised. Stress or depression can weaken the immune response, as the immune system interacts with the nervous and endocrine system.

Reproductive capacity is ideal in early twenties for producing healthy babies, but in our culture more women are delaying childbirth into the 30s. Reproductive capacity declines with age. Fertility problems increase dramatically in mid-30s, showing as many as 26per cent of women having fertility problems. The ova seem to deteriorate with age, and as the numbers of ova decline, fertility drops. Age also affects sperm, as sperm concentration decreases after age 40. Reproductive technologies (IVF, donor insemination) can help, but success drops with age.

Health and fitness varies with SES, as the economically advantaged and well-educated tend to hold good health over most of their adult lives, and the health of lower-income people with less education steadily declines. This relates to several things: stressful life events, crowding, pollution, diet, exercise, substance abuse, supportive social relationships, and affordable health care.

- Nutrition in the US has suffered as high-fat, high-calorie foods are more available, and fast-paced lifestyles have led to less exercise.
  - Overweight and obesity- 20per cent of Americans are obese. It is higher among low-SES ethnic minorities (24per cent Hispanic adults, 30per cent African Americans, 50per cent Native-Americans) Gender factors in: 5-7per cent more women are obese than men (ironic, since women are more weight-conscious). Overweight affects another 41per cent of Americans. Americans are the heaviest people in the world. Obesity rates rise steadily from 25 to 60.
  - The obesity epidemic- the rise in obesity began in the late 1980s, until today 61per cent of Americans have a weight problem. Why?
- Changing food environment and lifestyle
  - Availability of cheap fat and sugar – high-fructose corn syrup is

6X as sweet as table sugar and so is cheaper to use in manufacturing. Also palm oil from Malaysia is cheaper and tastier than other vegetable oils but it is highly saturated. Putting these products in fast food made them cheaper and more calorie-dense.

- Portion supersizing has attracted more customers to fast food chains, at the expense of health. The calories in McDonald's fries rose from 320 in 1970s to 610 today. And adults are more likely to clean their plates!
- Increasingly busy lives once women entered the labour force, the day of the home-cooked meal declined. As the economy faltered, adults worked more hours and days, and eating out increased, as did other convenience foods. Snack foods increased, too. Dietary fat increased from 19 to 38per cent!
- Declining rates of physical activity were seen due to sedentary jobs, and more time spent at the job, TV as the primary leisure activity.
- Misguided information about healthy weight, exercise and diet lulled the American people to sleep around this issue.

• Combating the obesity epidemic is a national concern, since obesity is responsible for $100 billion in health costs. Social efforts are needed to turn this around:
  - Government funding to support public education
  - Priorities on parks and rec centers in low-income neighbourhoods
  - Laws that mandate posting calorie, sugar and fat contents of foods sold
  - Special tax on foods high in calories, sugar, or fat
  - Incentives to schools/ workplaces for healthy eating and daily exercise, weight management programmes
  - Causes include declining Basal metabolic rate (BMR) which is the amount of energy the body needs at complete rest. This declines as numbers of active muscle cells drop (which happens with an increasingly sedentary lifestyle.) Excess weight is associated with many health problems: high blood pressure, circulation problems, atherosclerosis, stroke, diabetes, live and gallbladder disease, arthritis, sleep and digestive disorders, cancer, early death. This doesn't even include the stigmatization of the illness. Obese people are less likely to find mates, to be rented apartments, to get financial aid for college, to be offered jobs. 40per cent of Americans say they are trying to lose weight. Many of those are in the normal range, but the focus on thinness creates unrealistic expectations about desirable weight. There can develop unrealistic anxiety about one's body if reality isn't figured in.

  - Treatment should begin in early adulthood, but lifestyle changes are hard to maintain, as 95per cent of people who start a weight programme return to their original weight within 5 years. These things effect long-term change:
- Well-balanced diet low in fat, plus exercise
- Keeping a record of what is eaten
- Social support
- Teaching problem-solving skills to deal with temptations and frustration
- Extended intervention
  - Dietary fat – 60per cent of Americans eat too much fat in their diets. It should make up no more than 30per cent of total calories. Fat consumption may have a role in breast cancer or colon cancer. Fat builds up through cholesterol into plaque on arterial walls. It is especially a factor in African Americans incidence of heart disease. Exercise can create chemical byproducts that help eliminate cholesterol.
  - Saturated fat generally comes from meat and dairy products, and is solid at room temperature. This is related to CVD.
  - Unsaturated fat comes in the form of vegetable oils.
- Exercise- 20-30 minutes of vigorous aerobic exercise can protect against obesity, enhance the immune system, and aid in mental outlook. Only 15-20per cent of Americans exercise at this level. 30per cent are not active at all. This is more of a problem for women and low-SES adults. Exercise reduces body fat and builds muscle, which requires more calories to sustain, so it is good for many reasons. It links to reduced cancer, prevents diabetes, reduces CVD, and increases resistance to stress. It reduces anxiety, depression, improves mood, enhances alertness and energy. As outlook improves, it enhances immune function.
- Substance abuse puts people at risk as it increases risk of accident, affects cardiac function, liver function, and increases the natural deterioration of aging.
  - Cigarette smoking is a problem for 25per cent of Americans but that has declined from 40per cent in 1965. Even so the decline is mostly with college-educated people. Blue-collar people still smoke at high rates. Most smokers started before age 21, showing how vulnerable teens are in choosing habits that have lifetime consequences. Smoking causes less oxygenation to tissues, and makes the heart rate and blood pressure rise. Long-term effects are reduced night vision, rapid wrinkling of the skin, loss of bone, lower sperm count, higher rates of impotence in

men. Later effects are higher risk of heart attack, stroke, cancer of the mouth, throat, larynx, esophagus, lungs, pancreas, kidneys, and bladder. Smoking is the most preventable cause of death in industrialized nations. This is dose-related, as more cigarettes smoked, greater the chance of premature death. Quitting has fast effects on health- as risks return to original levels within 3-8 years after quitting. Like overeating, however, the recidivism rate after quitting is high- 70-80per cent return to smoking within one year.

- Alcohol is a problem for 13per cent of men and 3per cent of women in the US. One third of heavy drinkers are alcoholics- people who cannot limit their alcohol use. Men show signs as early as the teens and early 20s. 80per cent are also heavy smokers, increasing their health risks enormously. There is a genetic connection with alcohol use, but it doesn't condemn a person to drink. And as many of 50per cent of hospitalized alcoholics do not have a family history. Risk is higher for certain ethnic groups, however, particularly for Native Americans, as well as those in poverty. Alcohol acts as a depressant, impairing the judgement of the brain. It initially reduces anxiety, so it is used as a social lubricant, but as it wears off it produces anxiety, leading to drinking to relieve symptoms of withdrawal. Consequences include liver disease, CVD, pancreatic inflammation, GI tract irritation, bone marrow problems, some cancers. Later is causes brain damage, leading to dementia, confusion, apathy, impaired memory. 40per cent of highway fatalities involve drinkers who are drinking and driving. Half of convicted felons are alcoholics. Alcohol is related to date rape and domestic violence. The best treatments include family and personal counseling, group support, and aversion therapy. AA is a powerful support in the community once a person leaves hospital environment. 50per cent of alcoholics in recover relapse within a few months.

- Sexuality is actively explored in the young adult years, although most people have had sex within their teen years.
  - Heterosexual attitudes and behaviour has changed a lot in the past generation as people are more casually sexual than in the past. The media promotes the idea that people are more sexually active than in the past, but often young people find that their first sexual experiences aren't all that the movie images portray. Partners tend to be similar in age, education, ethnicity, and religion. Most people meet through workplace, families or friends, not through ads or at bars. People do have more partners, as 1/3

of adults over age 50 have had 5+ partners, and ½ of people age 30-50 have had that many partners. There tends to be a sort of serial monogamy, though. Most college students say they do want to settle down with one exclusive partner. Americans aren't having sex as often as one would think, either. One third of 18- to 59-year olds say they have sex twice a week, another third have sex a few times a month, and 1/3 have it a few times a year or not at all. What affects frequency is: age, cohabiting or married, how long the couple has been together. Sexual activity increases through the twenties, and declines in the 30s, often due to the demands of family and jobs. Most (80per cent) say they feel satisfied emotionally and physically, though. Satisfaction is greater for married people (88per cent) and it declines as numbers of partners increases! Sexual problems include lack of interest in sex and inability to achieve orgasm, and this is mainly a problem for women. For men the problems are climaxing too early, and anxiety about performance. A past with abuse or poor sexual experiences links to sexual dysfunctions.

- Sex differences in attitudes towards sexuality relate to evolutionary dynamics- the urge to continue the species relates to how we display our sexuality. Sperm are plentiful and ova are less numerous, so women tend to be picky about finding a partner who will support her with resources and commitment while she takes care of babies. We also model the behaviours we have seen in our parents and other adults as we grew up. There is still more stigma attached to women having numerous partners than men, who actually get admiration for their sexual success. Men do expect more sexual pleasure and offer less commitment than most women want. Adultery is viewed differently by men and women, too. Men are more upset by a partner's sexual activity, and women are more upset by their partner's emotional connection to another woman. Men and women come closer to the mean as they age, however. Pubertal hormones are powerful motivators.
- Homosexual attitudes and behaviour are changing as concerns about health care and AIDS are prevalent in this group. Attitudes have become more accepting as gay images are seen more commonly in the media. Men are more negative towards homosexuals than women, as homophobia is more common for men. 2.8per cent of men and 1.4per cent of females are homosexual or bisexual, but many do not identify themselves as such. Patterns for couples are similar as for heterosexuals: similar

demographics, greater sexual satisfaction in committed relationships, frequency of sex is not high. They are more likely to live in cities and college towns where attitudes are more accepting and likelihood of finding partners is higher. They tend to be well educated.

- Sexually transmitted disease is most common in adolescence, but is still prevalent in early adulthood as adults are exploring partners. It is more common in women, since transmission to women is easier than to men. AIDS is concentrated among gay men and IV drug users. So gay men have changed many sexual practices, such as limiting their number of partners and using condoms regularly. So rate of infection is declining, but AIDS is the fifth-leading cause of death among young adults. It is spreading fastest in impoverished areas, associated with poor health in general, poor education, high stress and hopelessness. Women are at high risk, as incidence in women has risen from 7per cent to 19per cent of cases of AIDS.
- Sexual coercion- 13per cent of women have endured rape, intercourse by force, threat, or due to lack of ability to give consent (unconscious, mental retardation). Nearly half have endured other forms of sexual aggression. Most (8/10) victims are under 30. Most of the time the perpetrators are known to the victims. This occurs to all SES, ethnic groups, walks of life. Characteristics of the perpetrator are more predictive of attack than any characteristics of the victim. These perpetrators: believe in traditional gender roles, approve of violence against women, accept rape myths (women really want it, it's romantic) Many of these men deny what they do is rape: 44per cent of college women say they have been coerced to have sex, but only 19per cent of men say they have gotten sex through force. Perpetrators view normal friendliness as sexual come-on, and resistance as desire. They deny their own responsibility, and say the woman brought it on herself, so he's not responsible. Cultures that strongly stereotype according to gender, and raise boys to be dominant, competitive, aggressive, and women to be submissive, cooperative, and passive, have greater incidences of rape. Social acceptance of violence figures in here, too. Greater exposure to pornography, particularly violent pornography relates to assault, since it desensitizes men to the pain they are causing the victim.
- Consequences of rape are similar to survivors of extreme trauma: shock, confusion, withdrawal, psychological numbing. This develops into disturbed sleep, depression, chronic fatigue, anxiety,

suicidal thoughts. If coercion is chronic, in the context of a relationship, the victim often feels at more risk if she tries to leave. This is a relevant fear, since the chances of a woman being murdered by her abusing partner increase 70per cent if she leaves. This is why domestic shelters' locations are kept secret. As many as half the victims are physically injured. Some get STDs, and 5per cent get pregnant. They may engage in unhealthy behaviours and addictions as a distraction from their internal pain.
  - Prevention and treatment require the victim to call out for help, and many feel that is a huge risk. But if they are seen in medical clinics for other things, sometimes the safety of the environment allows them to speak out. There are safe houses, legal aid, and economic support for the victims and their children. Therapy is essential for overcoming the long-term effects of rape or assault. Some social programmes that can help are:
- Routine screening for victimization
- Validation of the experience
- Safety planning
- Preventing sexual coercion
  - Reduce gender stereotyping and inequalities
  - Mandate treatment for men who assault women
  - Expand interventions for children who have witnessed violence between adults
  - Teach women to take precautions that lower the risk of sexual assault
  - Menstrual cycle is central to women's lives, with concurrent health concerns.
- Premenstrual syndrome (PMS) is an array of physical and psychological symptoms that appear 6-10 days before menstruation. These may include abdominal cramps, fluid retention, tender breasts, backache, headache, fatigues, irritability, depression. It may become a problem after age 20, and 40per cent of women have some form of it, although it is usually mild. 10per cent have severe enough symptoms to interfere with regular activities. It may have a genetic substrate. Treatments deal with the symptoms, but sometimes include antidepressants. This is still a controversial topic, as many feminists believe this issue has been overblown, used by women to avoid responsibility for their lives.
- Psychological stress involves adverse life events, daily hassles, environmental conditions that wear out one's coping skills at a certain point. There are clear effects on health from unmitigated stress. It involves the classic fight or flight response, with all the attendant

physiological responses: raised blood pressure, cardiovascular disease, impaired immune function, GI tract problems. Young adulthood is a time of great adaptation to new roles and jobs, so there is a lot of stress involved – even for happy events, such as weddings, and babies. Stress management is easier as adults shift into middle age, since greater life experience tends to put things into a more manageable perspective. Older adults also have a greater sense of personal control of their lives. Some things that can buffer stress are: social support, exercise, control of substances, learning coping skills.

- Fostering a healthy adult life
  - Engage in healthy eating
  - Maintain a reasonable body weight
  - Keep physically fit
  - Control alcohol intake, do not smoke
  - Engage in responsible sexual behaviour
  - Manage stress

COGNITIVE DEVELOPMENT

Changes in the Structure of Thought

- Postformal thought is cognitive development past Piaget's formal operational stage. Thinking becomes restructured in adulthood, as life is rarely as clear and emotionally manageable as one thinks it will be in adolescence.
- Perry's theory – after interviewing college students at the end of each year of college, Perry found that students gradually changed their thinking in the face of reality and adult responsibility.
  - Dualistic thinking is representative of younger students- dividing information, values, and authority into right and wrong, good and bad, we and they. Truth is compared to abstract standards, and authority figures are respected simply because of their authority base.
  - Relativistic thinking occurs as students age and become aware of the diversity of opinions on any topic. Now they see knowledge as embedded in a framework of thought. Now they recognize there is little absolute truth, but relative truths, based on context. Now thinking becomes more flexible, tolerant, and realistic.
  - This transition in thinking may be unique to people pursuing extended education, with all the diversity that they face in that environment. The underlying theme is adaptive cognition- thought that is less constrained by the need to find one answer to a question and it more responsive to context.

- Schaie's theory regards the goals of mental activity- the shift from acquiring knowledge to using it.
  - Acquisitive stage (childhood and adolescence) is the time when people are acquiring knowledge. They develop enhanced processing abilities, strategies for use of information, and ways to combine and integrate it.
  - Achieving stage (early adulthood) is when people adapt their cognitive skills to particular situations: job, marriage, childbearing, that affect long-term goals. Now they are applying knowledge to real life problems. These are problems that don't have a single right solution. How a person negotiates getting his/her needs met, and cooperates with others sets a trajectory for the remaining life course.
  - Responsibility stage (middle adulthood) develops as adults expand their responsibilities to others- mentoring at work, raising children, taking care of elderly parents. Now reasoning has to do with social obligations, setting boundaries, knowing when and how to let go of circumstances that one can't change.
  - Executive stage is the most advanced of this type of thinking- it characterizes people whose responsibilities have become very complex. Job responsibilities affect others, require monitoring of others' progress in the context of the business mission. So it requires that they understand the dynamics of the institutional structure, incoming information, goals, and personal needs of employees, or family members.
  - Reintegrative stage (late adulthood) involves people at retirement, re-examining and reintegrating their interests and values to produce a satisfying quality of life. No longer do they have to consider decisions in terms of consequences to assessing what they want and whether their life has offered them meaning. They become selective about how they spend time and who they spend it with. Each choice holds weight.
- Labouvie-Vief's theory involves the transition from adolescent perception of all the possibilities to adult perception of the practical and realistic.
  - Pragmatic thought is a structural advance in which logic becomes a tool for solving real-world problems. This change is motivated by the need to specialize. When adults choose a career path, they eliminate all the alternative possibilities. They fine-tune their learning for that particular environment and its demands. The advantage of this is that it opens new doors to higher levels of expertise and competence. Now they accept inconsistencies of

life and people and develop thinking that accepts imperfection and compromise. This includes awareness of multiple truths, integration of logic with reality, and tolerance for the gap between the ideal and the real.

Information Processing: Expertise and Creativity

Expertise is the acquisition of extensive knowledge in a field or endeavor, due to specialization coming from selection of a major or occupation. Becoming an expert has great effects on how we process information. Experts remember and reason more quickly and effectively. They know more domain-specific concepts and represents them in deeper ways. So experts approach problems with goals in mind, linking information and problems in complex patterns that are unseen to a novice. Experts have such knowledge that they arrive at solutions quickly because they use more automatic processing in the realm of their expertise. Expertise links to creativity, since they are directed at solving problems and meeting specific needs. Adult creativity has the ability to formulate new problems and ask significant questions that haven't been suggested before. There is a movement from problem solving to problem finding. It seems to require 10 years to develop master-level creativity. Creative accomplishments rise in early adulthood, peak in late thirties or early forties, and gradually decline. There are differences based on when a person found their career interest, as well as specific area of expertise. Not all experts are creative. It requires innovative thinking style, tolerance of ambiguity, special drive to succeed, and a willingness to experiment and try again in the face of failure. It requires much time and energy, so for many women, family responsibilities squeeze it out.

Changes in mental abilities- cross-sectional studies show a peak in intelligence test performance at 35, followed by a drop into old age. But using long-term longitudinal studies of a group, test scores show an age-related increase. Longitudinal studies show an increase in intellectual ability around age 50, into the 60s, with a gradual drop after that. Cohort effects seem to be responsible, as each new generation had better education, nutrition, and information available to them. Not all intellectual abilities follow this pattern, but it is consistent over large groups.

College experience is described by many people as their most influential period of adulthood. Not only are students exploring and developing careers, they are exploring their values, social skills and are being exposed to diversity on many levels. 75per cent of US graduates enroll in some form of college.

- Psychological impact of attending college- attitudes and values broaden. They show increasing interest in performing arts, social issues, and develop greater tolerance for different values and issues of different people. Moral reasoning expands into concern for less fortunate people. Along with that comes a greater self-understanding, higher self-esteem. These developments occur as students get more involved in academic and non-academic pursuits. Living in a dorm makes a difference, since students get completely immersed in the atmosphere of the college. Commuting students need some comparable way of getting connected.

- Dropping out of college- 45per cent of college students at two-year institutions and 26per cent of those in 4-year institutions drop out, most in the first year. People drop out for a number of reasons: lack of motivation, poor adaptation to college demands, unwillingness to meet with mentors, teachers who could encourage them. The more connected a student becomes in the first months, the more chance they have to complete school.

Vocational choice is a major element of identity development. Work offers self-respect, a group of like-minded people to connect with, a certain economic status, lifestyle.

- Selecting a vocation occurs over years as children think about what they want to be when they grow up.
  - Fantasy period- in early and middle childhood children fantasize about different jobs. They think about what life would be like if they were a teacher, actress, pilot.
  - Tentative period – early and middle adolescence stirs adolescents to think about careers in more complex, realistic ways. They consider what they are interested in and what skills they have and what values they hold.
  - Realistic period- late adolescence and early adulthood- the realities of adulthood press in on youth and they narrow their options. They explore the possibilities, gather information, and finally crystallize their choices by considering the educational demands of various careers.
- Factors influencing vocational choice
  - Personality (Holland's theory) interacts with job choice since we try to find jobs that fit our personalities. This relationship isn't strong, but it is consistent. We do hold more than one personality type and have flexibility to learn various jobs, but we'll be more successful in a job environment that fits our interests and abilities. Many factors influence the jobs we strive for- economics, family responsibilities, educational opportunities.
  - Investigative person- interested in science
  - Social person- likes interacting with people, human services, teaching
  - Realistic person- mechanical occupations outside

- Artistic person- needs individual expression in arts, music
- Conventional person- likes structure, material possessions, social status, business, quality control
- Enterprising person-adventurous, persuasive, leader, drawn to sales or politics
- Family influences are powerful, simply because what a student sees in his/her family is what seems doable and familiar. Youth aspirations correlate closely with jobs of the parents. This has to do with educational aspirations and successes. The best predictor of occupational status (white collar, blue collar) is years of schooling completed. High SES parents can also network for their kids, getting them summer jobs and helping them see the work in a meaningful way. These parents also stress independence, so their children will tend to seek higher status jobs to please them.
- Teachers can influence a student's choice of field, simply by their enthusiasm and grounded insights into what it takes to be successful. This is especially true for students from low SES families.
- Gender stereotypes held women back in numbers of career tracks until the past 20 years. Women have gained training in occupations that were generally held by men. Even so, there is not equal representation in many career fields: engineering, physicians, law. Women are still concentrated in traditionally feminine professions: writing, social work, education, and nursing. They do not rise to the same level of production as men, either. This probably has to do with gender-based messages to girls- resulting in girls having less confidence and underestimating their abilities. Women's career aspirations decline in college. They rethink their careers to include flexibility that will allow starting a family. Even women gifted in math tend to choose medicine or a health profession rather than engineering, math or physical science. Women who do press on in their goals have four things in common:
- A college that values the accomplishments of women and enhances women's experiences.
- Frequent interaction with faculty or mentors in their field.
- Opportunity to test abilities in a supportive environment.
- Models of successful women who have managed the family-career conflict.
- Access to vocational information helps students to find their way in a real work world. Many students don't have a clear idea what

it will take to make their dreams come true. They may not realize what they need to complete a degree and when they shift majors or schools they lose credits and delay their graduation.

- Vocational preparation of non-college bound young adults is essential, since finding a job after high school is difficult in the skilled workforce of the US. Unemployment in this group reaches 20per cent.
- Work-study apprenticeships in Germany are successful in training students who don't care to go to college, but can learn complex jobs with mentors. Businesses provide financial support, since the programme guarantees well-trained employees. Apprentices pass qualifying exams and become certified as skilled workers, earning union wages. This allows young people to establish themselves in a well-paid career with benefits and advancement possibilities. A similar programme could be useful in the US to allow for smoother transitions from school to work for youth who aren't going to college.

5

Attention Development in Adults

ADULT ATTENTION DEFICIT HYPERACTIVITY DISORDER

Adult attention deficit hyperactivity disorder (also referred to as adult ADHD or simply ADHD in adults, formerly AADD) is theneurobiological condition of attention deficit hyperactivity disorder (ADHD) in adults.

About one-third to two-thirds of children with symptoms from early childhood continue to demonstrate notable ADHD symptoms throughout life.

Three subtypes of ADHD are identified in the DSM-IV as:

- Predominantly Inattentive (ADHD-PI)
- Predominantly Hyperactive (ADHD-PH)
- Combined type (ADHD-C)

In later life, the hyperactive/impulsive subtype manifests less frequently. The hyperactivity symptoms tend to turn more into "inner restlessness", starting in adolescence and carrying on in adulthood.

Adult ADHD is typically marked by inattentiveness, difficulty getting work done, procrastination and organizational problems. Specifically, adults with ADHD present with persistent difficulties in following directions, remembering information, concentrating, organizing tasks, completing work within specified time frames and appearing timely in appointments. These difficulties affect several different areas of an ADHD adult's life, causing emotional, social, vocational, marital, legal, financial or academic problems. As a result, low self-esteem is commonly developed. However, given the right guidance and coaching, these traits of ADHD could also lead to career success.

Diagnosis of the condition follows after one or several assessment interviews by a clinician including:

- Examination of personal history
- Observational evidence from family members or close friends
- Academic reports, often going back to school years
- etc., as well as evaluation to diagnose additional possible conditions which often coexist with ADHD, called comorbidities or comorbid disorders. The condition is highly heritable, and while its exact causes

are not fully known, genetic or environmental factors are understood to play a part. ADHD is a childhood-onset condition, usually requiring symptoms to have been present before age 12 for a diagnosis. Children under treatment will migrate to adult health services if necessary as they transit into adulthood, however diagnosis of adults involves full examination of their history.

Successful treatment of ADHD is usually based on a combination of medication, cognitive behavioural therapy, and coaching or skills training. Medium-to-high intensity physical exercise, improved sleep and improved and targeted nutrition are also known to have a positive effect. Within school and work, reasonable accommodations may be put in place to help the individual work more efficiently and productively.

CLASSIFICATION

The DSM-IV, or Diagnostic and Statistical Manual of Mental Disorders, 2000 edition, defines three types of ADHD:

1. A Predominantly Inattentive type
2. A Predominantly Hyperactive-Impulsive type
3. A Combined type, that displays symptoms from both types

To meet the diagnostic criteria of ADHD, an individual must display:

- At least six inattentive-type symptoms for the inattentive type
- At least six hyperactive-type symptoms for the hyperactive-impulsive type
- All of the above to have the combined type

The symptoms need to have been present since before the individual was seven years old, and must have interfered with at least two spheres of his or her functioning (at home and at school or work, for example) over the last six months. The DSM-IV criteria for ADHD are, however, tailored towards the type of symptoms that children would show, and might therefore underestimate the prevalence of ADHD in adults. In 2013, the newer DSM-V reviewed some of these criteria, with more lenient requirements for the diagnosis, specially in adults.

SIGNS AND SYMPTOMS

ADHD is a chronic condition, beginning in early childhood and persisting throughout a person's lifetime. It is estimated that 33-66per cent of children with ADHD will continue to have significant ADHD-related symptoms persisting into adulthood, resulting in a significant impact on education, employment, and interpersonal relationships.

Individuals with ADHD exhibit deficiencies in self-regulation and self-motivation which in turn foster problematic characteristics such as distractibility, procrastination, disorganization and misprioritization. They are often perceived by others as chaotic, with a tendency to need high stimulation to be less distracted and function effectively. The learning potential and overall intelligence of an adult with ADHD, however, are no different from the potential and intelligence of adults who do not have the disorder.

Whereas teachers and caregivers responsible for children are often attuned to the symptoms of ADHD, employers and others who interact with adults are far less likely to regard such behaviours as a symptom. In part, this is because symptoms do change with maturity;adults who have ADHD are less likely to exhibit obvious hyperactive behaviours. Instead they may report constant mental activity and inner restlessness, as their hyperactivity internalizes.

Symptoms of ADHD can vary widely between individuals and throughout the lifetime of an individual. As the neurobiology of ADHD is becoming increasingly understood, it is becoming evident that difficulties exhibited by individuals with ADHD are due to problems with the parts of the brain responsible for executive functions. These result in problems with sustaining attention, planning, organization, prioritization, time blindness, impulse control and decision making.

The difficulties generated by these deficiencies can range from moderate to extreme, resulting in the inability to effectively structure their lives, plan daily tasks, or think of and act accordingly even when aware of potential consequences.

These lead to poor performance in school and work, followed by underachievement in these areas. In young adults, poor driving record with traffic violations as well as histories of alcoholism or substance abuse may surface. The difficulty is often due to the ADHD person's observed behaviour (*e.g.* the impulsive types, who may insult their boss for instance, resulting in dismissal), despite genuinely trying to avoid these and knowing that it can get them in trouble. Often, the ADHD person will miss things that an adult of similar age and experience should catch onto or know. These lapses can lead others to label the individuals with ADHD as "lazy" or "stupid" or "inconsiderate".

As problems accumulate, a negativistic self-view becomes established and a vicious circle of failure is set up. Up to 80per cent of adults may have some form of psychiatriccomorbidity such as depression or anxiety. Many with ADHD also have associated learning disabilities, such as dyslexia, which contributes to their difficulties.

Studies on adults with ADHD have shown that, more than often, they experience self stigma and depression in childhood, commonly resulting from feeling neglected and different from their peers. These problems may play a role to the high levels of depression, substance abuse, and relationship problems that affect adults with ADHD later in life.

Inattentive-type (ADHD-PI)	Hyperactive/Impulsive-type (ADHD-PH)
In children:	
• Forgetful during daily activities	In children:
• Easily distracted by extraneous stimuli	• Squirms and fidgets (with hands and/or feet)
• Losing important items (*e.g.* pencils, homework, toys, etc.)	• Cannot sit still
• Always asking for attention, but	• Cannot play quietly or engage in leisurely activities
• Not listening and not responding to name being called out	• Talks excessively
• Unable to focus on tasks at hand, cannot sustain attention in activities	• Runs and climbs excessively
• Avoids or dislikes tasks requiring sustained mental effort	• Always on the go, as if "driven by a motor"
• Makes careless mistakes by failing to pay attention to details	• Cannot wait for their turn
• Difficulty organizing tasks and activities	• Blurts out answers
• Fails to follow-through on complex instructions and tasks (*e.g.* home work, chores, etc.)	• Intrudes on others and interrupts conversations
In adults, these evolve into:	In adults:
• Avoiding tasks or jobs that require concentration	• Chooses highly active, stimulating jobs
• Procrastination	• Avoids situations with low physical activity or sedentary work
• Difficulty initiating tasks	
• Difficulty organizing details required for a task	• May choose to work long hours or two jobs
• Difficulty recalling details required for a task	• Seeks constant activity
• Difficulty multitasking	• Easily bored
• Poor time management, losing track of time	• Impatient
• Indecision and doubt	• Intolerant and frustrated, easily irritated
• Hesitation of execution	• Impulsive, snap decisions and irresponsible behaviours
• Difficulty persevering or completing and following through on tasks	• Loses temper easily, angers quickly
• Delayed stop and transition of concentration from one task to another	• The tendency to hyperfocus on particularly stimulating or emotionally engaging tasks.

DIAGNOSIS

The diagnosis of ADHD in adults requires retrospectively establishing whether the symptoms were also present in childhood, even if not previously recognized. As with othermental disorders such as schizophrenia there is no objective "test" that diagnoses ADHD. Rather, it is a combination of a careful history of symptoms up to early childhood, including corroborating evidence from family members, previous report cards, etc. The screening tests also seek to rule out other conditions or differential diagnoses such asdepression, anxiety, or substance abuse. Other diseases such as hyperthyroidism may exhibit symptoms similar to those of ADHD, and it is imperative to rule these out as well.Asperger syndrome, a condition on the autism spectrum, is sometimes mistaken for ADHD, due to impairments in executive functioning found in some people with Asperger syndrome. However, Asperger syndrome also typically involves difficulties in social interaction, restricted and repetitive patterns of behaviour and interests, and problems withsensory processing, including hypersensitivity. Along with this, the quality of diagnosing an adult with ADHD can often be skewed being that the majority of adults with ADHD also have other complications, ranging from anxiety and depression to substance abuse.

Assessment of adult patients seeking a possible diagnosis can be better than in children due to the adult's greater ability to provide their own history, input, and insight. However, it has been noted that many individuals, particularly those with high intelligence, develop coping strategies that mask ADHD impairments and therefore they do not seek diagnosis and treatment.

Formal tests and assessment instruments such as IQ tests, standardized achievement tests, or neuropsychological tests typically are not helpful for identifying people with ADHD. Furthermore, no currently available physiological or medical measure is definitive diagnostically. However, psycho-educational and medical tests are helpful in ruling in or out other conditions (*e.g.* learning disabilities, mental retardation, allergies) that may be associated with ADHD-like behaviours.

United States medical and mental health professionals follow the Diagnostic and Statistical Manual of Mental Disorders (DSM) of the American Psychiatric Association;the International Classification of Diseases (ICD) published by the World Health Organisation (WHO) is often used by health professionals elsewhere. Periodic updates incorporate changes in knowledge and treatments. For example, under DSM-IV (published in 1994, with corrections and minor changes in 2000), the diagnostic criteria for ADHD in adults broadly follow the same as in children, but the proposed revision for the DSM-5 differentiates the presentation of ADHD for children and adults for several symptoms.

It should be noted that every normal individual exhibits ADHD-like symptoms occasionally (when tired or stressed, for example) but for a positive diagnosis to be received, the symptoms should be present from childhood and persistently interfere with functioning in multiple spheres of an individual's life: work, school, and interpersonal relationships. The symptoms that individuals exhibit as children are still present in adulthood, but manifest differently as most adults develop compensatory mechanisms to adapt to their environment.

PATHOPHYSIOLOGY

Over the last 30 years, research into ADHD has greatly accelerated. There is no single, unified theory that explains the cause of ADHD and research is ongoing. Genetic factors are presumed important, and it has been suggested that environmental factors may affect how symptoms manifest.

It is becoming increasingly accepted that individuals with ADHD have difficulty with "executive functioning". In higher organisms, such as humans, these functions are thought to reside in the frontal lobes. They enable recall of tasks that need accomplishing, organization to accomplish these tasks, assessment of consequences of actions, prioritization of thoughts and actions, keeping track of time, awareness of interactions with surroundings, the ability to focus despite competing stimuli, and adaptation to changing situations.

Several lines of research based on structural and/or functional imaging techniques, stimulant drugs, psychological interventions have identified alterations in the dopaminergicand adrenergic pathways of individuals with ADHD. In particular, areas of the prefrontal cortex appear to be the most affected. Dopamine and norepinephrine areneurotransmitters playing an important role in brain function. The uptake transporters for dopamine and norepinephrine are overly active and clear these neurotransmitters from the synapse a lot faster than in normal individuals. This is thought to increase processing latency and salience, and diminished working memory.

TREATMENT

Treatment for adult ADHD may combine medication and behavioural, cognitive, or vocational interventions. Treatment often begins with medication selected to address the symptoms of ADHD, along with any comorbid conditions that may be present. Medication alone, while effective in correcting the physiological symptoms of ADHD, will not address the paucity of skills which many adults will have failed to acquire because of their ADHD (*e.g.*, one might regain ability to focus with medication, but skills such as organizing, prioritizing and effectively communicating have taken others time to cultivate).

MEDICATIONS

Stimulants, the first line medications in adult ADHD are typically formulated in immediate and long-acting formulations.

Methylphenidate, a stimulant, with short and long-acting formulations, is often the first-line therapy and appears effective. In the short term, methylphenidate is well tolerated. However, long term studies have not been conducted in adults and concerns about increases in blood pressure have not been established. Methylphenidate increases concentrations of dopamine and norepinephrine in the synaptic cleft, promoting increased neurotransmission. It acts to block the dopamine and norepinephrine reuptake transporters, thus slowing the removal at which these neurotransmitters are cleared from the synapses.

Amphetamine and its derivatives, prototype stimulants, are likewise available in immediate and long-acting formulations. Amphetamines act by multiple mechanisms including reuptake inhibition, displacement of transmitters from vesicles, reversal of uptake transporters and reversible MAO inhibition. Thus amphetamines actively increases the release of these neurotransmitters into the synaptic cleft. They may have a better side-effect profile than methylphenidate cardiovascularly and potentially better tolerated.

The non-stimulant atomoxetine (Strattera), is also an effective treatment for adult ADHD. Although atomoxetine has a half life similar to stimulants it exhibits delayed onset of therapeutic effects similar to antidepressants. Unlike the stimulants which are controlled substances, atomoxetine lacks abuse potential. It is particularly effective for those with the predominantly inattentive concentration type of attention deficit due to being primarily a norepinephrine reuptake inhibitor. It is often prescribed in adults who cannot tolerate the side effects of amphetamines or methylphenidate. It is also approved for ADHD by the US Food and Drug Administration. A rare but potentially severe side effect includes liver damage and increased suicidal ideation.

Bupropion and desipramine are two antidepressants that have demonstrated some evidence of effectiveness in the management of ADHD particularly when there is comorbidmajor depression, although antidepressants have lower treatment effect sizes.

PSYCHOSOCIAL THERAPY

Treatment of adult ADHD may also include forms of stress management or relaxation training.

Research has shown that, alongside medication, psychological interventions in adults can be effective in reducing symptomatic deficiencies. Emerging evidence suggests a possible role for cognitive behavioural therapy (CBT) alongside medication in the treatment of adult ADHD.

For most adults, the psychosocial therapy is not effective. For this reason, medications are the first line of therapies. The medications that are prescribed for adults come in both stimulant and non-stimulant form. Although the drug therapies are effective for adults, the benefits should be discussed with the patient's physician to ensure the benefits of the medications outweigh the risk. If medication is unwanted or not an option, increasing exercise and changing one's diet may help alleviate some of the symptoms such as hyperactivity.

EPIDEMIOLOGY

In North America and Europe, it is estimated that three to five per cent of adults have ADHD, but only about ten per cent of those have received a formal diagnosis. It has been estimated that 5per cent of the global population has ADHD (including cases not yet diagnosed). In the context of the World Health Organization World Mental Health Survey Initiative, researchers screened more than 11,000 people aged 18 to 44 years in ten countries in the Americas, Europe and the Middle East. On this basis they estimated the adult ADHD proportion of the population to average 3.5 per cent with a range of 1.2 to 7.3 per cent, with a significantly lower prevalence in low-income countries (1.9per cent) compared to high-income countries (4.2per cent). The researchers concluded that adult ADHD often co-occurs with other disorders, and that it is associated with considerable role disability. Although they found that few adults are treated for ADHD itself, in many instances treatment is given for the co-occurring disorders.

HISTORY

In the 1970s researchers began to realize that the condition now known as ADHD did not always disappear in adolescence, as was once thought. At about the same time, some of the symptoms were also noted in many parents of the children under treatment. The condition was formally recognized as afflicting adults in 1978, often informally called adult ADD, since symptoms associated with hyperactivity are generally less pronounced.

Early work on disorders of attention was conducted by Alexander Crichton in 1798 writing about "mental restlessness". The underlying condition came to be recognized from the early 1900s by Sir George Still. Efficacy of medications on symptoms was discovered during the 1930s and research continued throughout the twentieth century. ADHD in adults began to be studied from the early 1970s and research has increased as worldwide interest in the condition has grown.

SOCIETY AND CULTURE

ADHD in adults, as with children, is recognized as an impairment that may constitute a disability under U.S. federal disability non-discrimination laws, including such laws as theRehabilitation Act of 1973 and the Americans With Disabilities Act (ADA, 2008 revision), if the disorder substantially limits one or more of an individual's major life activities. For adults whose ADHD does constitute a disability, workplaces have a duty to provide reasonable accommodations, and educational institutions have a duty to provide appropriate academic adjustments or modifications, to help the individual work more efficiently and productively.

In a 2004 study it was estimated that the yearly income discrepancy for adults with ADHD was $10,791 less per year than high school graduate counterparts and $4,334 lower for college graduate counterparts. The study estimates a total loss in productivity in the United States of over $77 billion

USD. By contrast, loss estimations are $58 billion for drug abuse, $85 billion for alcohol abuse and $43 billion for depression.

CONTROVERSY

ADHD controversies include concerns about its existence as a disorder, its causes, the methods by which ADHD is diagnosed and treated including the use of stimulant medications in children, possible overdiagnosis, misdiagnosis as ADHD leading to undertreatment of the real underlying disease, alleged hegemonic practices of the American Psychiatric Association and negative stereotypes of children diagnosed with ADHD. These controversies have surrounded the subject since at least the 1970s.

DEVELOPMENTAL TETHERS LINK CHILDHOOD TRAITS TO ADULT OUTCOMES

Developmental psychology has focused on mechanisms, both external and internal to the child, that shape, refine, and reinforce patterns of development over time. Developmental trajectories are the pathways children take from infancy (with all of the promise and risk that it holds) into adulthood and beyond. For most children, these trajectories travel through a happy medium, producing adolescents and young adults who can flexibly adapt to their environments and lead successful, independent lives. Even when examining young children who appear at elevated risk for maladaptation, the same positive trajectory holds true for the majority of children. For example, even among very shy children, the majority do not go on to have social anxiety disorder. This pattern may act as the developmental equivalent of the statistical construct of regression to the mean. Over the course of time, development appears to smooth away the jagged edges of early risk through naturally occurring maturational, experiential, and social processes.

However, for a subset of children the risks evident early in life persist, calcifying into a pattern of maladaptation through childhood and into adulthood. Since children appear to be more open to prevention and intervention, over time it becomes increasingly more difficult to redirect maladaptive trajectories. Thus it is exceedingly important to identify and target the mechanisms at play early in life.

These mechanisms — developmental tethers — bind children to specific trajectories and resist the normal ameliorative or "smoothing away" process. From our lab's perspective, developmental tethers grow out the child's individual early traits or biases. These biases provoke an environmental response. The child processes and interprets these responses and frames subsequent behaviours based on the conclusions drawn. This can become cyclical, growing progressively more entrenched (and biased) with each successive iteration.

Our work has focused on attention as one such tether, specifically examining the role attention biases to threat may play in increasing risk for anxiety, particularly in children with extreme temperamental traits. We focus on behavioural inhibition, a trait that is rooted in biology, is evident in the first year of life, and is associated with up to a four-fold increase in risk for clinical anxiety by adolescence. This work takes advantage of neuroscience research that has carefully plotted the neural structures that support attention and emotion, coupled with our knowledge of how developmental processes unfold over time. As a result, we are now in a position to identify and target discrete brain-based attention mechanisms for intervention that may prove to be efficient, effective, and widely disseminable supplements to traditional forms of treatment, such as cognitive behavioural therapy (CBT).

ATTENTION IS A CENTRAL GUIDE TO THE CHILD'S ENVIRONMENT

From birth, individuals are bombarded with more sensory stimuli than one could ever hope to process and respond to. As such, we must learn to selectively attend to those aspects of the environment that support our current goals. At the same time, however, we must also remain open to unexpected, yet salient, events that can (and, perhaps, even should) disrupt our current plans. The famed neuroscientist Joseph LeDoux (1994) formulated the iconic example of the hiker moving through the forest who must closely attend to the path's route while also noting the unexpected and unwanted appearance of snakes. This delicate balancing act requires sophisticated neural systems that can monitor and direct flexible, goal-directed behaviour.

This balancing act of attending to goals while responding to unexpected information is strongly rooted in neural development and emerges slowly over time. For example, under the right circumstances young infants are captured by salient stimuli in their visual world. This can be seen when infants fixate on a toy hanging over head from a mobile. Once captured, the infant may be incapable of disengaging and looking way — leading to a great deal of frustration. This phenomena, known as "sticky fixation", begins to dissipate at approximately three to four months of age, with the maturation of the superior colliculus — a small region nestled in the midbrain.

Over the course of early childhood, increasingly more sophisticated systems come on line so that the child is no longer beholden to external forces (exogenous control) and can now willfully direct his or her attention (endogenous control). This is an exceedingly complex relation, instantiated in rich neural interconnections across multiple brain regions.

As a result, we often focus on a subset of this network that we believe most clearly reflects a specific component of the link between attention and socioemotional development. For example, the anterior cingulate cortex (ACC) subserves cognitive control functions associated with monitoring the effectiveness, efficiency, and meaning of behaviour and performance. The ACC is considered a transition zone between the limbic and frontal cortex, linking together the emotional processing of objects and events (rooted in the limbic system) with top-down control mechanisms (often localized to the frontal cortex).

When examining attention biases to threat and the emergence of anxiety, the focus is often on the amygdala and the ventrolateral prefrontal cortex (vlPFC). We view the amygdala as a structure centrally involved in salience detection and stimulus-reinforcement learning. The vlPFC is thought to adjust goal-directed behaviour based on threat-salience information. Differences in amygdala and vlPFC activity thereby reflect both the level of threat perceived during specific events as well as the cognitive demands of the activity at hand. However, before this interplay can take place, attention acts as a gate keeper — determining which events are allowed to "enter" this network.

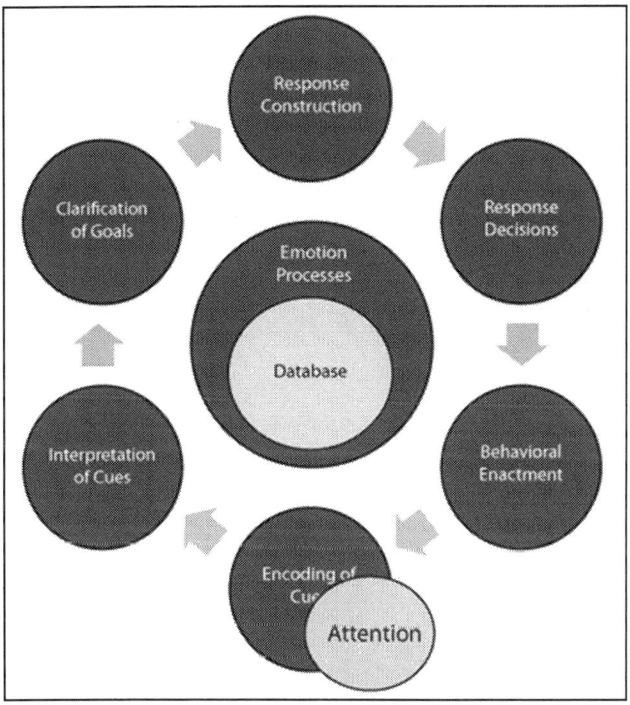

Fig. This modified representation of Crick and Dodge's (1994) social information processing model depicts the steps by which individuals encode, process, and act on information from the environment.

Information processing models lay out the means by which children take in, interpret, and respond to their environment. Children must first encode a small subset of the myriad of incoming cues. They then interpret these cues, often in light of how they guide or clarify goal selection. Finally, potential responses are generated, one is chosen, and the choice is then enacted. Serving as the 'database' for this progression is a store of memories, social knowledge, acquired rules governing behaviours, and past emotional experiences. A simplified illustration of Crick and Dodge's model.

One can envision a young child entering the loud and boisterous school playground with these small processing units rotating sight unseen in the mind. He must pick out from the din of voices the location and identity of potential playmates (cue encoding). From among the multiple groups, he must choose which one to approach. If he is smart, he will avoid the bullying group that teased him last week (cue interpretation based on current goals and past events) and instead approach the small group with a like-minded interest in trucks and cars.

A small circle representing attention in its gate-keeping role. Attention acts as a filter allowing only a small subset of potential cues into the system. Without this filter, the system would almost immediately become overwhelmed and collapse. It is the small frightened child frozen in place by the crushing, indistinguishable buzz of the school playground. As noted above, a nimble attentional filter ensures that the system remains flexible — remaining on target to reach set goals and blocking out distracters, while still able to respond to important unexpected events. This is LeDoux's snake in the path or our small child's bully in the playground. The danger comes when the attentional filter is biased — seeing more snakes or bullies than may actually exist.

ATTENTION BIASES AND THE LINK TO ANXIETY

An exciting new area of research suggests that in anxious adults the balance of activity within the fronto-limbic network may be shifted, preferentially responding to threat-related events. Due to this shift, or bias, in the filter, anxious individuals detect threat in their environment more often, and at lower levels of intensity, than do their non-anxious counterparts. Anxious adults then respond in the most logical manner by retreating from the threat and avoiding in the future any situations in which they may once again encounter this threat. Unfortunately, when attention biases to threat are exceedingly high, the individual's social world can shrink and become distorted, leading to maladaptive behaviours, social withdrawal, and, in some cases, clinical levels of anxiety.

Thus, attention mechanisms may play a pivotal role in shaping the individual's experienced environment from the first days of life. If this view is correct, early life individual differences in attention should be associated with diverging trajectories of socioemotional development during early childhood — potentially extending into adolescence. This process may be most acute in children at risk for anxiety. Much of the focus has been on children at risk due to the temperamental trait of behavioural inhibition.

Kagan and colleagues were the first to describe behavioural inhibition as a salient temperamental type. Behavioural inhibition is the tendency to display signs of fear and wariness in response to unfamiliar stimuli and this trait is marked by heightened vigilance, motor quieting, and withdrawal from novelty. As behaviourally inhibited children mature, they increasingly fear social circumstances, displaying poorly regulated social behaviour and increased social reticence. This, in turn, leads to peer rejection, low self-esteem, and poor social competence. In prospective research, behavioural inhibition emerges as one of the strongest predictors of risk for later anxiety.

Behavioural inhibition and anxiety share important similarities at the behavioural level, such as hypervigilance towards threat and a tendency to avoid social stressors. They also share similar biological antecedents. Kagan has argued that behaviourally inhibited children have a lowered threshold for amygdala arousal when faced with novelty. This limbic hyperarousal impacts subsequent neural processes and, in turn, shapes social behaviour.

As a first examination of attention as a developmental tether, my colleagues and I characterized infants at 9-months of age for high or low levels of sustained attention. We then observed trajectories of behavioural inhibition through age 7 years and social discomfort at age 14 years. We found that children with low levels of sustained attention showed increasing levels of behavioural inhibition over childhood. In addition, initial behavioural inhibition predicted adolescent functioning only in the children with low levels of sustained attention. The observed developmental trajectories may be a reflection of the important gatekeeper role that attention plays in day-to-day psychological processes, influencing the initiation, deployment, and termination of a wide range of behaviour and neural functions.

Given this initial empirical foundation, we then looked to see if children with a history of behavioural inhibition also display attention biases to threat. In doing so, we carried out a series of studies using the standard task employed to quantify attention biases in anxious adults. In a dot-probe task, two visual stimuli, one threat-related and one neutral, are shown briefly on each trial, and their removal is followed by a small probe in the location just occupied by one of the stimuli. Participants are required to respond as fast as possible to the probe Attention bias towards threat is revealed when participants are faster to respond to probes that replace threat-related rather than neutral stimuli. Recent work has found consistent patterns of bias to threat in anxious children and adults. In addition, testing within the fMRI environment has also shown disturbances in both frontal (*i.e.*, vlPFC) and limbic (*i.e.*, amygdala) regions in clinically anxious adolescents.

My colleagues and I presented a standard dot probe task to adolescents who had been followed since infancy and who were characterized with regard to behavioural inhibition. We found that these adolescents showed a significant bias towards threat. Pointing to attention's role as a developmental tether, early behavioural inhibition predicted levels of social withdrawal in adolescence only for those participants who displayed a bias towards threat. In a follow-up study with an independent cohort of young children (age 5 years), we again found that early behavioural inhibition only predicted later social maladjustment in the presence of attention biases to threat. Importantly, these data suggest that the relations between attention and social development are evident, and remarkably similar in form, both before and after the expected developmental window for the emergence of anxiety. These data also point to the role that early attention mechanisms may play in shaping broad patterns of functioning by acting as a tether between early temperamental biases and subsequent social outcomes.

ATTENTION AS A TARGET FOR INTERVENTION FOR ANXIETY

Building on these findings a number of laboratories are now examining attention as a direct target of intervention for anxiety. This view treats attention bias as a causal mechanism of anxiety and not simply a symptom of the disorder. If proven effective, this new line of research may greatly enhance our ability to influence the information processing biases at the heart of anxiety.

A great deal of research has examined mechanisms traditionally thought to shape developmental trajectories, such as parenting, social environment, and genetic predisposition. These studies have greatly improved our understanding of developmental risk and will help us identify those children most vulnerable to anxiety. However, they do not always provide a clear or simple path for intervention.

For example, while we know that parenting style plays an important role in ameliorating or exacerbating early temperamental biases, designing, implementing, and assessing effective parenting interventions is exceedingly difficult and costly. Even applying gold-standard evidence-based interventions such as cognitive-behaviour therapy (CBT) face difficulties as they rely on highly trained practitioners and must be tailored for use with young children. Indeed, remission rates with first-line treatments hover at only 50per cent. Thus, the challenge is to identify an intervention that can effectively target individuals vulnerable to anxiety, is amenable to use with even young children, and can be widely implemented.

Recent work has therefore focused on attention bias modification (ABM) as a new mechanism for intervention. In ABM protocols employing the dot-probe task, the target location is systematically manipulated so that the targets always appear at the location opposite the threat cue. Since attending to systematic contingencies can assist in task performance, an implicitly learned bias away from the threat cue is gradually induced. MacLeod and Hagan (1992) provided initial suggestive evidence for causality, and a series of other studies extend this evidence. The results show promise: in a small study Schmidt et al found that after training, 72per cent of patients in the active treatment condition, relative to 11per cent of patients in the placebo, no longer met DSM-IV criteria for Social Anxiety Disorder (SAD). Recent work has found promising results in clinically anxious children.

Work with ABM is in its infancy and many deep questions remain. These include: What processes are affected by ABM? How do these processes influence the deep-seated behavioural patterns seen in anxiety? How long do the effects of ABM persist? Can ABM be used effectively as a preventive tool? Finally, how do ABM-linked effects interact with the normative developmental trajectories of attention? My laboratory is one of many now working to address these questions. Indeed, our current NIMH-funded study is examining the impact of ABM on social behaviour, anxious symptoms, and the neural correlates of attention in children at temperamental risk for anxiety.

Systematic research on ABM protocols are only now emerging. owever, if proven effective ABM holds the promise of a portable, efficient, easily-implemented intervention that can be used with very young children. This would increase our ability to ameliorate suffering and broaden access to treatment across geographic location, socioeconomic status, and age. Initial proof of concept studies, like the one we are carrying out, are crucial for merging theoretical promise with actual empirical data.

DEVELOPING ATTENTION: BEHAVIOURAL AND BRAIN MECHANISMS

Few life changes are as dramatic as the development that occurs between infancy and elementary school, with locomotion, language, and voluntary control as the most obvious behaviour changes. We also know that the brain changes in size, connectivity, and synaptic density during this period. What is least explored is exactly how these brain changes support behavioural change. Our research traces the development of attention networks that support the mechanisms of self-regulation, allowing children to control their emotions and behaviour. In this chapter, we first outline the connection between attention and self-regulation. We examine measurement of individual differences in attention in adults. The heart of the paper summarizes the relation of early temperament (7 months) to later temperament and attention (age: 7 years). We show how changes in mechanisms of control over this period relate to genes and to the environment provided by the caregiver. Finally, we examine training studies that influence some of the same brain connections that change during development.

During infancy, the caregiver provides much of the child's regulation. Soothing by holding and rocking or by orienting of attention is a common practice for control of distress. Holding supports the child's focus on the external physical environment, and the social world of interaction with the caregiver provides a means of raising and lowering sensory stimulation. This process allows the caregiver to accommodate the child to controls appropriate for a given culture and environment. External controls on arousal, distress, and sensory input eventually become internalized as toddlers come to control their own emotional and cognitive levels through self-regulation. Success in the development of self-regulation has many advantages for the child's future.

ATTENTION AND SELF-REGULATION

Starting at about the age of 3 years, parents can answer questions about their children's ability to control their own emotions and behaviour. For example, caregivers answer questions such as when playing alone, how often is your child distracted? How often does your child look immediately when you point? The answers are aggregated to form scales measuring attention focusing, inhibitory control, low intensity pleasure, and perceptual sensitivity. These are summarized in a higher order scale called effortful control (EC). Effortful control has been studied in relation to many important achievements of childhood. For example, empathy is strongly related to EC, with children high in EC showing greater empathy.

Imaging the human brain has revealed brain networks related to specific aspects of attention, including obtaining and maintaining the alert state, orienting to sensory stimuli, and resolving conflict among competing responses.

The alerting network is modulated by the brain's norepinephrine system and involves major nodes in frontal and parietal cortex. The alert state is critical to high level performance. Phasic changes in alertness can be produced by the presentation of a signal warning of an impending target. This leads to a rapid change from a resting state to one of increased receptivity to the target. The orienting network interacts with sensory systems to improve the priority of information relevant to task performance. The orienting network exerts much of the control over other brain networks during infancy and early childhood.

The executive network is involved in resolving competing actions in tasks where there is conflict. The executive network includes the anterior cingulate cortex, anterior insula, areas of the midprefrontal cortex, and the underlying striatum. Regulation occurs by enhancing activity in networks related to our goals and inhibiting activity in conflicting networks. These controls operate through long connections between the nodes of the executive network and cognitive and emotional areas of the frontal and posterior brain. In this way, the executive network is important for voluntary control and self-regulation. As mentioned previously, effortful control is a higher order temperamental factor assessing self-regulation that is obtained from parent report questionnaires. In childhood, performance on conflict related cognitive tasks is positively related to measures of children's effortful control. During childhood and in adulthood, effortful control and self-regulation are correlated with school performance and with indices of life success, including health, income, and successful human relationships.

MEASURING INDIVIDUAL DIFFERENCES IN EXECUTIVE ATTENTION

There are individual differences in the efficiency of each of the three attentional networks. The attention network test (ANT) was devised as a means of measuring these differences. The task requires the person to press one key if a central arrow points to the left and another if it points to the right. Conflict is introduced by having surrounding flanker arrows point in either the same (congruent) or the opposite (incongruent) direction. Cues presented prior to the target provide information on where or when the target will occur. Three scores are computed that are related to the performance of each individual in alerting, orienting, and executive control. In our work, we have used the ANT to examine the efficiency of brain networks underlying attention. A children's version of this test is very similar to the adult test but replaces the arrows with animal figures.

Studies have shown moderate reliability of conflict scores and lower reliability for the orienting and alerting scores, but recent revisions of the ANT provide better measures of orienting and alerting that may improve these results. The attentional networks involve different cortical brain areas, and scores on the ANT are related to distinct white matter pathways as well as structural differences in cortical thickness. Thus, the attentional networks show independent anatomy and connectivity. However, the ANT and its various revisions show significant interaction among networks. The networks communicate and work together in many situations, even though their anatomy is mostly distinct. The dorsal part of the anterior cingulate cortex (ACC) is involved in the regulation of conflict in cognitive tasks, while the more ventral part of the cingulate is involved in regulation of emotion. One way to examine regulation is to image the structural connections of different parts of the cingulate using diffusion tensor imaging (DTI). This form of imaging traces diffusion of water molecules in long myelinated fibres and provides a means of examining the physical connections present in the brain. DTI studies have shown that the dorsal (cognitive) part of the ACC is connected primarily to parietal and frontal lobes, while the ventral (emotional) part of the ACC has strong connections to subcortical limbic areas.

The executive attention network also includes the underlying striatum and adjacent areas of the midprefrontal cortex. There is evidence that the anterior insula is involved particularly in switching between tasks, while adjacent midprefrontal cortex is important during complex decision making. Comparative anatomical studies point to important differences in the evolution of cingulate connectivity between non-human primates and humans. Anatomical studies show the great expansion of white matter, which has increased more in recent evolution than has the neo-cortex itself. One type of projection cell called the von Economo neuron is found only in the anterior cingulate and a related area of the anterior insula, two brain areas that are active together even when the person is resting and not performing a task. It is thought that von Economo neurons are important in communication between the cingulate and other brain areas. This neuron is not present at all in monkeys and there are many more such neurons present in adult humans than in great apes. Moreover, there is some evidence that the frequency of the neuron increases in development between infancy and later childhood.

PRINCIPLES OF DEVELOPMENT OF SELF-REGULATION

CONTROL SYSTEMS

Some individuals have stronger activations and connectivity in brain areas related to self-regulation than others and are thus better able to exercise the various functions of self-regulation. Moreover, childhood assessments of self-regulation as measured by the ability to delay rewards and by observer reports of the child's self-control predict performance as adults. How do these individual differences arise?

To investigate this question, we have run a longitudinal study of the development of attentional networks starting in infancy (7 months), and now the children are 7 years of age. In our longitudinal study, we have found evidence of both behavioural and neural mechanisms of self-regulation. The earliest form of regulation appeared to come from the orienting rather than the executive network. This conclusion was based on several findings. First, parent reports of their child's orienting to the environment were correlated with reports of their positive and negative affect. Moreover, direct tests were done on the role of orienting to novel objects in soothing. Distressed infants, while orienting was maintained showed a reduction in overt signs of distress, but the distress returned when orienting was broken.

Second, in our longitudinal study, we observed that children of 7 months showed evidence of behaviour related to self-regulation. When confronted with novel objects, some infants oriented for a long period before reaching towards them. This tendency for a cautious reach was positively correlated with the number of anticipations infants made in orienting to a repetitive sequence of visual events. This striking observation showed that infants fast in orienting to repetitive visual sequences, often in anticipation of the object, exercised stronger controls over whether and when they reached for an object by moving towards it slowly. At the time, we did not know if rapid orienting to repetitive locations was controlled by the executive or the orienting network, but because ours was a longitudinal study, we later found that anticipations at 7 months were more closely related to orienting at 4 years than to the executive network. We have confirmed this idea in our examination of the children at 7 years. The time that infants examined a novel toy before starting to reach for it, their overall latency to reach, and the total time they examined the toy were all significantly correlated with the orienting network at the age of 7.

Lewkowicz and Hansen-Tift provided dramatic evidence that orienting can demonstrate a high level of discrimination in attending environmental events. Infants prior to 6 months and after one year oriented primarily to the eyes of pictures of faces, just as adults do, but between 6 and 12 months when language learning was prominent they were more likely to orient to the mouth. This shows direction of attention by orienting, but it does not let us know whether this control also involves the executive network.

Resting state brain imaging data have also indicated that the orienting system shows greater connectivity during infancy than do brain areas associated with the executive network. In the first week of life, resting state data show an important hub in infants in the ACC/SMA area. Although this hub shows the largest number of connections in infancy,;it is much less strongly activated than hubs found in adults. Fransson et al. also report a hub area in the left parietal lobe during infancy. Menon indicates a substantial increase in connectivity between core areas of what he calls the salience network, but we term the executive network (ACC and insula) between childhood (7–9 years) and adulthood (20 years).

He finds no significant developmental change in connections between lateral parietal and frontal areas (orienting network). This imaging data provides further support for the slow development of control from the ACC and the early dominance of the orienting network.

In addition, most hubs for information processing in the infant brain are closely related to sensory and motor brain areas that would be targets of the orienting network. While there is evidence that some of these resting state studies may be confounded by greater movement that can occur in younger subjects, in our view it seems unlikely that this artifact will change the conclusions discussed above. However, the problems that occur with any one imaging method support the approach of relating different imaging methods and establishing their connections to behaviour as we have sought to do in this chapter.

We think the relatively slow development of long-term connections to distant brain areas allows the executive network to provide more control at later ages. Indeed direct evidence on this point came from a study of 7-month-old infants viewing visual displays. They oriented longer when the display was in error and this behaviour was associated with a set of scalp electrodes at the frontal midline which localized to the anterior cingulate, an important node of the executive network. However, the lack of connections of the cingulate to remote areas was shown in an inability to use error to control behaviour. The most frequent adult response to a self-made error is to slow down during the next trial. We traced the evidence for this kind of control and found that it emerged around three years of age and was not found at the age of 2.

The growing behavioural influence of executive control is shown in an MRI study of the resolution of conflict in the flanker task by 725 children from 4 to 21 years. From 4 to 8 years, ability to resolve conflict was positively related to the size of the anterior cingulate. Beyond the age of 8, the connectivity of the anterior cingulate was correlated with the speed of response. The brain and behaviour correlation in early childhood was similar to our finding that flanker task performance showed a specific improvement in children of 6–8 years, but reaction time in the task continued to improve until adulthood. A different study used emotional responses to a fear face during a rewarded go/no-go task to explore the role of brain connectivity in regulation of the amygdala from the ventral anterior cingulate. They found a significant correlation between age and the efficiency of connectivity between the ventral ACC and amygdala during the presentation of fear faces.

The major change in connectivity took place between ages 5 and 7. These studies show substantial overlap in age between development of purely cognitive and emotional self-regulation. We do not believe that the flanker task and emotional go/no-go tasks index the full development of control mechanisms, since more complex tasks may show longer periods of development, but these studies do provide strong confirmation of growing executive system control during early childhood and the close correspondence of brain connectivity to behavioural performance.

In summary, we have discovered a transition between the brain networks responsible for control at 7 months and those at 4 years and later. At 7 months, control involves the orienting network, but by 4 years the executive network dominates. Behaviourally, the orienting network involves sensory stimulation and we believe this is a major reason why infants show control by external stimulation provided by caregivers and sensory events. We also do not believe that control through orienting ends with the preschool transition. We view adults as having dual control. Looking away from disturbing or highly arousing events is clearly a major coping strategy in adults. However, the growing influence of executive control allows the person's internally controlled goals to become generally dominant.

CONTROL OF EMOTION AND COGNITION

The structural connectivity of the anterior cingulate reflects its control functions. The ventral portion of the ACC and adjacent orbital frontal cortex connects mainly to limbic regions and its function is thought to be related to control of emotions. The more dorsal part of the cingulate connects more strongly to cortical areas in the frontal and parietal lobes. This is reflected in evidence of increased connectivity between the dorsal ACC and auditory areas when attending to speech, while a switch to visual input is reflected in increased connectivity between the ACC and occipital lobe. The developmental data cited in the last section support separate functions for the ventral and dorsal ACC and show they both develop strongly between 5 and 8 years of age.

We want to understand the origins of cognitive and emotional controls in the developing infant and child. As mentioned previously, one important function of the anterior cingulate is to play a role in the detection of error. Error detection found at 7 months may reflect either the cognitive or emotional aspects related to the violation of expectation. However, studies using high density scalp EEG at 4–6 years suggest that the resolution of conflict at 4 years involves primarily ventral areas of the cingulate;later more dorsal areas become involved. In addition, studies of resting state MRI in infancy suggest a node in the midprefrontal cortex adjacent to emotional parts of the ACC. This evidence fits with the idea that emotional control develops more quickly than cognitive control during early life, although there is strong overlap in their later development. While the data are not completely clear on this point, it is of obvious importance to parents in fostering the development of these controls.

EARLY TEMPERAMENT PREDICTS LATER CONTROL

By temperament, we mean constitutionally based individual differences in reactivity and self-regulation. At 7 months, we used a parent report scale, the Infant Behaviour Questionnaire (IBQ), which heavily weighs reactive responses of the infant, although it does provide a measure of orienting that involves an early control network.

PREDICTING ATTENTION NETWORKS

We found surprisingly high and significant correlations between temperament measures at 7 months and performance on the attention network test at 7 years. Our surprise reflects the fact that these correlations are found over an extended time course during which there is considerable neural maturation and they also involve parent report during infancy and behaviour in a cognitive reaction time task (ANT) during childhood. These correlations must be regarded as tentative, however, since they involve only sixteen of the seventy infants who remained in the study when the ANT was measured at 7 years of age. The small remaining sample is partly self-selected (some loss resulting from moving away may have been involuntary) from the larger number of infants involved at 7 months.

Separate aspects of temperament were related to each of the attention networks. For a correlation matrix, see Table 1, and in what follows we report significant correlations. Infants' perceptual sensitivity to the environment (.56) and duration of orienting (.55) were correlated with ANT scores of the alerting network at the age of 7 years. While we did not predict that parent ratings of orienting would be related to the alerting network rather than the orienting network, this may reflect dependence of orienting on alertness during infancy when sleep occupies so much of the day.

Infant approach behaviour as rated by parents were correlated with ANT scores for the orienting network at the age of 7. As we have seen previously, orienting as reported by parents and measured in the laboratory can be used to control emotional reactivity in infancy, and this aspect seems to predict the skill of taking in sensory information later in life. Soothability as reported by the parent may reflect both the child's propensity and the parent's skill. This could mean that the parents' ability to provide emotional soothing to the child is an important determinant of cognition via the orienting network.

The scales of infant smiling and laughter (".60), vocal reactivity (".64), and cuddliness (".64) were negatively correlated with the ability to resolve conflict and, in addition, the higher order factor of positive affect that contains these scales was also negatively correlated with ANT conflict at 7 years. Multiple regression indicates that these factors could account for about 50 per cent of the variance in the difference between reaction time in incongruent and congruent flankers.

In addition, negative affect measured in infancy is correlated with the total errors found in the ANT at the age of 7. It is interesting that positive affect was related to the speed of the children's response, which may largely reflect the efficiency of white matter connections, while negative affect predicted the errors that arise due to competition from the incompatible flankers.

Many older ideas of temperament are based on stability between childhood and adults traits. However, Rothbart and Derryberry suggested that we should expect temperament to change as new neural systems come on line. They recognize that there is stability, but change is be expected as neural systems and connections are established. A number of the temperament correlations between infancy and childhood in the previous literature support the ability to predict control in children from infant emotion.

Putnam et al. found that positive emotion in infancy is related to later parent reports of their child's effortful control and that infant surgency (smiling and laughter and approach) predicted high effortful control in toddlers. Komsi et al. also found that infant smiling and laughter predicted effortful control in children when they were 5 years old. In addition, the overall orienting measure in infancy predicted 7-year-old soothability, effortful control, and interest.

Thus, both ANT cognitive tests and parent reported effortful control support the relation of early reactive emotion in infancy to control systems of childhood. The correlations found between parent reported temperament at 7 months and ANT performance at 7 years were as high or higher than those found between temperament at the two ages.

It is possible these high correlations are due to the unique nature of the 16 families who persisted from 7 months to 7 years. Comparison of those infants who remained in the study until the age of 7 with those who dropped out did not reveal any striking differences, although there was some evidence that the parents continuing with the study were more committed to timely submission of questionnaires than those who dropped out. Moreover, we found neither significant demographic nor behavioural differences between the 16 persistent families and those who were involved at 7 years but not at 7 months.

However, the 16 children who had participated at 7 months were faster in ANT performance than the new recruits. Since faster speed of responding is frequently related to better overall performance, this finding suggests that the 16 children who persisted from time 1 were relatively high performing children. This effect was probably not due to practice, since a direct comparison of performance on the ANT at the age of 7 of children who had also taken the test at the age of 6 and those who had not practiced it previously showed no differences in speed.

The speed differences may have reflected recruitment of lower SES families at the age of 7 years than we had previously recruited or other unknown characteristics of the persistent families. A more interesting possibility is that early positive emotional reactivity reflects a particularly predictive feature of child behaviour. One possible mechanism for the strong influence of early positive emotion on later control is that more reactive children in infancy come to control their positive emotions more strongly and that this transfers to cognitive control as measured by the ANT.

ROLE OF GENETIC VARIATION

We have pursued two strategies to help understand how genes are related to the individual efficiency of attention networks. One approach involves adults and uses the association of attentional networks with particular neuromodulators.

These associations have led to identification of candidate genes that relate to each network. The results were summarized by Green et al. and are shown in Table 2. A number of other results have qualified the view of Green et al. somewhat. It seems clear that serotonin as well as dopamine can influence the executive attention network and that there are interactions between dopaminergic and cholinergic genes at the molecular level that modify the degree of independence between them. Nonetheless, the scheme in Table 2 provides a degree of organization and prediction that is often lacking in studies of genetic influences on cognition and behaviour.

In our longitudinal study, we examined genetic variation in twelve genes that had been related to attention in adult studies. The children had been evaluated when they were 7 months old, and genotyping took place when they returned to the laboratory at 18–20 months. We also genotyped all of the children at 7 years. We compared the results at two ages to be sure of high replication of our classifications. We found supportive evidence for some of the genes discussed in Table 2. The COMT gene was related to number of anticipatory looks at 7 and 18 months. The DRD4 7 repeat allele was not related to our attention measures in infancy or among toddlers but did relate to effortful control at the age of 4. This discontinuity likely reflected the change in networks of control from orienting to executive control that we found between 2 and 4 years of age.

In addition, parenting quality at 18–20 months was examined through observation of caregiver-child interactions in which the children played with toys in the presence of one of their caregivers. Raters reviewed videotapes of the caregiver-child interaction and rated the parent on five dimensions of parenting quality according to a schedule developed by NICHD: support, autonomy, stimulation, lack of hostility, and confidence in the child. According to their scores, parents were divided at the median into two groups: one showing a higher quality of parenting and the other a lower quality.

We reported previously that variations in COMT, SNAP25, CHRNA4, and DRD4 were related to elements of emotion during infancy (age of 7 months) and during the toddler period (18–20 months). COMT was related to positive affect including smiling and laughter and high intensity pleasure at 7 months. SNAP 25 was related to negative affect, mainly distress at 7 and 18 months. CHRNA 4 was related to effortful control at 18 months and DRD4 was related to sensation seeking at 18 months.

However, unlike the temperament measure of emotion to which the genetic variations were often related, there was little evidence that the genetic variations by themselves predicted behaviour at 7 years on the ANT. A recent meta-analysis of studies of twins indicates that genetic factors that influence cognition at one point are largely different from those at later times. Our studies suggest that shifts in control networks and gene X environment interactions may be among the reasons for this lack of prediction in early life.

SIMULATING DEVELOPMENT THROUGH TRAINING

Development in the title of this chapter refers both to changes in attention through the natural maturation of the brain and to our efforts to develop attention through training. Below we discuss similarities between the development of white matter pathways between infancy and childhood with the influence of meditation training on adult white matter. It is our hope that efforts to train attention may help us to better understand the process of infant and child development. As we have seen, parenting influences this development, and we hope to better inform parents about what can be done to improve this process.

The developmental process through which attention networks and self-regulation mature is very complex. There are many changes in brain structure and function that may be related to the multiple changes in voluntary behaviour in early development. As discussed previously, an increasingly popular way of tracing brain changes is to use resting state MRI to characterize how the brain changes in development. In our recent work, we have tried to relate behaviour changes to changes in functional connectivity.

The changes in connectivity during development reported in resting state MRI studies involve functional connectivity based upon correlations between BOLD activity in separated brain areas. There is also evidence of actual physical changes in the white matter thought to underlie these correlations. Our recent training work with adults using diffusion tensor imaging (DTI) has uncovered white matter changes that have some similarities to those found in development. Changes in connectivity surrounding the ACC have been shown to be critical to improved reaction time in the flanker task during development. Training adults might thus allow us to uncover how connections developing during childhood support the changes in self- control between infancy and adulthood.

During development, there is a large change in the physical connections between brain areas. The density of axons in pathways connecting brain areas increases, followed by an increase in the myelin sheath that surrounds the axons and provides insulation. Together, these changes result in more efficient connections. Fractional anisotropy (FA) is the main index for measuring the integrity of white matter fibres when using DTI.

In our work, we studied FA in college students before and after a form of mindfulness meditation called integrated body mind training (IBMT) in comparison to a control group given the same amount of relaxation training. We found clear improvement in the executive attention network after only five days of training. After two to four weeks of training, we found significantly greater change in FA following meditation training than following the relaxation training control. This change was found in all white matter tracts surrounding the ACC, but not in other brain areas. This was particularly striking because one of these pathways, the anterior corona radiata, has previously been reported to be correlated with individual differences in the ability to resolve conflict using the ANT.

These alterations in FA could originate from several factors, such as changes in myelination, axon density, axonal membrane integrity, axon diameter, intravoxel coherence of fibre orientation, and others. Several DTI studies have examined axial diffusivity (AD) and radial diffusivity (RD), the most important indices associated with FA, to understand the mechanisms of FA change.

Changes in AD are associated with axon morphological changes, with lower AD value indicating higher axonal density. In contrast, RD relates to the myelin insulation surrounding the axons. Decreases in RD imply increased myelination, while increases represent demyelination.

In our study, we investigated AD and RD where FA indicated that integrity of white matter fibres was enhanced in the IBMT group more than control group. We found that after two weeks of training, there were changes in axonal density but not in myelination.

In some areas, these changes in axonal density were correlated with improved mood and affect as measured by self-report. After 4 weeks of training, we found evidence of myelination changes. Our studies also found that reaction time in the attention network test and specifically the executive network was improved more by IBMT training than by the control. Since the developmental changes in childhood first involve changes in axonal density and only later myelination, our training may provide changes that are somewhat similar to those found in development. If so, it might be possible to use training to study how physical changes in connectivity alter aspects of control, including reaction time, control of affect, stress reduction, and other changes found with training.

FUTURE DIRECTIONS

The work described here has barely begun to open up a window on the dramatic changes in control between infancy and childhood. Some changes in the size and connectivity of brain areas related to cognitive and emotional control have been documented by resting state and task related MRI methods. More work needs to be done in these areas.

Moreover, we are at the very beginning of understanding the joint role of caregivers and genetic endowment in creating the brain networks of control. We have clear evidence that parents can rate in infancy critical aspects of their child's emotions and behaviour that seem to exert influence on the development of control and in some cases we know that specific genes are important, but confirmation and extension of these ideas are critical to understand what environments and experiences will foster self-regulation. Research is starting to provide ideas as to the epigenetic basis of environmental influence, and these need to be expanded and applied to the development of self-regulation.

It is important that specific interventions can influence connectivity even into adulthood. More studies are needed to connect brain changes fostered by learning with specific behavioural gains and then to determine if there are more than superficial similarities between adult development through specific interventions and the changes that take place in early child development. We think the small scale and tentative steps outlined in this report point the way to the types of studies that can lead to improved understanding of how specific brain changes support the child's developing abilities for self-regulation.

6

Social Cognitive Development during Adolescence

INTRODUCTION

Adolescence is the transitional period between late childhood and the beginning of adulthood, and marks the beginning of the reproductive lifespan in humans. Adolescence involves sexual maturity in terms of hormones and physical development of the body, and is also characterised by an increase in the complexity of group interactions and thus social behaviour. Adolescence is a period of development and consolidation of the social self, of one's identity and understanding of the self in relation to the social world. Anecdotal evidence and self-report data suggest that children seem to become progressively self-conscious and concerned with other people's opinions as they go through puberty and the period of adolescence.

The psychosocial context of adolescents is markedly different to that of children and adults. Relationships with peers, family and society go through distinct changes during this time. Adolescents begin to assert more autonomous control over their decisions, emotions and actions, and start to disengage from parental control. At the same time, the school context involves an intense socialisation process during which adolescents become increasingly aware of the perspectives of classmates, teachers and other societal influences.

Recent evidence has shown that the brain goes through a remodelling process during adolescence. It is possible that neural plasticity facilitates the development of social cognitive skills required during the period of adolescence.

DEVELOPMENT OF THE ADOLESCENT BRAIN

Recent structural MRI studies have demonstrated that the brain undergoes considerable development during adolescence. Both cross-sectional and longitudinal data demonstrate that changes in the frontal and parietal regions are especially pronounced and prolonged. Grey matter (GM) development in these areas is non-linear, in contrast to its linear development in the occipital lobes. The volume of GM in the frontal lobes increases during childhood with a peak occurring at around 12 years for males and 11 years for females, roughly coinciding with the age of puberty onset. This is followed by a decline in GM volume during adolescence.

Similarly, parietal lobe GM volume increases during the pre-adolescent stage to a peak at around 12 years for males and 10 years for females, and is followed by a decline during adolescence. While frontal and parietal cortex development is relatively rapid during adolescence, GM in the superior temporal cortex, including superior temporal sulcus (STS), reaches a peak at around 16 years and then follows a steady decline, not reaching maturity until relatively late. At the same time, there is an increase in prefrontal cortex (PFC) and parietal cortex white matter (WM) density from puberty onset, throughout adolescence and into adulthood.

Earlier post-mortem investigations of human brain development revealed that two main cellular processes occur in the frontal cortex during adolescence: synaptogenesis followed by synaptic pruning;and axonal myelination. Myelinated axons appear white in MR images, whereas non-myelinated matter appears grey.

Thus, the increase in WM seen in certain brain areas in MRI images during childhood and adolescence is thought to reflect the increase in myelination in those areas. The decrease in GM during adolescence might simply be a consequence of the increase in WM (since there is no increase in total brain volume). However, the non-linearity of GM development suggests it does not simply reflect the consequences of increased WM. Instead, it has been suggested that the pattern of GM development reflects, at least in part, the synaptic reorganisation that takes place during that period. The combined effect of these maturational processes might be to fine-tune neural circuitry in the PFC and other cortical regions, and thus increase efficiency of the cognitive systems they subserve.

CHANGES IN COGNITION: DEVELOPMENT OF EXECUTIVE FUNCTION

Structural development of these cortical regions may influence cognitive functioning during adolescence. A combination of behavioural and fMRI studies have demonstrated development of executive functions, that is, cognitive skills that enable the control and coordination of thoughts and behaviour, which are generally associated with the PFC. Behavioural studies of performance on tasks including inhibitory control, processing speed, prospective memory, working memory, decision-making and risk-taking continue to develop during adolescence. fMRI studies have shown that performance changes in executive function tasks are related to PFC development.

NEURAL PLASTICITY AND THE DEVELOPMENT OF INTELLIGENCE

A recent longitudinal MRI study of participants aged between 3 and 29 years revealed that the trajectory of change in cortical thickness is associated with the development of IQ. The relationship between cortical thickness and IQ, as indexed by Wechsler intelligence scales, was found to vary with age. Stratification of participants into three IQ bands (average, high and superior IQ) indicated that the maximum trajectory differences between groups were in superior frontal gyrus bilaterally extending into the medial PFC. The developmental shift in trajectory was most pronounced for the most intelligent children and adolescents: the children with the highest IQ had a thinner cortex in early childhood but cortical thickness then increased, peaking at around age 11, and then underwent the most dramatic cortical thinning thereafter. Shaw and colleagues proposed that intelligence levels relate to how the cortex changes during development.

While several studies have investigated the development of executive function in adolescence, as yet, few have looked at the development of social cognition during this period. In the next section, we describe studies that have focussed on the development of socio-emotional processing during adolescence.

DEVELOPMENT OF SOCIAL COGNITION

EMOTION PROCESSING IN ADOLESCENCE

The environmental and biological changes at adolescence lead to new social encounters and heightened awareness and interest in other people. The importance of evaluating other people may be associated with increased attention to socially salient stimuli, particularly faces, and the processing of emotional information. Recognition of facial expressions of emotion is one area of social cognition that has been investigated during adolescence. The amygdala, a brain region associated with emotion processing, was found to be significantly activated in response to the perception of fearful facial expressions in an fMRI study of adolescents aged between 12 and 17 years.

The perception of happy faces compared with neutral was associated with significant bilateral amygdalar activation in a group of 12 adolescents aged 13–17 years. Sex-differences in amygdala-mediated cognitive development have also been reported to occur during adolescence. While the left amygdala responded to fearful facial expressions in all children, left amygdala activity decreased over the adolescent period in females but not in males. Females also demonstrated greater activation of the dorsolateral PFC over this period, whereas males demonstrated less activation in this region with age. These findings were taken as evidence for an association between cerebral maturation and increased regulation of emotional behaviour;the latter mediated by prefrontal systems. A similar result was found in a recent study by Yurgelun-Todd and Killgore (2006) in a study of facial emotion processing in adolescents. In this study, bilateral prefrontal activity increased with age (from 8 to 15 years) for girls, whereas only the activity in right PFC was correlated with age in boys. It is possible that functional maturation associated with face emotion processing may be modulated by gender-specific hormonal profiles.

The effect of age on amygdala response to fearful facial expressions was addressed byThomas and colleagues (2001). Adults (mean age 24 years) relative to children (mean age 11 years) demonstrated greater amygdala activation to fearful facial expressions, whereas children relative to adults showed greater amygdala activation to neutral faces. It was argued that the children perceived the neutral faces as more ambiguous than the fearful facial expressions, with resulting increases in amygdala activation to the neutral faces. Age-related differences in neural strategies for emotion processing have been shown in an fMRI study of a group of adolescents (aged 7–17 years) and a group of adults who viewed faces showing emotional expressions.

While viewing faces with fearful emotional expressions, compared with adults, adolescents exhibited greater activation of the amygdala, orbitofrontal cortex (OFC) and anterior cingulate cortex (ACC). When subjects were asked to switch their attention between a salient emotional property of the face, like thinking about how afraid it makes them feel, and a non-emotional property, such as how wide the nose is, adults, but not adolescents, selectively engaged and disengaged OFC. In other words, the adult brain better modulated OFC activity based on attention demands, while the adolescent brain better modulated activity based on the demands of emotion. On the other hand, when there were no attentional demands, emotional content of the stimuli induced higher activity in ACC, OFC and amygdala in the adolescents compared with the adults. These fMRI results suggest that both the brain's emotion processing and cognitive appraisal systems develop during adolescence. This development has previously been interpreted in the context of the Social Information Processing Network (SIPN) model.

The SIPN model posits that social information processing occurs by way of three interacting neural 'nodes', which afford the detection of social stimuli that are then integrated to a larger emotional and cognitive framework. Nelson and colleagues propose that the 'detection node', comprising the intraparietal sulcus, STS, fusiform face area as well as temporal and occipital regions, deciphers social properties of the stimulus such as biological motion. The 'affective node,' including limbic areas of the brain including the amygdala, ventral striatum, hypothalamus and OFC, processes the emotional significance of the social stimulus. Finally, the 'cognitive-regulatory node', consisting of much of the PFC, is responsible for theory of mind, impulse inhibition and goal-directed behaviour. Development during adolescence of the nodes, the connections between them, the innervation by gonadal steroid receptors and the maturation of the neural substrates themselves, are proposed to explain development of social cognitive behaviours.

THE IMAGINARY AUDIENCE

The emergence of the social self seems to be marked by a period of heightened self-consciousness, during which adolescents are thought to become increasingly preoccupied with other people's concerns about their actions, thoughts and appearance. This development has been described in terms of phases of egocentrism during childhood and adolescence and is based on Piaget's stages of cognitive growth. It is proposed that after children develop internal representations of objects and referential thinking during early childhood, they reach the stage of the 'emergence of concrete operations'. Between the ages of 7 and 11 years, children's abilities to deal with classes and hierarchies are proposed to be restricted to concrete, physical entities and do not extend to abstract thought. Children of this age group therefore manifest an inability to distinguish between a mental construction and perceptual phenomena. By age 11, the emergence of 'formal operational thought' enables children to differentiate between the perception of an object and their own mental construction of it, allowing them to objectify their own thoughts and reason about them. Piaget proposed that this new form of thinking allows children at early adolescence to conceptualise other people's thoughts and take their perspectives.

The development of adolescent egocentrism is therefore thought to be a dialectic process: it is the ability to represent other people's thoughts as distinct from their own and therefore decentre themselves that also drives the new form of egocentrism. In other words, as soon as they are able to understand that other people have distinct thoughts and perspectives, they become preoccupied with the notion that other people's thoughts are focused on their own behaviour or appearance. Elkind's original theoretical model of adolescent egocentrism delineates two ideation patterns thought to arise as a consequence, and to characterise common adolescent social behaviours: the 'imaginary audience' and the 'personal fable'. The notion of the imaginary audience refers to adolescents' beliefs that they are the object of other people's scrutiny. According to Elkind's theory, this belief results in increased self-consciousness, a tendency to anticipate the reactions of other people in relation to the self, and a feeling of being the focus of attention, regardless of whether a real audience exists or not in the situation. The personal fable, a related construct, denotes adolescents' convictions of their own personal uniqueness, giving rise to the sense of being 'special'.

Since this original account of adolescent egocentrism, social psychological studies have investigated the imaginary audience with questionnaires and qualitative approaches. The exact age, validity and explanation of Elkind's account of adolescent egocentrism have been challenged, and the theory has since evolved.

PERSPECTIVE TAKING

The ability to take another's perspective is crucial for successful social communication. Reasoning about others, and understanding what they think, feel or believe, involves stepping into their 'mental shoes' and taking their perspective. The distinction between the phenomenal and representational levels of self-other relationships is worth noting. As detailed by Frith and de Vignemont (2005) and Vogeley and colleagues (2004), one can take different perspectives in terms of spatial representations, such that the locations of other entities in space are represented by the beholder in different reference frames. In an egocentric frame of reference, the location of an object is represented in relation to the subject, *i.e.* in relation to the personal agent (*e.g.* is the line on your right or left?), whereas in the allocentric frame of reference, the location of one object in relation to another object is represented by the agent (*e.g.* is the line on the right or left of the square?). Thus, while the egocentric perspective relates that which is seen to the agent who sees it, the allocentric perspective is independent of the agent's position. At the phenomenal level, however, the first-person perspective (1PP) (*e.g.* is the line on your right or left?) and the third-person perspective (3PP) (*e.g.* is the line on his right or left?) are both centred on an agent. Perspective taking at this phenomenal level requires 'the translocation of the egocentric viewpoint' from the 1PP to the 3PP.

Perspective taking includes awareness of one's own subjective space or mental states ('first-person perspective' or 1PP) and the ability to ascribe locations, mental states or emotions to another person ('third-person perspective' or 3PP). Perspective taking is related to first-order theory of mind in that it involves surmising what another person is thinking or feeling. It requires the ability to distinguish the self from someone else and appreciate another's intentions or beliefs. The ability to adopt another's viewpoint may underpin the ability to read other minds and understand another's feelings. Thus, emotional perspective taking, considering how 'she' would feel rather than how 'I' would feel necessitates a shift in the egocentric perspective, from one's own to another person's egocentric perspective.

MECHANISMS OF PERSPECTIVE TAKING

There is currently much debate surrounding the mechanism of perspective taking. How do we automatically switch roles from the self to the other in everyday social interactions? One prevalent view is that we understand others by mentally simulating their actions. In support of this 'simulation theory', a growing body of evidence from neurophysiological studies has demonstrated that common brain areas are activated both when we execute an action and when we observe another person perform the same action. Simulation theorists draw on the existence of a mirror neuron system to suggest that simulating other people's actions is an ontogenic precursor to understanding their thoughts and emotions. On the other side of the debate is 'theory theory', or the idea that we use a common sense psychological theory, or folk psychology, to understand other minds, rather than internally simulating them.

PERSPECTIVE TAKING AND THE BRAIN

The brain regions that undergo the most significant development during adolescence overlap with those that have been linked to the ability to take other people's perspectives and infer mental states. Functional neuroimaging studies have revealed that medial PFC, IPL and STS are associated with making the distinction between 3PP and 1PP at the motor, visuo-spatial, conceptual and emotional level. While these have shown common activations in 1PP and 3PP conditions in prefrontal and parietal areas, and common deactivations in areas such as lateral superior temporal cortex, differential activity between the two perspective conditions has also been reported. Taking someone else's perspective, whether it involves thinking about how another person would think or feel, or imagining them making an action, relative to one's own perspective, was associated with increased activity in medial superior frontal gyrus, left STS, left temporal pole and right IPL.

IPL has also been implicated in the distinction between self and other at the sensorimotor level as well as at a higher social cognitive level. In line with simulation theory, therefore, common neural networks are recruited for 1PP and 3PP. However, Vogeley and colleagues (2001) suggest that the differential brain activity implies that simulation cannot be the only mechanism at play. Perhaps the distinct brain regions activated in 3PP and 1PP indicate who the agent is in the interaction.

The medial PFC also plays a role in differentiating between the self and an unknown other such as George W. Bush, and between the self and a personally known other such as a close friend. Medial PFC has been consistently associated with mentalising. Mentalising refers to the inferences we naturally make about other people's intentions, beliefs and desires, which we then use to predict and make sense of their behaviour. A number of neuroimaging studies, using a wide range of tasks, have reported activation in what seems to be a highly circumscribed mentalising network, comprising the medial PFC, STS especially around the temporo-parietal junction (TPJ), and the temporal poles adjacent to the amygdala.

Recently, using fMRI, Aichhorn and colleagues (2006) investigated whether, like social perspective taking and theory of mind, visual perspective taking is associated with medial PFC activity. They developed a paradigm that strictly necessitated a shift of perspective in a computerised visuo-spatial task. The results demonstrated that medial PFC was not involved in visual perspective taking, but that posterior regions of the STS and TPJ were involved in judging what another can see. Drawing on results of differential neural networks shown to be involved in visual compared with social perspective taking in various studies, Aichhorn and colleagues (2006) suggested that different aspects of theory of mind are required in different types of perspective taking. They suggest that the dorsal posterior STS/TPJ region is involved in realising that minds represent the world differently and storing 'cold' facts about the mind. Medial PFC, on they other hand, is proposed to be involved representing 'hot' information such as predicting the emotional consequences of behaviour.

DEVELOPMENT OF PERSPECTIVE TAKING DURING ADOLESCENCE

A large body of research has focussed on the development of theory of mind during childhood and its impairment in autism. Since Piaget's studies using the three mountain problem, only a handful of social psychology studies have investigated perspective taking in early to middle childhood and, to our knowledge, none has considered its development during adolescence. Studies have shown that theory of mind develops in infancy by the age of 5 years. So, what are the cognitive consequences of the continued development of its underlying neural circuitry? Clearly, the development of associated abilities will be subtle. Given that the social environment dramatically changes during adolescence, and that the brain undergoes a restructuring process, it might be expected that social cognitive abilities such as perspective taking develop during adolescence. We therefore investigated development of perspective taking during adolescence.

SUBJECTS

We recruited 107 right-handed participants, comprising 30 pre-adolescent children (12 males, mean age 8.6 years, s.d. = 0.46), 40 adolescents (19 males, mean age 12.8 years, s.d. = 1.20) and 37 adults (19 males, mean age 24.0 years, s.d. = 4.05). The study was approved by the local ethics committee. Written consent was obtained from each participant, and from his or her parent or guardian for subjects under 16.

PERSPECTIVE TAKING TASK

The task involved answering questions that required the participant to imagine either how s/he would feel (for 1PP scenarios), or how a protagonist (for 3PP scenarios) would feel in various scenarios. The participant was asked to choose as quickly as possible one of two emotional faces in answer to each question (from a total of five possible emotional faces). Each participant's non-directional reaction time difference between 3PP and 1PP (ΔRT) was calculated and analysed using a one-way ANOVA to test the effects of age and gender on ΔRT.

RESULTS: DEVELOPMENT OF EFFICIENCY FOR PERSPECTIVE TAKING

While there was no significant effect of gender, there was a significant main effect of age group showing that ΔRT decreased significantly with age ($F(2,104) = 10.82; P<0.0001$;Table 1). Post hocBonferroni tests indicated that the mean ΔRT was significantly larger in pre-adolescents compared with adults ($P<0.0001$) and in adolescents compared with adults ($P < 0.005$).

ΔRT was plotted to investigate directionality. As shown in the graph, ΔRT among both groups of younger participants was larger and spread almost equally in both directions (*i.e.* 3PP > 1PP and 1PP> 3PP), whereas among adults there was little difference with ΔRT values clustering around the zero mark of the difference scale (*i.e.* 3PP = 1PP). This finding suggests that the efficiency, or strategy,of perspective taking develops during adolescence, perhaps in parallel with the underlying neural circuitry.

DISCUSSION

The synaptic reorganisation in the frontal and parietal cortices during adolescence is likely to have implications for social cognitive processes that depend on these brain regions, such as mentalising, perspective taking and related processes. This conjecture is supported by the findings from our perspective taking study. If we assume that, among the age groups tested, adults are most experienced in social interaction and have mature frontal and parietal neural circuitry, then a low difference in ΔRT (3PP = 1PP) is likely to indicate the highest proficiency in perspective taking. In contrast, the most pronounced difference in RT between 1PP and 3PP, seen in the pre-adolescent group, would therefore indicate relatively inefficient processing. It might be speculated therefore, that prior to adolescence, the unsystematic direction of ΔRT reflects an immature cognitive mechanism for perspective taking.

Whether this response pattern among pre-adolescents is a result of a relative difficulty in differentiating between the first- and third-person, or that children of this age group are less inclined, or find it more difficult, to step into another person's 'mental shoes', requires further investigation. The differences between age groups may also be influenced by differences in social experience. Compared with children and adolescents, adults are generally more skilled at instinctively inferring the perspectives of other people. Perhaps adults show no difference between RTs for 1PP and 3PP as a result of their mature neural circuitry supporting social cognition, as well as their greater social experience.

We have described how neuroimaging and behavioural data demonstrate that executive functions, recognition of facial emotions and emotional perspective taking develop during adolescence, in terms of cognitive and neural strategies. This may be interpreted in terms of the SIPN model. Executive function abilities such as risk assessment, decision making and impulse inhibition, and social cognitive abilities such as facial emotion recognition and perspective taking, are associated with components of the three nodes of the SIPN, including PFC, amygdala and STS. These social cognitive processes show development, while the neural substrates themselves show plasticity in terms of actual structure or changes in activity with age in the social cognitive tasks we have reviewed.

However, the SIPN is perhaps also limiting as it neglects the role of the parietal cortex. Parietal cortex (particularly IPL) undergoes a developmental trajectory similar to that of PFC and is associated with processes related to social cognition, such as perspective taking in the motor, conceptual and emotional domains and imitation of other people's actions. Parietal development has already been linked to the improvement in abstract reasoning skills during adolescence. Further investigations are required to determine how parietal development influences social cognitive development, and which regions are particularly involved.

New studies might consider what mechanisms are directing social cognitive development. The SIPN proposes a 'multi-step' route, in which neurally based nodes process social stimuli in a sequential manner. Somewhere in this route, however, between detecting that a stimulus is animate and imbuing it with emotional significance, the brain must assign it to the correct agent. In other words, in the framework of the SIPN, an additional 'agency node' linked to IPL might be involved in distinguishing whether the action is related to the self or to another before the limbic node would process approach or avoidance decisions and before the cognitive-regulatory node would perform higher level social processing. Indeed, as mentioned above, IPL seems to be involved in distinguishing between self and other, in terms of imagining how someone would think or feel, making an action or imagining making an action.

A recent behavioural study demonstrated that, like perspective taking, the ability to imagine making an action develops during adolescence. Two motor imagery tasks thought to tap action representations were administered to 40 young adolescents (24 males;mean age 13.1 years) and 33 adults (15 males;mean age 27.5 years). The tasks relied on the chronometry of executed (E) and imagined (I) hand actions. Typically, the timing of E and I are highly correlated owing to representations of motor constraints. However, the correlation between E and I is significantly lower for parietal lesion patients, children with developmental co-ordination disorder and adults with schizophrenia. The results of our study showed that there was a significant increase in the execution imagery time correlation between adolescence and adulthood, perhaps reflecting refinement of the action representation in the parietal cortex system. While parietal cortex is involved in storing representations of one's own actions and differentiating between self and other, it has been proposed that STS is associated with the prediction of actions based on past actions, while medial PFC is involved in anticipating future consequences of actions based on internal mental states (Frith, in press). We know from executive function studies that the ability to suppress impulses develops during adolescence, perhaps in line with PFC maturation.

As the ability to inhibit one's own impulses develops and the ability to understand other people's mental states is refined, a change in the strategy for perspective taking might take place. Perhaps children and young adolescents exert relatively poor inhibition over their own egocentric bias, and therefore rely on predicting other people's emotional perspectives based on the consequences of their own past actions. Maturation of PFC circuitry might facilitate a strategic shift such that older adolescents and adults can predict the feelings of other people based on how they anticipate the other person would feel if s/he were to make the action in the given scenario. Development of IPL might enable older adolescents and adults to keep the self/other distinction intact, while in pre-adolescents, immature circuitry in the area might lead to a blurring between 1PP and 3PP and the imposition of the self-perspective onto the other.

7

Adult Intellectual Development

Fluid and Crystallized Intelligence are the factors that make up our general intelligence. Fluid Intelligence is our basic information processing. It has the 'fluid' quality of being directable to almost any situation and gives the ability to find meaning in confusion and solve new problems. Crystallized Intelligence is one's investment in particular areas of acquired knowledge, experience and practical skills;it also includes our language and social skills.

For most people Fluid Intelligence ceases to develop after the age of about twenty and starts to fall after the age of 25, unless an appropriate intervention is made to continue the mind's active development. On the other hand, many dimensions of Crystallized Intelligence typically continue to develop throughout the life span, particularly in the individual's chosen domain of work experience. But this can limit the individual to a perspective within narrow boundaries;creativity and wisdom demand a much wider perspective, in which a range of domains are interlinked.

By using the techniques of Mind Development, the development of both Fluid and Crystallized Intelligence can be restarted and accelerated or broadened, even if the individual is of middle age, so he or she can have the boundless energy of youth and achieve the wisdom of the aged.

There is particular need for the widespread inclusion of more cognitively stimulating educational and entertainment activities for young people, as teenagers have lower IQs than their counterparts of 30 years ago. Tests carried out in 1980 and again in 2008 show that the IQ score of an average 14-year-old dropped by more than two points over the period.

Among those in the upper half of the intelligence scale, a group that is typically dominated by children from middle class families, performance was even worse, with an average IQ score six points below what it was 28 years ago. The trend marks an abrupt reversal of the so-called "Flynn effect" which has seen IQ scores rise year on year, among all age groups, in most industrialized countries throughout the past century. Youth culture is more visually orientated around computer games than they are in terms of reading and holding conversations.

This chapter will describe the stages that an individual passes through as the mind develops its faculties of intelligence, from birth through to maturity. It will indicate the points at which development may become arrested, and also show the potential that exists in human beings for much greater mind development than is customarily the case, given appropriate stimulation and training.

The future prosperity of our society depends on the standard of education rising, to develop to a high level all the kinds of intelligence of which a person is capable - not just for children at school but as an ongoing lifetime process of adult development. In this way, we have the potential to create a much saner, happier and more exciting world to live in.

CHILD VS. ADULT INTELLIGENCE

Over 90 years ago, Binet and Simon delineated two different methods of assessing intelligence. These were the psychological method (which concentrates mostly on intellectual processes, such as memory and abstract reasoning) and the pedagogical method (which concentrates on assessing what an individual knows).

The main concern of Binet and Simon was to predict elementary school performance independently from the social and economic background of the individual student. As a result, they settled on the psychological method, and they spawned an intelligence assessment paradigm which has been substantially unchanged from their original tests.

With few exceptions, the development of adult intelligence assessment instruments proceeded along the same lines of the Binet-Simon tests. Nevertheless, the difficulty of items was increased for older examinees. Thus, extant adult intelligence tests were created as little more than upward extensions of the original Binet-Simon scales.

The Binet-Simon tests are quite effective in predicting school success in both primary and secondary educational environments. However, they have been found to be much less predictive of success in post-secondary academic and occupational domains. Such a discrepancy provokes fundamental questions about intelligence.

One highly debated question asks whether college success is actually dependent on currently used forms of measured intelligence, or if present measures of intelligence are inadequately sampling the wider domain of adult intellect. One possible answer to this question lies in questioning the preference of the psychological method over the pedagogical method for assessing adult intellect. Recent research across the fields of education, cognitive science, and adult development suggests that much of adult intellect is indeed not adequately sampled by extant intelligence measures and might be better assessed through the pedagogical method.

Several lines of research have also converged on a redefinition of adult intellect that places a greater emphasis on content (knowledge) over process. Substantial strides have been made in delineating knowledge aspects of intellectual performance which are divergent from traditional measures of intelligence and in demonstrating that adult performance is greatly influence by prior topic and domain knowledge. Even some older testing literature seems to indicate that the knowledge measured by the Graduate Records Examination—Advanced topic exams is comparable or better indicator of future graduate school success and post-graduate performance than traditional aptitude measures.

KNOWLEDGE AND INTELLIGENCE

When an adult is presented with a completely novel problem (*e.g.*, memorizing a random set of numbers or letters), the basic intellectual processes are typically implicated in predicting which individuals will be successful in solving problems. The dilemma for adult intellectual assessment is that the adult is rarely presented with a completely novel problem in the real world of academic or occupational endeavors.

Rather, the problems which an adult is asked to solve almost inevitably draw greatly on the his/her accumulated knowledge and skills—one does not build a house by only memorizing physics formulae. For an adult, intellect is better conceptualized by the tasks that the person can accomplish and the skills that he/she has developed rather than the number of digits which can be stored in working memory or the number of syllogistic reasoning items which can be correctly evaluated. Thus, the content of the intellect is at least as important as the processes of intellect in determining an adult's real-world problem solving efficacy.

From the artificial intelligence field, researchers have discarded the idea of a useful General Problem Solver in favour of knowledge-based expert systems. This is because no amount of processing power can achieve real-world problem solving proficiency without an extensive set of domain-relevant knowledge structures. Gregory (1994) describes the difference between such concepts as "potential intelligence" (knowledge) and "kinetic intelligence" (process). Similarly, Schank and Birnbaum (1994) say that "what makes someone intelligent is what he/she knows."

One line of relevant educational research is from the examination of expert-novice differences which indicates that the typical expert is found to mainly differ from the novice in terms of experience and the knowledge structures that are developed through that experience rather than in terms of intellectual processes.

Additional research from developmental and gerontological perspectives has also shown that various aspects of adult intellectual functioning are greatly determined by knowledge structures and less influenced by the kinds of process measures which have been shown to decline with age over adult development.

SHIFTING PARADIGMS

By bringing together a variety of sources of research evidence, it is clear that our current methods of assessing adult intellect are insufficient. When we are confronted with situations in which the intellectual performance of adults must be predicted (*e.g.* continuing education or adult learning programmes), we must begin to take account of what they know in addition to the traditional assessment of intellectual processes.

Because adults are quite diverse in their knowledge structures (*e.g.*, a physicist may know many different things than a carpenter), the challenge for educational assessment researchers in the future will be to develop batteries of tests that can be used to assess different sources of intellectual knowledge for different individuals. When adult knowledge structures are broadly examined with tests such as the Advanced Placement AP and College Level Exam Programme CLEP, it may be possible to improve such things as the prediction of adult performance in specific educational endeavors, the placement of individuals, and adult educational counseling.

INTELLECTUAL DEVELOPMENT: AGE 17–45

Does intelligence increase or decrease during adulthood? This question has plagued psychologists for decades. Crosssectional studies of IQ tend to show that young adults perform better than middleaged or older adults, while longitudinal studies of IQ appear to indicate that people increase in intelligence through the decades, at least until their 50s. But the issue of intellectual development in adulthood is not so straightforward or simple. The results of the crosssectional studies—younger adults, as a group, do better on IQ tests—may be due more tocohort influences, such as longer schooling or greater exposure to television than that enjoyed by the previous generation, than to aging influences.

The results of the longitudinal studies—over time, persons do better on IQ tests—may be due to the effects of practice, increased comfort taking such tests, or the tendency for those who remain in the studies to perform better than those who drop out.

Attempts to measure IQ are complicated by the fact that there are different types of intelligence. Crystallized intelligence is the ability to use learned information collected throughout a lifetime, andfluid intelligence is the ability to think abstractly and deal with novel situations. Young adults tend to score higher on tests of fluid intelligence, while middle adults tend to score higher on tests of crystallized intelligence. Variables unique to young, middle, and older adults complicate any comparison of IQs among the groups. All things considered, the results of traditional IQ tests suggest that intelligence usually continues at least at the same level through young and middle adulthood.

THINKING PATTERNS

Young adult thinking, especially in a person's early 20s, resembles adolescent thinking in many ways. Many young people see life from an idealistic point of view, in which marriage is a fairy tale where lovers live happily ever after, political leaders never lie or distort the truth, and salespeople always have consumers' best interests in mind. People in their 20s have not always had the benefit of multiple life experiences, so they may still view the world from a naively trusting and black- or- white perspective. This is not to say that young adults do not question their world, challenge rules, or handle conflicts. These, and more, are normal developmental tasks that lead to realistic thinking and recognition of life's ambiguities. But until young adults reach that level of thinking, they may want absolute answers from absolute authorities.

Many young adults—particularly those who have attended college—develop the ability to reason logically, solve theoretical problems, and think abstractly. They have reached Piaget's formal operations stage of cognitive development. During this stage, individuals can also classify and compare objects and ideas, systematically seek solutions to problems, and consider future possibilities.

As young adults confront and work through the gray areas of life, some may go on to develop postformal thinking, or practical street smarts. Developing the wisdom associated with postformal thinking is a lifelong process, which begins in the teenage years and is fully realized in the older adult years.

PIAGET'S STAGES OF COGNITIVE DEVELOPMENT

Jean Piaget, a child psychologist, traced four broad stages in the logical and cognitive development of children, in his studies from the 1930s to the '70s. The first stage, from birth to two years, is the stage of Sensori-Motor intelligence: the infant's coordination of reflexes and sensori-motor repetition, leading up to basic recall of absent objects and to an experimental search for new means to achieve pleasurable ends, bounded by what the child can physically perform and observe being performed.

During the course of a child's cognitive development there are changes in the way that the individual represents (*i.e.* stores and retrieves) information that is perceived through the senses. A small infant is limited to the actions which it can make upon the immediate world surrounding it, when it first learns to separate the world into 'me' and 'not me', discovering its body schema. From then on its learning consists of developing and revising that schema as it performs more operations on the outside world and learns from the effects that result.

It is hard to imagine how a baby thinks. It cannot think in pictures of objects because it has not really discovered what objects are yet, or what properties they have, in a real enough way to picture them. Instead it remembers things as a kind of 'muscle memory' (in the sensori-motor kinesthetic system) using an internal representation of the 'feel' of things to code the information. Before 4 or 5 years of age traumatic memories and their accompanying considerations and decisions that affect future behaviour, are not available to recall in the way that an adult recalls, like a full-perceptic movie, but rather in terms of emotional body-centered feelings of needs and wants, or fears and pains, although there will be an element of auditory and visual imagery particularly accompanying poignant moments. There will be hardly any visual representation of the first eighteen months, until the infant becomes ambulatory and starts to walk and talk.

The second stage, of the toddler up to 5 years, is the stage of Pre-logical intuitivethought. This is a period of 'magical thinking' in the sense that he easily confuses apparent or imagined events with real events. He would, if allowed, jump out of a window expecting to fly, because he has seen birds fly. It is something of a 'dream world'; a toy car is very much the real thing to a toddler. This is a state commonly regressed to by those on hallucinogenic drugs.

In normal development, at about the age of five, a relatively sudden transition occurs. Control passes from the mammalian brain (with schemata based on classical conditioning) to the fully human brain (a structure operating on associative, operant and cognitive processes). After this transition, many lower order mechanisms become inhibited and they are replaced by higher order cortical mechanisms, which operate cognitively. As part of this transition, language begins to function as a vehicle for logical thought at the concrete level, rather than solely a means to serve social and emotional needs. The predominant mode of representation of the world has become auditory, with memories featuring received commands.

The third stage, between 6 - 12, is Concrete Operational thought, when the child can symbolize (*i.e.* can make a concrete mental image of) operations, without having to do them physically. The child has developed realistic internal imaging of the world around him, so that by 7 or 8 years of age a concrete visual mode of representation has become the predominant way of thinking about and remembering experience, alongside kinesthetic and auditory representations. He learns to classify and relate, and to measure distances and quantities, and thereby performs constructive thinking. Contact with the environment is maintained during such mental operations, because by reversing them, a return to the perceived form is always possible. A child will build and knock down Lego constructions. Concrete operations are the foundation upon which more abstract intellectual operations can be built. Young children and those restricted to concrete operations tend to focus attention on only one salient aspect of an object, situation or problem at a time, to the exclusion of other potentially relevant aspects. Piaget called this tendency 'centration.'

Pretty soon though, the child's world widens further still, until it includes information which isn't easily represented using pictures. (Try imaging a concept like 'freedom' or 'fairness'). When this happens, the child becomes more likely to use symbolic representation, including inner speech, using words as formalized symbols which 'stand for' the concepts. This is the beginning of the conceptual, auditory digital stage of development. At this point the child's own decisions and intentions may be expressed as inner speech, whereas before they were 'felt' intentions. This is the beginning of conceptual cognitive ability, which is developed through effective education.

The fourth stage, that takes place from age 12 (given sufficient IQ, education and stimuli) to adulthood, is Formal Operations. This is a more objective way of perceiving the world with the ability to focus simultaneously on several aspects of a problem - this is 'decentration.' Even adults, before they obtain the full abilities of formal operations - or if (as is common) they do not develop that far - continue with a centrated, single-minded point of view, intolerant of alternatives. Adult centration is the rule rather than the exception. The centrated person has tunnel vision when it comes to the world of ideas;the decentrated person is open to considering new ideas from all directions.

Typically, a person of average intelligence (which is only 100 by definition) would remain below the sub-stage 1 of Formal Operations, predominantly using Concrete Operations. A higher level of mental maturity would only be manifest in emotionally neutral situations or in a domain specific manner, perhaps in the context of work requiring concentrated problem solving. When "off duty" or when under emotional pressure most people would tend to regress to the level of Concrete Operational thought, and under severe pressure to the Pre-Logical thinking of Stage 2.

Only about 17per cent of the population, those with an IQ above 110, use Formal Operations on an everyday basis. And only about 5per cent of the population reach the final stage of Formal Operations, true formal thought, and probably about 2per cent continue to develop at the Postformal Level. Of them, about 0.1per cent go on to complete this process. This is mainly because a person needs to be in an educational or otherwise stimulating environment, until he or she is about thirty. Most university students leave university after gaining a first degree at between the ages of twenty-two to twenty-four, so the process of Postformal development all but ceases, unless they continue to work in an intellectually stimulating environment.

Having a wealth of concrete information which he is unable to understand, the person attempts to rearrange this information in order to simplify it. He discovers he can do this by keeping some variables constant, while he experiments with the others. The person induces generalized laws which he can apply to data of the most diverse kinds. The person can think about thoughts, classify classifications, and 'operate on operations' and so conceive of general laws behind the array of particular instances. Hypotheses can be made and tested, and implications deduced, through scientific experiment.

To summarize, the baby's mode of representation is primarily kinesthetic, at the sensori-motor stage of development. By 4 years of age, during the pre-logical stage, the predominant representation has become auditory. The child then develops realistic internal imaging of the world around him, so that by 7 or 8 years of age a concrete visual mode of representation has become predominant. Conceptual thought as inner speech then develops and by 10 years of age at the earliest, or more typically 12-14 years, the young person is ready, given sufficient and competent schooling, to develop towards Formal operations.

Note: The following research showed that subjects with a high IQ pass through the Piagetian stages more rapidly. One hundred nine fifth and seventh graders, classified as either bright or average, were tested to determine the relationship of intelligence (as defined by scores on psychometrically derived tasks) and developmental precocity (defined in terms of Piagetian theory). Specific measures used were the Iowa Tests of Basic Skills, Raven's Standard Progressive Matrices, and Piagetian tasks (conservation of volume, displacement, the balance, and the period of a pendulum). The major finding was that students who scored higher on psychometric measures of intelligence were also developmentally advanced in Piaget's sequence of cognitive developmental stages. The finding did not contradict Piagetian theory since out-of-sequence successes were not observed.

Very bright (mean IQ = 152) third graders were compared with both average IQ third graders and average IQ sixth graders on perceptual, cognitive, and affective perspective-taking tasks. The role-taking skills of the intellectually-gifted children were more similar to those of their mental age mates than to those of their chronological age mates on both the cognitive and affective tasks. On the perceptual task, the bright children's performance fell between that of the two comparison groups. The results provide evidence that gifted children are advanced in thinking about both the social and physical worlds, and have implications for educational issues such as curriculum development and acceleration vs. enrichment.

Jean Piaget offers a helpful description of developmental stages as they relate to learning. Gifted students are often in his "formal operations" stage when their peers are still in his "pre-operational" or "concrete operations" stages. When a child is developmentally advanced he/she has different learning abilities and needs. This is where Bloom's Taxonomy can be a particularly useful. Students in the "formal operations" developmental stage need learning experiences at the upper end of Bloom's Taxonomy. Essentially all assignments should offer the student the opportunity to utilize higher level thinking skills like analysis, synthesis and evaluation, as defined by Bloom.

Piaget has written that somewhere around puberty, given sufficient educational stimulus the thinking process changes from concrete operations to formal operations. Neurological change is not the only change at this time;the social environment of an adolescent plays a major role along with quality of education being another key factor. Children construct reality out of their experience with the environment. As children grow older and their thought process matures they can construct reality more closer to that of an adult.

PIAGET'S THEORY OF COGNITIVE DEVELOPMENT

Piaget's theory of cognitive development is a comprehensive theory about the nature and development of human intelligence. Piagetbelieved that one's childhood plays a vital and active role in a person's development. Piaget's idea is primarily known as adevelopmental stage theory. The theory deals with the nature of knowledge itself and how humans gradually come to acquire, construct, and use it. To Piaget, cognitive development was a progressive reorganization of mental processes resulting from biological maturation and environmental experience. He believed that children construct an understanding of the world around them, experience discrepancies between what they already know and what they discover in their environment, then adjust their ideas accordingly.

Moreover, Piaget claimed that cognitive development is at the center of the human organism, and language is contingent on knowledge and understanding acquired through cognitive development. Piaget's earlier work received the greatest attention. Many parents have been encouraged to provide a rich, supportive environment for their child's natural propensity to grow and learn. Child-centered classrooms and "open education" are direct applications of Piaget's views. Despite its huge success, Piaget's theory has some limitations that Piaget recognized himself: for example, the theory supports sharp stages rather than continuous development (decalage).

NATURE OF INTELLIGENCE: OPERATIVE AND FIGURATIVE

Piaget noted that reality is a dynamic system of continuous change and, as such, is defined in reference to the two conditions that define dynamic systems. Specifically, he argued that reality involves transformations and states. Transformations refer to all manners of changes that a thing or person can undergo. States refer to the conditions or the appearances in which things or persons can be found between transformations. For example, there might be changes in shape or form (for instance, liquids are reshaped as they are transferred from one vessel to another, and similarly humans change in their characteristics as they grow older), in size (for example, a series of coins on a table might be placed close to each other or far apart), or in placement or location in space and time (*e.g.*, various objects or persons might be found at one place at one time and at a different place at another time). Thus, Piaget argued, if human intelligence is to be adaptive, it must have functions to represent both the transformational and the static aspects of reality. He proposed that operative intelligence is responsible for the representation and manipulation of the dynamic or transformational aspects of reality, and that figurative intelligence is responsible for the representation of the static aspects of reality.

Operative intelligence is the active aspect of intelligence. It involves all actions, overt or covert, undertaken in order to follow, recover, or anticipate the transformations of the objects or persons of interest. Figurative intelligence is the more or less static aspect of intelligence, involving all means of representation used to retain in mind the states (*i.e.*, successive forms, shapes, or locations) that intervene between transformations. That is, it involves perception, imitation, mental imagery, drawing, and language.Therefore, the figurative aspects of intelligence derive their meaning from the operative aspects of intelligence, because states cannot exist independently of the transformations that interconnect them. Piaget stated that the figurative or the representational aspects of intelligence are subservient to its operative and dynamic aspects, and therefore, that understanding essentially derives from the operative aspect of intelligence.

At any time, operative intelligence frames how the world is understood and it changes if understanding is not successful. Piaget stated that this process of understanding and change involves two basic functions: assimilation and accommodation.

ASSIMILATION AND ACCOMMODATION

Through his study of the field of education, Piaget focused on two processes, which he named assimilation and accommodation. To Piaget, assimilation meant integrating external elements into structures of lives or environments, or those we could have through experience. Assimilation is how humans perceive and adapt to new information.

It is the process of fitting new information into pre-existing cognitive schemas. Assimilation in which new experiences are reinterpreted to fit into, or assimilate with, old ideas.It occurs when humans are faced with new or unfamiliar information and refer to previously learned information in order to make sense of it. In contrast, accommodation is the process of taking new information in one's environment and altering pre-existing schemas in order to fit in the new information. This happens when the existing schema (knowledge) does not work, and needs to be changed to deal with a new object or situation. Accommodation is imperative because it is how people will continue to interpret new concepts, schemas, frameworks, and more. Piaget believed that the human brain has been programmed through evolution to bring equilibrium, which is what he believed ultimately influences structures by the internal and external processes through assimilation and accommodation.

Piaget's understanding was that assimilation and accommodation cannot exist without the other. They are two sides of a coin. To assimilate an object into an existing mental schema, one first needs to take into account or accommodate to the particularities of this object to a certain extent. For instance, to recognize (assimilate) an apple as an apple, one must first focus (accommodate) on the contour of this object. To do this, one needs to roughly recognize the size of the object.

Development increases the balance, or equilibration, between these two functions. When in balance with each other, assimilation and accommodation generate mental schemas of the operative intelligence. When one function dominates over the other, they generate representations which belong to figurative intelligence.

SENSORIMOTOR STAGE

Cognitive development is Jean Piaget's theory. Through a series of stages, Piaget proposed four stages of cognitive development: the sensorimotor, preoperational, concrete operational and formal operational period. The sensorimotor stage is the first of the four stages in cognitive development which "extends from birth to the acquisition of language". In this stage, infants progressively construct knowledge and understanding of the world by coordinating experiences (such as vision and hearing) with physical interactions with objects (such as grasping, sucking, and stepping). Infants gain knowledge of the world from the physical actions they perform within it. They progress from reflexive, instinctual action at birth to the beginning of symbolic thought towards the end of the stage.

Children learn that they are separated from the environment. They have aspect of environment, even though they may be outside the reach of a child's senses. In this stage, according to Piaget, the development of object permanence is one of the most important accomplishments. Object permanence is a child's understanding that objects continue to exist even though he or she cannot be seen or heard. Peek-a-boo is a good test for that. By the end of the sensorimotor period, children develop a permanent sense of self and object.

US Navy 100406-N-7478G-346 Operations Specialist 2nd Class Reginald Harlmon and Electronics Technician 3rd Class Maura Schulze play peek-a-boo with a child in the Children's Ward at Hospital Likas

Piaget divided the sensorimotor stage into six sub-stages".

Sub-Stage	Age	Description
1 Simple Reflexes	Birth-6 weeks	"Coordination of sensation and action through reflexive behaviors". Three primary reflexes are described by Piaget: sucking of objects in the mouth, following moving or interesting objects with the eyes, and closing of the hand when an object makes contact with the palm (palmar grasp). Over the first six weeks of life, these reflexes begin to become voluntary actions. For example, the palmar reflex becomes intentional grasping.
2 First habits and primary circular reactions phase	6 weeks - 4 month s	"Coordination of sensation and two types of schema: habits (reflex) and primary circular reactions (reproduction of an event that initially occurred by chance). The main focus is still on the infant's body".As an example of this type of reaction, an infant might repeat the motion of passing their hand before their face. Also at this phase, passive reactions, caused by classical or operant conditioning, can begin.
3 Secondary circular reactions phase	4–8 monhs	Development of habits. "Infants become more object-oriented, moving beyond self-preoccupation; repeat actions that bring interesting or pleasurable results". This stage is associated primarily with the development of coordination between vision and prehension. Three new abilities occur at this stage: intentional grasping for a desired object, secondary circular reactions, and differentiations between ends and means. At this stage, infants will intentionally grasp the air in the direction of a desired object, often to the amusement of friends and family. Secondary circular reactions, or the repetition of an action involving an external object begin; for example, moving a switch to turn on a light repeatedly. The differentiation between means and ends also occurs. This is perhaps one of the most important stages of a child's growth as it signifies the dawn of logic.
4 Coordination of secondary circular reactions stages	8–12 mont hs	"Coordination of vision and touch—hand-eye coordination; coordination of schemas and intentionality".This stage is associated primarily with the development of logic and the coordination between means and ends. This is an extremely important stage of development, holding what Piaget calls the "first properintelligence". Also, this stage marks the beginning of goal orientation, the deliberate planning of steps to meet an objective.
5 Tertiary circular reactions, novelty, and curiosity	12–18 mont hs	"Infants become intrigued by the many properties of objects and by the many things they can make happen to objects; they experiment with new behavior". This stage is associated primarily with the discovery of new means to meet goals. Piaget describes the child at this juncture as the "young scientist," conducting pseudo-experiments to discover new methods of meeting challenges.
6 Internalization of Schemas	18–24 mont hs	"Infants develop the ability to use primitive symbols and form enduring mental representations". This stage is associated primarily with the beginnings of insight, or true creativity. This marks the passage into the preoperational stage.

PRE-OPERATIONAL STAGE

Piaget's second stage, the pre-operational stage, starts when the child begins to learn to speak at age two and lasts up until the age of seven. During the Pre-operational Stage of cognitive development, Piaget noted that children do not yet understand concrete logic and cannot mentally manipulate information. Children's increase in playing and pretending takes place in this stage. However, the child still has trouble seeing things from different points of view. The children's play is mainly categorized by symbolic play and manipulating symbols. Such play is demonstrated by the idea of checkers being snacks, pieces of paper being plates, and a box being a table. Their observations of symbols exemplifies the idea of play with the absence of the actual objects involved. By observing sequences of play, Piaget was able to demonstrate that, towards the end of the second year, a qualitatively new kind of psychological functioning occurs, known as the Pre-operational Stage.

The pre-operational stage is sparse and logically inadequate in regard to mental operations. The child is able to form stable concepts as well as magical beliefs. The child, however, is still not able to perform operations, which are tasks that the child can do mentally, rather than physically. Thinking in this stage is still egocentric, meaning the child has difficulty seeing the viewpoint of others. The Pre-operational Stage is split into two substages: the symbolic function substage, and the intuitive thought substage. The symbolic function substage is when children are able to understand, represent, remember, and picture objects in their mind without having the object in front of them. The intuitive thought substage is when children tend to propose the questions of "why?" and "how come?" This stage is when children want the knowledge of knowing everything.

SYMBOLIC FUNCTION SUBSTAGE

At about two to four years of age, children cannot yet manipulate and transform information in a logical way. However, they now can think in images and symbols. Other examples of mental abilities are language and pretend play. Symbolic play is when children develop imaginary friends or role-play with friends. Children's play becomes more social and they assign roles to each other. Some examples of symbolic play include playing house, or having a tea party. Interestingly, the type of symbolic play in which children engage is connected with their level of creativity and ability to connect with others. Additionally, the quality of their symbolic play can have consequences on their later development. For example, young children whose symbolic play is of a violent nature tend to exhibit less prosocial behaviour and are more likely to display antisocial tendencies in later years.

In this stage, there are still limitations, such as egocentrism and precausal thinking.

Egocentrism occurs when a child is unable to distinguish between their own perspective and that of another person. Children tend to stick to their own viewpoint, rather than consider the view of others. Indeed, they are not even aware that such a concept as "different viewpoints" exists. Egocentrism can be seen in an experiment performed by Piaget and Swiss developmental psychologist Bärbel Inhelder, known as the three-mountain problem. In this experiment, three views of a mountain are shown to the child, who is asked what a traveling doll would see at the various angles. The child will consistently describe what they can see from the position from which they are seated, regardless of from what angle they are asked to take the doll's perspective. Egocentrism would also cause a child to believe, "I like Sesame Street, so Daddy must like Sesame Street, too".

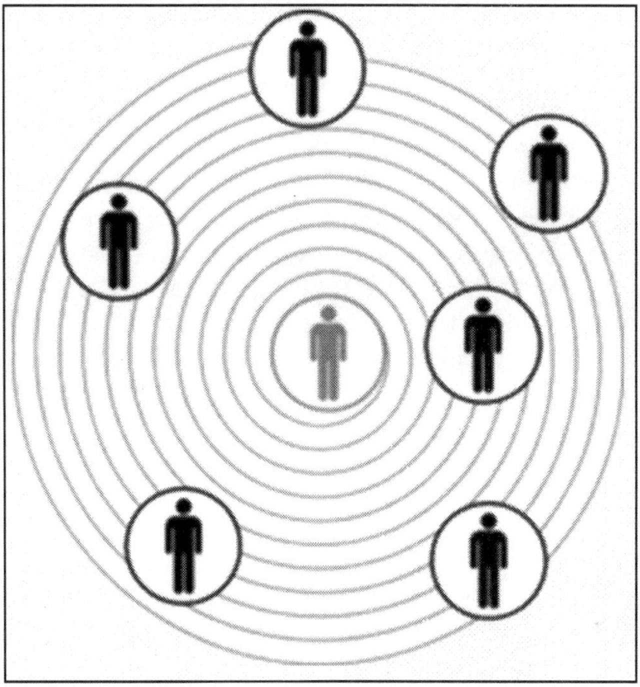

Fig. Egocentrism.

Similar to preoperational children's egocentric thinking is their structuring of a cause and effect relationships. Piaget coined the term "precausal thinking" to describe the way in which preoperational children use their own existing ideas or views, like in egocentrism, to explain cause-and-effect relationships. Three main concepts of causality as displayed by children in the preoperational stage include:animism, artificialism and transductive reasoning.

Animism is the belief that inanimate objects are capable of actions and have lifelike qualities. An example could be a child believing that the sidewalk was mad and made them fall down, or that the stars twinkle in the sky because they are happy. Artificialism refers to the belief that environmental characteristics can be attributed to human actions or interventions. For example, a child might say that it is windy outside because someone is blowing very hard, or the clouds are white because someone painted them that colour.

Finally, precausal thinking is categorized by transductive reasoning. Transductive reasoning is when a child fails to understand the true relationships between cause and effect. Unlike deductive or inductive reasoning (general to specific, or specific to general), transductive reasoning refers to when a child reasons from specific to specific, drawing a relationship between two separate events that are otherwise unrelated. For example, if a child hears the dog bark and then a balloon popped, the child would conclude that because the dog barked, the balloon popped.

INTUITIVE THOUGHT SUBSTAGE

At between about the ages of 4 and 7, children tend to become very curious and ask many questions, beginning the use of primitive reasoning. There is an emergence in the interest of reasoning and wanting to know why things are the way they are. Piaget called it the "intuitive substage" because children realize they have a vast amount of knowledge, but they are unaware of how they acquired it. Centration, conservation, irreversibility, class inclusion, and transitive inference are all characteristics of preoperative thought. Centration is the act of focusing all attention on one characteristic or dimension of a situation, whilst disregarding all others. Conservation is the awareness that altering a substance's appearance does not change its basic properties. Children at this stage are unaware of conservation and exhibit centration. Both centration and conservation can be more easily understood once familiarized with Piaget's most famous experimental task.

In this task, a child is presented with two identical beakers containing the same amount of liquid. The child usually notes that the beakers do contain the same amount of liquid. When one of the beakers is poured into a taller and thinner container, children who are younger than seven or eight years old typically say that the two beakers no longer contain the same amount of liquid, and that the taller container holds the larger quantity (centration), without taking into consideration the fact that both beakers were previously noted to contain the same amount of liquid. Due to superficial changes, the child was unable to comprehend that the properties of the substances continued to remain the same (conservation).

Irreversibility is a concept developed in this stage which is closely related to the ideas of centration and conservation. Irreversibility refers to when children are unable to mentally reverse a sequence of events. In the same beaker situation, the child does not realize that, if the sequence of events was reversed and the water from the tall beaker was poured back into its original beaker, then the same amount of water would exist. Another example of children's reliance on visual representations is their misunderstanding of "less than" or "more than". When two rows containing equal amounts of blocks are placed in front of a child, one row spread farther apart than the other, the child will think that the row spread farther contains more blocks.

Class inclusion refers to a kind of conceptual thinking that children in the preoperational stage cannot yet grasp. Children's inability to focus on two aspects of a situation at once inhibits them from understanding the principle that one category or class can contain several different subcategories or classes. For example, a four-year-old girl may be shown a picture of eight dogs and three cats. The girl knows what cats and dogs are, and she is aware that they are both animals. However, when asked, "Are there more dogs or animals?" she is likely to answer "more dogs". This is due to her difficulty focusing on the two subclasses and the larger class all at the same time. She may have been able to view the dogs as dogs or animals, but struggled when trying to classify them as both, simultaneously. Similar to this is concept relating to intuitive thought, known as "transitive inference".

Transitive inference is using previous knowledge to determine the missing piece, using basic logic. Children in the preoperational stage lack this logic. An example of transitive inference would be when a child is presented with the information "A" is greater than "B" and "B" is greater than "C". This child may have difficulty here understanding that "A" is also greater than "C".

CONCRETE OPERATIONAL STAGE

The concrete operational stage is the third stage of Piaget's theory of cognitive development. This stage, which follows the preoperational stage, occurs between the ages of 7 and 11 (preadolescence) years, and is characterized by the appropriate use of logic. During this stage, a child's thought processes become more mature and "adult like". They start solving problems in a more logical fashion. Abstract, hypothetical thinking is not yet developed in the child, and children can only solve problems that apply to concrete events or objects.

At this stage, the children undergo a transition where the child learns rules such as conservation. Piaget determined that children are able to incorporateInductive reasoning. Inductive reasoning involves drawing inferences from observations in order to make a generalization. In contrast, children struggle with deductive reasoning, which involves using a generalized principle in order to try to predict the outcome of an event. Children in this stage commonly experience difficulties with figuring out logic in their heads. For example, a child will understand that "A is more than B" and "B is more than C". However, when asked "is A more than C?", the child might not be able to logically figure the question out in their heads.

Two other important processes in the concrete operational stage are logic and the elimination of egocentrism.

Egocentrism is the inability to consider or understand a perspective other than one's own. It is the phase where the thought and morality of the child is completely self focused. During this stage, the child acquires the ability to view things from another individual's perspective, even if they think that perspective is incorrect. For instance, show a child a comic in which Jane puts a doll under a box, leaves the room, and then Melissa moves the doll to a drawer, and Jane comes back. A child in the concrete operations stage will say that Jane will still think it's under the box even though the child knows it is in the drawer.

Children in this stage can, however, only solve problems that apply to actual (concrete) objects or events, and not abstract concepts or hypothetical tasks. Understanding and knowing how to use full common sense has not yet been completely adapted.

Piaget determined that children in the concrete operational stage were able to incorporate inductive logic. On the other hand, children at this age have difficulty using deductive logic, which involves using a general principle to predict the outcome of a specific event. This includes mental reversibility. An example of this is being able to reverse the order of relationships between mental categories. For example, a child might be able to recognize that his or her dog is a Labrador, that a Labrador is a dog, and that a dog is an animal, and draw conclusions from the information available, as well as apply all these processes to hypothetical situations.

The abstract quality of the adolescent's thought at the formal operational level is evident in the adolescent's verbal problem solving ability. The logical quality of the adolescent's thought is when children are more likely to solve problems in a trial-and-error fashion. Adolescents begin to think more as a scientist thinks, devising plans to solve problems and systematically test opinions. They use hypothetical-deductive reasoning, which means that they develop hypotheses or best guesses, and systematically deduce, or conclude, which is the best path to follow in solving the problem. During this stage the adolescent is able to understand love, logical proofs and values. During this stage the young person begins to entertain possibilities for the future and is fascinated with what they can be.

Adolescents also are changing cognitively by the way that they think about social matters. Adolescent egocentrism governs the way that adolescents think about social matters, and is the heightened self-consciousness in them as they are, which is reflected in their sense of personal uniqueness and invincibility. Adolescent egocentrism can be dissected into two types of social thinking, imaginary audience that involves attention-getting behaviour, and personal fable, which involves an adolescent's sense of personal uniqueness and invincibility. These two types of social thinking begin to affect a child's egocentrism in the concrete stage. However, it carries over to the formal operational stage when they are then faced with abstract thought and fully logical thinking.

TESTING FOR CONCRETE OPERATIONS

Piagetian tests are well known and practiced to test for concrete operations. The most prevalent tests are those for conservation. There are some important aspects that the experimenter must take into account when performing experiments with these children.

One example of an experiment for testing conservation is an experimenter will have two glasses that are the same size, fill them to the same level with liquid, which the child will acknowledge is the same. Then, the experimenter will pour the liquid from one of the small glasses into a tall, thin glass. The experimenter will then ask the child if the taller glass has more liquid, less liquid, or the same amount of liquid. The child will then give his answer. The experimenter will ask the child why he gave his answer, or why he thinks that is.

- *Justification:* After the child has answered the question being posed, the experimenter must ask why the child gave that answer. This is important because the answers they give can help the experimenter to assess the child's developmental age.
- *Number of times asking:* Some argue that if a child is asked if the amount of liquid in the first set of glasses is equal then, after pouring the water into the taller glass, the experimenter asks again about the amount of liquid, the children will start to doubt their original answer. They may start to think that the original levels were not equal, which will influence their second answer.
- *Word Choice:* The phrasing that the experimenter uses may affect how the child answers. If, in the liquid and glass example, the experimenter asks, "Which of these glasses has more liquid?", the child may think that his thoughts of them being the same is wrong because the adult is saying that one must have more. Alternatively, if the experimenter asks, "Are these equal?", then the child is more likely to say that they are, because the experimenter is implying that they are.

FORMAL OPERATIONAL STAGE

The final stage is known as the formal operational stage (adolescence and into adulthood, roughly ages 11 to approximately 15-20): Intelligence is demonstrated through the logical use of symbols related to abstract concepts. This form of thought includes "assumptions that have no necessary relation to reality." At this point, the person is capable of hypothetical and deductive reasoning. During this time, people develop the ability to think about abstract concepts.

Piaget stated that "hypothetico-deductive reasoning" becomes important during the formal operational stage. This type of thinking involves hypothetical "what-if" situations that are not always rooted in reality, *i.e.* counterfactual thinking. It is often required in science and mathematics.

- Abstract thought emerges during the formal operational stage.

Children tend to think very concretely and specifically in earlier stages, and begin to consider possible outcomes and consequences of actions.

- Metacognition, the capacity for "thinking about thinking" that allows adolescents and adults to reason about their thought processes and monitor them.
- Problem-solving is demonstrated when children use trial-and-error to solve problems. The ability to systematically solve a problem in a logical and methodical way emerges.

While children in primary school years mostly used inductive reasoning, drawing general conclusions from personal experiences and specific facts, adolescents become capable of deductive reasoning, in which they draw specific conclusions from abstract concepts using logic. This capability results from their capacity to think hypothetically.

"However, research has shown that not all persons in all cultures reach formal operations, and most people do not use formal operations in all aspects of their lives".

EXPERIMENTS

Piaget and his colleagues conducted several experiments to assess formal operational thought.

In one of the experiments, Piaget evaluated the cognitive capabilities of children of different ages through the use of a scale and varying weights. The task was to balance the scale by hooking weights on the ends of the scale. To successfully complete the task, the children must use formal operational thought to realize that the distance of the weights from the center and the heaviness of the weights both affected the balance.

A heavier weight has to be placed closer to the center of the scale, and a lighter weight has to be placed farther from the center, so that the two weights balance each other. While 3- to 5- year olds could not at all comprehend the concept of balancing, children by the age of 7 could balance the scale by placing the same weights on both ends, but they failed to realize the importance of the location. By age 10, children could think about location but failed to use logic and instead used trial-and-error. Finally, by age 13 and 14, in early adolescence, some children more clearly understood the relationship between weight and distance and could successfully implement their hypothesis.

THE STAGES AND CAUSATION

Piaget sees children's conception of causation as a march from "primitive" conceptions of cause to those of a more scientific, rigorous, and mechanical nature. These primitive concepts are characterized as supernatural, with a decidedly non-natural or non-mechanical tone. Piaget has as his most basic assumption that babies are phenomenists. That is, their knowledge "consists of assimilating things to schemas" from their own action such that they appear, from the child's point of view, "to have qualities which, in fact, stem from the organism". Consequently, these "subjective conceptions," so prevalent during Piaget's first stage of development, are dashed upon discovering deeper empirical truths.

Piaget gives the example of a child believing that the moon and stars follow him on a night walk. Upon learning that such is the case for his friends, he must separate his self from the object, resulting in a theory that the moon is immobile, or moves independently of other agents.

The second stage, from around three to eight years of age, is characterized by a mix of this type of magical, animistic, or "non-natural" conceptions of causation and mechanical or "naturalistic" causation. This conjunction of natural and non-natural causal explanations supposedly stems from experience itself, though Piaget does not make much of an attempt to describe the nature of the differences in conception. In his interviews with children, he asked questions specifically about natural phenomena, such as: "What makes clouds move?", "What makes the stars move?", "Why do rivers flow?" The nature of all the answers given, Piaget says, are such that these objects must perform their actions to "fulfill their obligations towards men". He calls this "moral explanation".

PRACTICAL APPLICATIONS

Parents can use Piaget's theory when deciding how to determine what to buy in order to support their child's growth. Teachers can also use Piaget's theory, for instance, when discussing whether the syllabus subjects are suitable for the level of students or not. For example, recent studies have shown that children in the same grade and of the same age perform differentially on tasks measuring basic addition and subtraction fluency. While children in the preoperational and concrete operational levels of cognitive development perform combined arithmetic operations (such as addition and subtraction) with similar accuracy, children in the concrete operational level of cognitive development have been able to perform both addition problems and subtraction problems with overall greater fluency.

The stage of cognitive growth of a person differ from another. It affects and influences how someone thinks about everything including flowers. A 7-month old infant, in the sensorimotor age, flowers are recognized by smelling, pulling and biting. A slightly older child has not realized that a flower is not fragrant, but similar to many children at her age, her egocentric, two handed curiosity will teach her.

In the formal operational stage of an adult, flowers are part of larger, logical scheme. They are used either to earn money or to create beauty. Cognitive development or thinking is an active process from the beginning to the end of life. Intellectual advancement happens because people at every age and developmental period looks for cognitive equilibrium. To achieve this balance, the easiest way is to understand the new experiences through the lens of the pre-existing ideas. Infants learn that new objects can be grabbed in the same way of familiar objects, and adults explain the day's headlines as evidence for their existing worldview.

However, the application of standardized Piagetian theory and procedures in different societies established widely varying results that lead some to speculate not only that some cultures produce more cognitive development than others but that without specific kinds of cultural experience, but also formal schooling, development might cease at certain level, such as concrete operational level. A procedure was done following methods developed in Geneva.

Participants were presented with two beakers of equal circumference and height, filled with equal amounts of water. The water from one beaker was transferred into another with taller and smaller circumference. The children and young adults from non-literate societies of a given age were more likely to think that the taller, thinner beaker had more water in it. On the other hand, an experiment on the effects of modifying testing procedures to match local cultural produced a different pattern of results.

POSTULATED PHYSICAL MECHANISMS UNDERLYING SCHEMAS AND STAGES

In 1967, Piaget considered the possibility of RNA molecules as likely embodiments of his still-abstract schemas (which he promoted as units of action)—though he did not come to any firm conclusion. At that time, due to work such as that of Swedish biochemist Holger Hydén, RNA concentrations had, indeed, been shown to correlate with learning, so the idea was quite plausible.

However, by the time of Piaget's death in 1980, this notion had lost favour. One main problem was over the protein which, it was assumed, such RNA would necessarily produce, and that did not fit in with observation. It was determined that only about 3per cent of RNA does code for protein. Hence, most of the remaining 97per cent (the "ncRNA") could theoretically be available to serve as Piagetian schemas (or other regulatory roles now under investigation). The issue has not yet been resolved experimentally, but its theoretical aspects were reviewed in 2008 — then developed further from the viewpoints of biophysics and epistemology.

Meanwhile, this RNA-based approach also unexpectedly offered explanations for various other bio-mysteries, thus providing some measure of corroboration.

RELATION TO PSYCHOMETRIC THEORIES OF INTELLIGENCE

Piaget designed a number of tasks to verify hypotheses arising from his theory. The tasks were not intended to measure individual differences, and they have no equivalent inpsychometric intelligence tests. Notwithstanding the different research traditions in which psychometric tests and Piagetian tasks were developed, the correlations between the two types of measures have been found to be consistently positive and generally moderate in magnitude. A common general factor underlies them. It has been shown that it is possible to construct a battery consisting of Piagetian tasks that is as good a measure of general intelligence as standard IQ tests.

CHALLENGES TO PIAGETIAN STAGE THEORY

Piagetian accounts of development have been challenged on several grounds. First, as Piaget himself noted, development does not always progress in the smooth manner his theory seems to predict. "Decalage," or progressive forms of cognitive developmental progression in a specific domain, suggest that the stage model is, at best, a useful approximation. Furthermore, studies have found that children may be able to learn concepts and capability of complex reasoning that supposedly represented in more advanced stages with relative ease. More broadly, Piaget's theory is "domain general," predicting that cognitive maturation occurs concurrently across different domains of knowledge (such as mathematics, logic, and understanding of physics or language). Piaget did not take into account variability in a child's performance notably how a child can differ in sophistication across several domains.

During the 1980s and 1990s, cognitive developmentalists were influenced by "neo-nativist" and evolutionary psychology ideas. These ideas de-emphasized domain general theories and emphasized domain specificity or modularity of mind. Modularity implies that different cognitive faculties may be largely independent of one another, and thus develop according to quite different timetables, which are "influenced by real world experiences". In this vein, some cognitive developmentalists argued that, rather than being domain general learners, children come equipped with domain specific theories, sometimes referred to as "core knowledge," which allows them to break into learning within that domain. For example, even young infants appear to be sensitive to some predictable regularities in the movement and interactions of objects (for example, an object cannot pass through another object), or in human behaviour (for example, a hand repeatedly reaching for an object has that object, not just a particular path of motion), as it becomes the building block of which more elaborate knowledge is constructed.

Piaget's theory has been said to undervalue the influence that culture has on cognitive development. Piaget demonstrates that a child goes through several stages of cognitive development and come to conclusions on their own but in reality, a child's sociocultural environment plays an important part in their cognitive development. Social interaction teaches the child about the world and helps them develop through the cognitive stages, which Piaget neglected to consider.

More recent work has strongly challenged some of the basic presumptions of the "core knowledge" school, and revised ideas of domain generality—but from a newer dynamic systems approach, not from a revised Piagetian perspective. Dynamic systems approaches harken to modern neuroscientific research that was not available to Piaget when he was constructing his theory. One important finding is that domain-specific knowledge is constructed as children develop and integrate knowledge. This enables the domain to improve the accuracy of the knowledge as well as organization of memories. However, this suggests more of a "smooth integration" of learning and development than either Piaget, or his neo-nativist critics, had envisioned. Additionally, some psychologists, such as Lev Vygotsky and Jerome Bruner, thought differently from Piaget, suggesting that language was more important for cognition development than Piaget implied.

POST-PIAGETIAN AND NEO-PIAGETIAN STAGES

In recent years, several theorists attempted to address concerns with Piaget's theory by developing new theories and models that can accommodate evidence which violates Piagetian predictions and postulates.

- The neo-Piagetian theories of cognitive development, advanced by Robbie Case, Andreas Demetriou, Graeme S. Halford, Kurt W. Fischer, Michael Lamport Commons, and Juan Pascual-Leone, attempted to integrate Piaget's theory with cognitive and differential theories of cognitive organization and development. Their aim was to better account for the cognitive factors of development and for intra-individual and inter-individual differences in cognitive development. They suggested that development along Piaget's stages is due to increasing working memory capacity and processing efficiency by "biological maturation". Moreover, Demetriou´s theory ascribes an important role to hypercognitive processes of "self-monitoring, self-recording, self-evaluation, and self-regulation", and it recognizes the operation of several relatively autonomous domains of thought (Demetriou, 1998;Demetriou, Mouyi, Spanoudis, 2010;Demetriou, 2003, p. 153).
- Piaget's theory stops at the formal operational stage, but other researchers have observed the thinking of adults is more nuanced than formal operational thought. This fifth stage has been named post formal thought or operation. Post formal stages have been proposed. Michael Commons presented evidence for four post formal stages: systematic, meta-systematic, paradigmatic, and cross-paradigmatic (Commons and

Richards, 2003, p. 206-208;Oliver, 2004, p. 31). There are many theorists, however, who have criticized "post formal thinking," because the concept lacks both theoretical and empirical verification. The term "integrative thinking" has been suggested for use instead.

- A "sentential" stage, said to occur before the early preoperational stage, has been proposed by Fischer, Biggs and Biggs, Commons, and Richards.
- Searching for a micro-physiological basis for human mental capacity, Traill proposed that there may be "pre-sensorimotor" stages ("$M''^{1}L$", "$M''^{2}L$", ...), which are developed in the womb and/or transmitted genetically.
- Jerome Bruner has expressed views on cognitive development in a "pragmatic orientation" in which humans actively use knowledge for practical applications, such as problem solving and understanding reality.
- Michael Lamport Commons proposed the model of hierarchical complexity (MHC) in two ways: "Horizontal Complexity" and "Vertical Complexity".
- Kieran Egan has proposed five stages of understanding: "somatic", "mythic", "romantic", "philosophic", and "ironic", which is developed through cognitive tools such as "stories", "binary oppositions", "fantasy" and "rhyme, rhythm, and meter" to enhance memorization to develop a long-lasting learning capacity.
- Lawrence Kohlberg developed three stages of moral development: "Preconventional", "Conventional" and "Postconventional".Each level is composed of two orientation stages, with a total of six orientation stages: (1) "Punishment-Obedience", (2) "Instrumental Relativist", (3) "Good Boy-Nice Girl", (4) "Law and Order", (5) "Social Contract", and (6) "Universal Ethical Principle".
- Andreas Demetriou has expressed Neo-Piagetian theories of cognitive development.
- Jane Loevinger's stages of ego development occur through "an evolution of stages". "First is the Presocial Stage followed by the Symbiotic Stage, Impulsive Stage, Self-Protective Stage, Conformist Stage, Self-Aware Level: Transition from Conformist to Conscientious Stage, Individualistic Level: Transition from Conscientious to the Autonomous Stage, Conformist Stage, and Integrated Stage".
- Ken Wilber has incorporated Piaget's theory in his multidisciplinary field of Integral Theory. The human consciousness is structured in hierarchical order and organized in "holon" chains or "Great Chain of Being", which are based on the level of spiritual and psychological development.

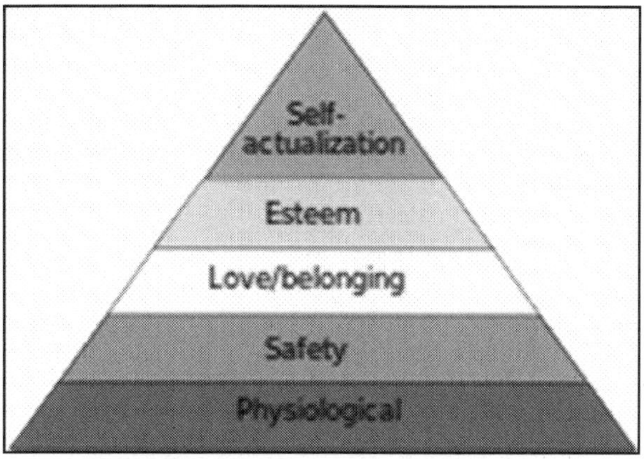

Fig. Maslow's Hierarchy of Needs.

- The process of initiation is a modification of Piaget's theory integrating Abraham Maslow's concept of self-actualization.
- Cheryl Armon has proposed five stages of " the Good Life": "Egoistic Hedonism", "Instrumental Hedonism", "Affective/Altruistic Mutuality", "Individuality", and "Autonomy/Community" (Andreoletti and Demick, 2003, p. 284).
- Christopher R. Hallpike proposed that human evolution of cognitive moral understanding had evolved from the beginning of time from its primitive state to the present time.
- Robert Kegan extended Piaget's developmental model to adults in describing the Constructive Developmental Framework.

THE FOUR LANGUAGES OF CONSCIOUS THOUGHT

You can consider your conscious thought processes - those which you can tune in to and observe as they happen - as being expressed in any or all of four thinking 'languages' or modalities, which are:

1. *Kinesthetic thought:* Experiencing bodily sensations, feelings and emotions, as reactions to a memory, immediate experience or imagined situation.
2. *Auditory thought:* Hearing others' speech, natural sounds and music, which are recalled from memory or imagined.
3. *Visual thought:* Seeing mental pictures, which are often fuzzy and fragmentary and which are recalled from memory or imagined.
4. *Verbal thought:* Speaking in your mental voice, just as if you were expressing your mental processes aloud in words, phrases and sentences - this is 'inner speech'.

For example you can think about your friend, lover or relative by saying that person's name in your mind, by forming a mental picture of that person, by sensing the person's tone of voice, or by tuning-in to the feeling response to the concept of that person. For much of your conscious thought, all four of these thinking languages come into play simultaneously. One may play a dominant role, since others may be suppressed, depending on your relationship to a particular subject (such as dislikes, fears, bad memories;or likes, compulsions, good memories).

Below the foreground of conscious thought is a continuous stream of preconsciousunseen mental activity, which organizes mental contents and controls actions 'without even thinking about it', like turning the page of a book. The four thinking languages are the means by which you project snapshots of the rapidly moving preconscious processes onto the 'screen' of your immediate attention.

You can capture some of these fleeting thoughts and translate them into conscious form, but the vast majority of them flow on invisibly and reliably without your conscious attention. The left-brain level of preconscious thought is quite capable of making decisions, of reasoning logically, and of directing a large share of your moment-to-moment actions, usually in the form of pre-programmed habitual patterns of behaviour. The right brain aspect of the preconscious is the basis for hunches, or intuitive thought processes, which seem to tell you what to do on a gut-feeling level, but offer no well worked-out verbal reasoning processes to substantiate the proposed course of action.

The preconscious thought stream, then, is the result of the conscious verbal left hemisphere and the non-verbal but aware right hemisphere, interfacing beneath the surface with the deeper Subconscious and the still deeper unconscious processes of both hemispheres. The preconscious emerges into consciousness in the form of the four thought languages: verbal, visual, auditory and kinesthetic. The content of the deeper subconscious may also erupt into consciousness, through the medium of a fifth language: that of metaphors and symbolic representations. This occurs most of all during dreaming, and twilight states of consciousness.

Suppression of the Subconscious (and by extension, repression of the unconscious) has the effect of reducing the perception of smell and taste, because these two senses are mediated by the more primitive (sub-cortical) centers of the brain which are the seat of the unconscious.

However, for those who have developed a high level of integration between the hemispheres, integration of the Subconscious has to a significant extent begun, so a further dimension of perception becomes apparent: the thought languages may be represented by taste, smell and colour, blending together in a synesthesia. Improved integration, then, enlarges the spotlight of the conscious mind, so that neither irrational thoughts nor useful intuitions are likely to pass by unnoticed, and the full wealth of the experience of life becomes open to view and may be appreciated.

If an adult is 'stuck' in a predominantly kinesthetic, auditory or visual mode of representation, this is a case of arrested development - he is at the concrete operational level of development, or maybe lower. At the primary school level, the education of children is best tailored to a child's major system of representation. However, to get a meaningful education at the secondary and tertiary level, an individual needs to be capable of a conceptual level of thinking, actively developing their Formal operations. Therefore the spoken and written modes of thinking should not be neglected in favour of the audio-visual methods of teaching, effective as they are;it should play an equal role through concentrated study and analysis of written materials and assignments involving creative writing and speaking.

ACHIEVING INDIVIDUATION

Moving beyond the Formal Operational stage of cognitive development, requires the achievement of Individuation. According to Jung, humans are not merely shaped by past events but strive for personal development as well. Part of the nature of humans is to be constantly developing, growing, and moving towards a balanced and complete level of development. Our present personality is determined by both who and what we have been and by the person we hope to become. The process of self-actualization is oriented towards the future. Jung's theory is based on the assumption that humans tend to move towards the fulfillment or realization of all their capabilities.

Achieving Individuation, or a fully harmonious and integrated personality, is a primary goal. To come to our full realization, we must become aware of and accept the full range of our being. This means that the public self that we present is only a small part of who and what we are. For Jung, both constructive and destructive forces exist in the human psyche, and to become integrated we must accept the dark side of our nature with our primitive impulses such as selfishness and greed. Acceptance of our 'dark side' or Shadow does not imply being dominated by this dimension of our being but simply recognizing that this is a part of our nature. At the end of the Individuation process, an individual is at least a 51per cent shareholder in his own mind. In that sense, he has integrated the Ego and the Shadow, and achieved sufficient Individuation to overcome the Superego, so he has majority control.

Jung says his method of active imagination involves a close attention to dream material and integration of the meanings they contain through some form of self-expression. Rigorous attention to, and integration of, unconscious material is the process by which adults begin to achieve Individuation. The process of using Mind Development techniques, such as facility with right brain mnemonics and creativity techniques, has a similar effect, because a student is continually drawing on the unconscious content of the right hemisphere and in the process discharging the energetic barrier that prevents integration.

Once a person has become a majority shareholder in his mind, then Self-Actualizing needs come to the fore: the student wonders about the remaining 49per cent. The inner-directed person does not derive his sense of value or identity solely from tradition nor from conformity to peer-group fashions, but from the resources of his own nature.

This orientation can only be achieved by an individual who is in the process of developing his own character, of becoming 'field-independent', his or her volition self-determined (based on self-knowledge) rather than the effect of manipulation or propitiation. The most original, creative and outstanding men and women are invariably of this type, and yet it is no 'elitist' type, for it is available to all human beings with the courage of their convictions. It is the way of life that takes 'individuation' as its goal: to manifest one's highest potential. To achieve Individuation and move beyond the stage of Formal Operations, the individual needs to become much more field-independent and inner-directed than is generally the case. There is a significant correlation between field-independence and IQ.

Field-dependents:

- Rely on the surrounding perceptual field.
- Have difficulty attending to, extracting, and using non-salient cues.
- Have difficulty providing structure to ambiguous information.
- Have difficulty restructuring new information and forging links with prior knowledge.
- Have difficulty retrieving information from long-term memory.
- Have a disposition to be other-directed.
- Have a tendency to be extraverted.
- Field-dependents tend to be extrinsically motivated.

Conversely, field-independents:

- Perceive objects as separate from the field.
- Can dis-embed relevant items from non-relevant items within the field.
- Provide structure when it is not inherent in the presented information.
- Reorganize information to provide a context for prior knowledge.
- Tend to be more efficient at retrieving items from memory.
- Have a disposition to be inner-directed.
- Have a tendency to be introverted.
- Field-Independents tend to be intrinsically motivated.

Note: Intrinsic motivation, or engaging in a task for its enjoyment value, is one of the most powerful forms of motivatio. It is associated with enhanced performance, improved conceptual and creative thinking, superior memory recall, positive affect, subsequent willingness to engage in other tasks, and better psychological and physical health - compared with extrinsic motivation, or engaging in a task to please others or to acquire an incentive.

Stages of Individuation parallel the stages of intellectual development, as described by Piaget and others. Achieving a substantial degree of Individuation and field-independence are necessary preconditions if one wishes to reach the Postformal Level of Operations and beyond.

COGNITIVE MATURITY

Maturity is completeness of growth and development. There are three components to this process: physical, psychological and cognitive. It is cognitive maturity that develops last, usually not reaching completion until the mid-twenties. Indeed, cognitive development continues until at least 30, given ongoing education or mental stimulus, and at later ages may be undertaken as a process of self-directed learning and development - such as with the Mind Development Courses - with corresponding benefits.

Cognitive maturity includes the following abilities:

- Mature judgement
- Seeing into the future
- Seeing how behaviour can affect future
- Associating cause and effect
- Moral intelligence
- Abstract thinking
- Seeing what is not obvious
- Planning and decision-making
- Rational behaviour and decision-making
- Rules of social conduct
- Understanding rules of social conduct

New MRI studies of the developing brain, clearly show that the physical development of the pre-frontal cortex is not complete until the mid-twenties. Before recent research revealed this startling new information, specialists had assumed that young people acted the way they do because of raging hormones, heredity, bad or good environmental factors, or a host of other reasons, all hopelessly commingled into a stew of influences that could probably never be understood. It is not that these other factors don't influence young people;the issue that underlies all of this, however, is an incompletely developed pre-frontal cortex that limits their ability to independently make mature decisions. Quite literally, they do not have the brain cell connections to make judgement calls.

POSTFORMAL OPERATIONS

Between the ages of 20 and 30, or earlier, if a student has a high IQ, especially if he is in a stimulating environment such as a university, or if he has a demanding profession or absorbing interest in which an extensive Knowledge Structure is required, a person who has obtained true Formal thought may continue to develop his or her intellect at the fifth stage of development, that of Postformal Operations. In the case of a person with a deviation IQ of 150+, he or she may start to develop Postformal Operations at 15 or earlier, and then continue to develop for another 10 to 15 years, if remaining in a stimulating environment.

With external help, such as our Mind Development Courses, the natural processes of development can be restarted even if the individual is well over the age of 30. Changes in environmental demands during adulthood, such as retraining for vocational needs, may also stimulate renewed development. Development ofCrystallized Intelligence over an increasingly broad range of life domains is then possible throughout life. This provides the contextual perspective from which original creativity and wisdom may arise, and maturity may also assist in the development of other kinds of intelligence, such as social, moral and emotional competence. A person aged over 30 is likely to have better problem solving ability than one under 30 with the same IQ, because of completion of maturation and increase of acquired crystallized intelligence.

If an adult has completed the stage of Formal Operations and reached full Formal Thought, the development of knowledge structures and intellectual development will continue at the Postformal level. On the other hand, without appropriate mental stimuli, adult intellectual development may not even reach to the level of Formal Operations yet alone achieving Individuation and Postformal development. Even university students may not have attained true Formal cognitive functionality and it appears the majority of the population function, most of the time, at the level of Concrete Operations. Furthermore, many people do not have a reliable ability to make Concrete Operations in an objective manner that is inner-directed enough to be free from the influence of their environmental conditioning and peer pressures.

But if the final stage of true Formal thought is reached, either naturally or through assisted intellectual development, there will be spontaneous attempts to increase mental capacity still further, to complete the process of maturation. This is Pierre de Chardin's point of ignition;a point at which a person has become sufficiently self-aware to attempt to direct his own course of mental evolution. He has developed metacognitive intelligence, in which the person is aware and in control of his own thinking processes.

Postformal thinking requires the ability to hold in the mind a complex array of differing information and viewpoints, in order to synthesize an overview. A variety of research suggests that people have the potential to gradually reach higher levels of mental complexity throughout the course of their lifespan. Mind Development Courses have the specific agenda of increasing the symbol space of the conscious mind as well as the speed at which it is accessed, in order to increase the capacity for cognitive complexity, with all the attendant benefits that ensue, including the increase of Fluid Intelligence.

Postformal thinking possesses an understanding of the relative, non-absolute nature of knowledge;it accepts contradiction as a basic aspect of reality;it includes the ability to focus simultaneously on several aspects of a problem, to see both sides and further implications and possibilities, and not to be identified in a solid way with only with one point of view. This is a 'broad perspective,' metacognitive viewpoint. Postformal thinkers are aware of paradox;they are capable of dialectic reasoning and are able to synthesize contradictory thoughts, emotions, and experiences.

Mind Development recognizes five levels of Postformal thought:

1. Dialectical reasoning:
2. In dialectics the resolution of two elements (thesis and antithesis) occurs due to contradiction or conflict resolving into a new thesis (and thus creating a new antithesis). Dialectic reasoning is a way of thinking which seeks to discover a whole new series of questions to be asked, rather than in finding 'once and for all' answers;it facilitates problem finding rather than just problem solving.
3. Problem finding:
4. Intelligence is the function of perceiving, posing and resolving problems. Problem finding means problem discovery - insight into what is missing in the existing picture of a situation. It is an aspect of divergent intelligence and requires initiative and creativity.
5. Relativistic operations:
6. Consideration of the relative, non-absolute nature of knowledge, which accepts contradiction as a basic aspect of reality.
7. Reflective judgement:
8. Beliefs are justified probabilistically using evidence and arguments; conclusions are defended as representing the most complete, most compelling, or most plausible understanding of an issue available to date, based on the current evidence.
9. Trialectic reasoning:
10. Postformal operations use a more flexible logic than formal thinking, containing fewer assumptions. Although this logic is 'weaker,' it allows the development of new kinds of thinking. Trialectics is the final stage of Postformal operations. Moving beyond Dialectic argument which is based on contradiction, we can look at the pros and cons of an argument trialectically, which includes the ability to think with Three Valued Logic: thesis and antithesis exist but are viewed in a qualitatively different way, and the resolution between them is through complementarity or cooperation, giving rise to a higher degree of insight, in which a new thesis is incorporated or synthesized.

At the fifth Level of Postformal operations, the Trialectic level, there is an integration of Convergent Intelligence (analytical focussing towards a single answer to a problem as required in IQ tests), Divergent Intelligence (the creative skill of looking wider than the obvious and asking new questions to generate novel and interesting ideas) and Practical Intelligence (knowledge about how to do things and relate effectively with the real world). I call this Trivergent Intelligence. This is a transitional phase towards thinking that is beyond Postformal operations.

METACOGNITION

Metacognition is thinking about thinking, knowing "what we know" and "what we don't know." Just as an executive's job is management of an organization, a thinker's job is management of thoughts. The basic metacognitive strategies are:

1. Connecting new information to former knowledge.
2. Selecting thinking strategies deliberately.
3. Planning, monitoring, and evaluating thinking processes.

A "thinking person" is in charge of their own behaviour. They determine when it is necessary to use metacognitive strategies. They monitor, control and judge their thinking. They figure out how and when to do a particular task or set of tasks, and then make sure that the tasks are done correctly.

Metacognition involves thinking and reasoning about one's own mental processes, such as memory, perception, calculation, association, etc. Metacognitive self-regulation is therefore central to intelligence. Most everybody with an IQ over 90 has some capacity for Metacognition, but a person's Metacognitive Intelligence increases dramatically if the person is able to achieve Formal and Postformal stages of mental development, and then it will continue to increase, until at least the age of 30.

Learning how to learn, developing a repertoire of thinking processes which can be applied to solve problems, is a major goal of education. When life presents situations that cannot be solved by learned responses, metacognitive behaviour is brought into play. Metacognitive skills are needed when habitual responses are not successful. Mind Development courses offer guidance in recognizing, and practice in applying, metacognitive strategies that help students successfully solve problems throughout their lives.

A specific type of multitasking behaviour that plays a key role in human cognition is called branching, and depends on the front-most region of the brain, the anterior prefrontal cortex, an area especially well-developed in humans compared to other primates and the area of brain responsible for Metacognition. Branching involves keeping a goal in mind over time (in working memory), while at the same time being able to change focus among tasks.

Take, for example, the field of study. Novice learners don't stop to evaluate their comprehension of the material. They generally don't examine the quality of their work or stop to make revisions as they go along. Satisfied with just scratching the surface, novice learners don't attempt to examine a problem in depth. They don't make connections or see the relevance of the material in their lives. Expert learners, on the other hand, apply metacognitive skills. They are aware of the goal of their studies: what they are intending to learn. At the same time as reading and understanding the material, they are aware of when they need to check for errors, the reason why they fail to comprehend, and how they may need to redirect their efforts. They realize there is more to discover about the subject than is contained in the written lines.

Formal operations of thought tend to overemphasize the power of pure logic in problem solving and underemphasize the pragmatic quality of real-life social or interpersonal situations. Formal thinking is therefore best suited for well-defined problems that call for scientific thinking and logical analysis and imply a single correct solution. It places a greater emphasis on problem solving than on analysis of situations and consequent discovery of problems.

Beyond the traditional Formal Operational level of intellectual development (which consists of symbol manipulation, reasoning, etc.), individuals can develop the ability to reason in situations beyond just a right or wrong answer (for example, moral actions) and take into account different perspectives. Whilst Formal thought perceives a system of organized complexity as being closed, simply reducible to its parts, Postformal thought is aware of the open aspects of a system - that the whole is more than the sum of its parts.

Once a person has reached the level of Postformal Operations, there is an integration of Emotion and Cognition. Postformal operations include the evaluation of the contextual relevance of emotional information when decision making. Along with the increase in Metacognitive Intelligence that accompanies Postformal operations, there is an increased ability for Introspection. Most people have some capacity for introspection, to look inward and reflect on one's self and one's own thoughts, but this capacity increases dramatically when a student attains the stages of Formal and Postformal Operations.

In recent years, Gardner's evaluation of multiple intelligences has identified (at least) seven specific intelligences linked to ways of learning, including spatial, body-kinesthetic, logical-mathematical and linguistic. Social intelligence has also been identified as a critical factor in personal development, as to be successful one needs to be able to relate well to others, to present oneself with clarity and authenticity, and communicate empathetically. An important aspect of social intelligence is Emotional intelligence: the ability to perceive, understand and regulate emotion in the self and others.

The question remains, how do people employ these many intelligences they may have in varying degrees? Whilst they may function on demand or at random, it is possible to develop a kind of meta-intelligence, by which a person rules over and helps to direct each specific capacity that they have. Meta-intelligence relates to awareness, adaptability, and the relative comparisons of different mental frameworks, models, and sets of behaviour. Obtaining a meta-view of one's own mental functions is a result of adult intellectual development. Ego strength and maturity enable an objective understanding of cause and effect that enhances the multiple intelligences that are not strictly cognitive.

The good news is that metacognitive growth continues after the age of twenty and certainly continues until, at least, the age of thirty. The bad news, however, is that it tends to become more Domain Specific during the adult phase of development. This is because the metacognitive processes, as they develop, are becoming progressively more dependent on Intermediate-Term Working Memory and specialist knowledge. In short, an adult has a higher level of meta-intelligence than a teenager, but it tends to be in several specific domains rather than Domain General. This can be countered by ongoing self-directed education and the tools to do this efficiently and well are provided by the Mind Development Courses.

An adult is rarely presented with a completely novel problem in the real world of academic or occupational endeavors. Rather, the problems which an adult is asked to solve almost inevitably draw greatly on his accumulated knowledge and skills. For an adult, intellect is better recognized by the range of tasks that the person can accomplish and the skills that he has developed, rather than by the abstract cognitive tasks typically included in IQ tests. He comes to increasingly rely on Crystallized Intelligence, thus the content of the intellect is at least as important as the processes of intellect in determining an adult's real-world problem solving efficiency.

SYSTEMS INTELLIGENCE

Emotional intelligence helps us to understand and manage our own emotions as well as other people's emotions towards us. Social intelligence is a super-set of emotional intelligence, incorporating our interactions with other people and how well we understand them. Systems intelligence takes a still broader view, to consider that human action always takes place in systemic settings consisting of both human and other interactive contextual elements.

Systems intelligent people understand why they act like they do - they understand their emotions. Systems intelligent people also understand social interactions and the importance of collaboration. Systems intelligence goes beyond emotional and social factors, however, to understand the broader context within which social interactions take place and to be intelligent about - and ultimately take responsibility for - the workings of the organizational system as a whole.

Systems intelligence is intelligent behaviour in the context of complex systems, which are often human in nature such as business organizations, or political, economic and societal interactions of a systemic, inter-relating and interactive nature. Systems intelligence is an innate trait in all humans. It is a capacity that all of us can reveal, if we recognize that the whole world around us is made of a complex web of relationships in which we play our part. If we act intelligently, we can influence positive outcomes, and help to avoid negative ones.

Systems intelligence in a person is developed through the following levels:

1. Being aware of the systemic environment in which one is operating, with an accompanying mental model of the system.
2. Being aware that possibilities for better outcomes - such as improved performance and productivity - stem from the interaction with oneself and the system.
3. Taking responsibility and managing improved and more productive ways of behaviour in the system.
4. Sustaining intelligent management of the system to produce positive results in the long term.
5. Initiating and leading organizations that are systems intelligent.

Levels 1 and 2 correlate with Formal Operations of cognitive ability. A person needs to have developed some level of detachment before he is able to see himself as part of a system. This detachment only comes with Formal Operations, even if the only goal is to conform. Until a person has the ideocentric viewpoint that comes with attaining the lower levels of Formal Operations, his effective Systems Intelligence is zero. Before a person has reached the level of Formal Operations, he is running on automatic, he can only conform to simple systems like the family, and he is not aware that he is part of a larger system.

Awareness that he is part of a system is only the first step, an individual will have to reach the level of Postformal Operations before he can have an impact and change a system in any but a minor way - and by this I mean a change for the better. Levels 3, 4 and 5 therefore correlate with the Postformal Levels.

Confirmation Bias apparently affects all of us. Simply put, we tend to first form an opinion, and then look at the evidence supporting that opinion. If evidence to the contrary is presented, we either downplay it or outright ignore it. Systems intelligence is all about acting in ways that take into account the true systems we participate in, in our daily lives. That is, "true" systems as opposed to systems we would like to believe we participate in. This strongly suggests that a systems intelligent person does his best to avoid confirmation bias.

Systems thinking as a method allows us to consciously assess evidence and reject any bias—including confirmation bias. Systems intelligence gives us the skill to recognize and reject confirmation bias, to act and react with a healthy amount of skepticism. This suggests that a systems intelligent person by nature strongly rejects pseudoscientific thinking, and exhibits a clear tendency to apply the scientific method: to be as objective, clear and rational as possible about the functions and interactions of the systems he plays a part in.

EXTELLIGENCE

Of course, individuals do not stand alone, they work with others in groups and share information. Individual thoughts may be shared with others and distributed by various means, while other information remains private (owned by one individual).

In the context of groups of people working together, it may be impossible to truly centralize executive functions, since each of the group's members possesses metacognitive intelligence and thus will automatically monitor their group's functioning. They can choose to cooperate or not with a named leader, and may even usurp the leader's control when necessary. There is distributed cognition within the group, between its members. They influence and depend on each other and each brings unique skills and knowledge to the table.

From the artificial intelligence field, researchers have discarded the idea of a General Problem Solver in favour of knowledge-based expert systems. This is because no amount of processing power can achieve real-world problem solving proficiency without an extensive set of domain-relevant knowledge structures. This cannot be accomplished alone, it requires a process of Distributed Cognition. Not all of one's intelligence occurs in one's own head;it needs to be combined with external resources of knowledge and understanding. This latter, external and distributed type of cognition is termed Extelligence. Like Metacognition, this is an important aspect of Crystallized Intelligence.

Of course, Extelligence begins with the transfer of learning. Learning is important because no one is born with the ability to function competently as an adult in society. The best learning experiences lead to transfer, defined as the ability to extend what has been learned in one context to new contexts. Educators hope that students will transfer learning from one problem to another within a course, from one year in school to another, between school and home, and from school to workplace. Assumptions about transfer accompany the belief that it is better to broadly educate people than simply train them to perform particular tasks.

A student who is stuck at the level of Concrete Operations can go through the motions of study, but his learning will be context specific and there will be little transfer to real life. Formal Operations are therefore a prerequisite for effective Mind Development. Unless a person has attained the level of Formal Operations all effective learning is situated in its original context: there is very little transfer from one context to another.

Our Extelligence is our capacity to utilize the cognitive capacities of significant others: our friends, our family, people at work and at our place of study, experts of various types, etc. And our capacities to use accredited instruments, adding machines, the Internet, libraries, works of reference etc., to extend our cognitive powers.

The term 'extelligence' was originated by Ian Stewart and Jack Cohen in their 1997 book Figments of Reality. It is a form of distributed intelligence. Whereas intelligence is based on the knowledge and cognitive processes within the brain, extelligence is based on the information, skills and understanding that one can readily access from external sources, the pooled sum of human knowledge.

Each individual can only access those parts of the total extelligence that is available, if they are willing and able to do so, and to contribute to it. There has to be an appreciation of what is out there, where to find it, and what it means in relation to the internal conceptual understanding. Extelligence is a metacognitive skill that does not usually develop to any great degree until a student has reached the level of further education.

Although creative individuals are often thought of as working in isolation, much of our intelligence and creativity results from interaction and collaboration with other individuals, with their ideas, writing, research and methodologies. We have to actively pursue and manage these relationships and the information that flows between us.

All people, except those with a very low IQ, have some capacity to make use of Extelligence, but people who have attained the stages of Formal and Postformal operations have a dramatically increased capacity to exploit Extelligence. It could be argued that the capacity to exploit Extelligence is a dimension of Metacognition.

Postformal thought takes advantage of the individual's full spectrum of knowledge, covering all the domains in which he has acquired knowledge, especially expert knowledge.

He can synthesize new solutions drawing upon domain-general rather than domain-specific expertise - and predict interaction between the domains - within the boundaries of his knowledge network, which as an Open System may be expanded and revised, and incorporate the research and conclusions of others as an (almost unlimited) extelligent resource. Developing the Knowledge Net is most important, if a student wishes to enhance his Postformal level of operations.

Extelligence, then, is a concept that helps to explain the development of a mind in intelligent species. Our Extelligence is much more complex even than our intelligence. The basis of Extelligence is a sharing of knowledge between humans. Extelligence is the intelligence we share. Extelligence involves everything that exceeds the intelligence of one human being.

EXTELLIGENCE AND EXFORMATION

The word Exformation is used by Tor N rretranders in his book The User Illusion, published in Danish in 1991 and in English in 1998. He argues that effective communication depends on a shared body of knowledge between the persons communicating. If someone is talking about cows, for example, what is said will be unintelligible unless the person listening has some idea what a cow is, what it is good for, and in what contexts they might encounter one. In using simply the word "cow," N rretranders says, the speaker has deliberately thrown away a huge body of contextual information, though it remains implied.

Language is any tool for transfer of information between two intelligent beings (or between intelligent agents within a system), dependent upon Exformation to be useful. With natural language many words are the results of complex calculations over hundreds or thousands of years (depth). A message has depth if it contains large quantities of Exformation. Exformation is a useful concept here - Exformation is a very beautiful expression. In order to access the Exformation that lies in our non-conscious, a skill that can hover between a conscious and a non-conscious state of mind needs to exist. It's said that the more Exformation you generate, the better your writing will be.

Transactive Memory is a process by which two or more people in a group develop a shared system for encoding, storing, and retrieving information and where each person is responsible for memorizing only part of the total information. Groups with well-developed Transactive Memory Systems recall more task-related knowledge and make fewer errors than groups lacking well-developed memory systems. There is Extelligence at the level of the individual agents within a group - the group itself then becomes a form of Extelligence. However, a group that is low in Exformation is low in Group Intelligence, it has a poor Transactive Memory System, and it is a poor source of Extelligence. From such a group, a student will not get Insights, he will only get Outsights... An Outsight is a statement believed by the person who utters it to be an important or profound Insight, but which is in fact regarded by its audience as so obvious or elementary that it reveals the speaker as hopelessly ignorant or slow-witted, at least relative to the relevant group. A student will not usually gain much Extelligence from a group that is low in Group Intelligence.

The key concepts of Cognitive Fluidity (mapping across domains);Extelligence (externalizing memory workloads);and Scaffolding (extending the mind into the material world), maximize cognitive abilities. A simple example of Scaffolding: if you always have a watch on your wrist, you as-good-as know the time as you've expanded your memory into the environment. In a ubiquitous computing environment the new intelligence is Extelligence, "knowledge and tools that are outside people's heads." In such an environment the user needs textual, visual and corporal literacy, *i.e.* an awareness of Extelligence and a working knowledge of all the senses.

One day, Networked Extelligence will replace or supersede learned intelligence - in other words, we may not know, but we will know how to know. Extelligence is the totality of intelligent expressions made by humans. It is the contextual and cultural analogue of internal, personal intelligence. In preliterate societies, poetry was a tool for Extelligence, and poems were aide memoires;today computers perform this service. Humankind has been using Intelligence to create Extelligence since the dawn of civilization.

To benefit maximally from Extelligence, an individual should have good Systems Intelligence, and in many cases Cultural Intelligence may also be a prerequisite. An individual should interact with a person or system that has a high level of Exformation, then using his experience and knowledge he is able to unfold the Exformation in the system. Exformation is perpendicular to information.

Exformation is everything we do not actually say but have in our heads when, or before, we say anything at all - whereas information is the measurable, demonstrable utterance we actually come out with. To communicate, you have to be able to express things in a way that matches the "Exformation" of the people you're talking to, then available Transactive Memory content will be high. Exformation-rich messages have depth in the sense that they call forth much with few symbols. The more Exformation shared by sender and receiver, the more compact a communication can be. Previous studies have provided evidence of the positive impact of Transactive Memory on group performances, such as the efficient storage and recall of knowledge. We make a fragment of the group thought-process portable and run it in our own reasoning and recall processes.

We as a species have been endowed by nature with an intelligence superior to all other species on Earth. However we have rarely applied more than a fraction of our potential for intelligence;we have abused technologies and engaged in enterprises that have allowed populations, pollution and use of resources to grow unchecked, creating vast ecological damage that threatens our very survival as a species. If we were as "dumb" as non-human species, nature would keep us better in check.

But are we smart enough to correct for our destructive ways, overriding certain behaviours encoded in our DNA that once served our survival, but are inappropriate in our modern circumstances? The situation may be tragic, because intelligence evolves slowly, much slower than the rate at which ecological destruction occurs by our own hands. There is, however, hope. Technology has led to environmental harm but can also lead us out of the malaise. By a concerted process of widespread propagation on the Internet, we can make available the extelligence and wisdom to moderate and turn around our destructive behavioural traits. Personal and cognitive development will play an important role in this urgent mission, since human nature - the root of human behaviour - will need to evolve very quickly indeed.

Note 1: Group intelligence refers to a process by which large numbers of people simultaneously converge upon the same point(s) of knowledge. James Surowiecki, in The Wisdom of Crowds, claims that, ironically, group intelligence requires independence of thought as well as superior judgement. Unlike herd behaviour, Group Intelligence - like crowd wisdom - is a uniquely human phenomenon. And, unlike the terms herd behaviour and herd mentality, Group Intelligence connotes more rational decision processes: based less upon emotional reactions and more upon knowledge and understanding.

Note 2: Cultural intelligence, cultural quotient or CQ, is a theory within management and organizational psychology, positing that understanding the impact of an individual's cultural background on their behaviour is essential for effective business, and measuring an individual's ability to engage successfully in any environment or social setting. First described by Christopher Earley and Soon Ang in Cultural Intelligence: Individual Interactions Across Cultures, CQ is measured on a scale, similar to that used to measure an individual's intelligence quotient. People with higher CQ are regarded as better able to successfully blend in to any environment, using more effective business practices, than those with a lower CQ.

Foreign cultures are everywhere - in other countries, certainly, but also in corporations, vocations and regions. Interacting with individuals within them demands perceptiveness and adaptability. And the people who have those traits in abundance aren't necessarily the ones who enjoy the greatest social success in familiar settings. Sometimes, people who are somewhat detached from their own culture can more easily adopt the mores and even the body language of an unfamiliar host. They're used to being observers and making a conscious effort to fit in.

Note 3: Social intelligence, according to the original definition of Edward Thorndike, is "the ability to understand and manage men and women, boys and girls, to act wisely in human relations." It is equivalent to interpersonal intelligence, one of the types of intelligences identified in Howard Gardner's theory of multiple intelligences. Some authors have restricted the definition to deal only with knowledge of social situations, perhaps more properly called social cognition.

EPISTEMIC INTELLIGENCE

Epistemology investigates the nature of knowledge, its presuppositions and foundations, and its extent and validity. The term epistemic cognition refers to an individual's process of acquiring knowledge. It includes the ways an individual monitors the epistemic nature of problems and the truth value of alternative solutions. It includes the individual's knowledge about the limits of knowing, the certainty of knowing, and the criteria for knowing. It also includes the strategies used to identify and choose between the form of solution required for different problem types.

Epistemic rationality considers the adequate justification of beliefs, to be able to decide, at least provisionally, those beliefs that are true, those beliefs that are false and those which we are insufficiently informed to decide upon. In other words, epistemology addresses the question, "How do we know what we know?" What are the basic assumptions and premises that influence perception? Epistemology is always and inevitably personal - no person's mind operates as a blank screen, objectively recording his or her experience. All experience is processed through personalized filters that interpret that experience on the basis of unconscious presuppositions. As a result, each person's reality is constructed via a subjective process that is influenced by a number of factors, including genetics, upbringing and education, cultural forces and life experiences.

In spite of its subjectivity, a person's reality is real to him or her. Since the epistemological process by which that personal reality is constructed tends to be unconscious, the product of perception is rarely evaluated. Rather, it is typically equated with objective truth and allowed to influence the person's cognition accordingly. Any change, therefore, which does not address these deeper epistemological issues tends to be only superficial.

Individual and developmental differences in what it means to know something, and hence in the criteria for justifying knowledge claims, have potentially wide-ranging implications. In providing support for a claim, young children have difficulty differentiating explanation of why a claim makes sense and evidence that the claim is true. Epistemic understanding progresses developmentally, but substantial variation remains among adults, with few adults achieving understanding of the complementary strengths and weaknesses of evidence and explanation in argument. Epistemic understanding shapes intellectual values and hence the disposition (as opposed to competence) to exercise intellectual skills. Only its most advanced levels support a disposition to engage in the intellectual effort that reasoned argument entails.

Patricia King and Karen Kitchener (1994) described a scale of Reflective Judgement composed of seven distinct epistemic levels:

Pre-Reflective Thinking (Pre-Conventional)

Individuals who reason in pre-reflectively justify their opinions in a simple fashion because they fail to perceive that answers to a question may contain some elements of uncertainty.

Level 1: Beliefs need no justification since there is assumed to be an absolute correspondence between what is believed and what is true. Alternative beliefs are not recognized. Typical statement: "I know what I have seen." Summary: What I observe to be true is true. This is termed the "copy view of knowledge," that knowledge is absolute.

Level 2: Beliefs are unexamined and unjustified or justified by their correspondence with the beliefs of an authority figure (such as a teacher or parent). Most issues are assumed to have a right answer, so there is little or no conflict in making decisions about disputed issues. Typical statement: "If it is on the news, it has to be true." Summary: There is a true reality that can be known, but not by everybody. Hence, the need for authorities who do know.

Level 3: In areas in which certain answers exist, beliefs are justified by reference to authorities' views. In areas in which answers do not exist, beliefs are defended as personal opinion since the link between evidence and beliefs is unclear. Typical statement: "When there is evidence that people can give to convince everybody one way or another, then it will be knowledge;until then, it's just a guess." Summary: Truth is temporarily inaccessible, even for authorities, but will be known at some point in time. In the meantime, rely on "feelings."

Quasi-Reflective Thinking (Conventional)

Individuals who reason in the middle levels of Reflective Judgement recognize that knowledge claims about ill-structured problems contain elements of uncertainty;thus, there is an understanding that some situations are truly problematic. The difficulty is in understanding how judgements ought to be made in light of this uncertainty. Often, individuals believe that while judgements ought to be based on evidence, valuation is individualistic and idiosyncratic. As such, individuals appear to believe that opinions are justified by making a judgement about the issue and then finding facts which support this conclusion;or by looking at all the conflicting evidence available and making a decision based on intuition, "gut instinct" or what "feels right;" or by choosing a given discipline or perspective on the topic and justifying a position based on the "rules of the game" for that discipline.

Level 4: Since there is no source of certainty for one's beliefs, beliefs are justified by giving reasons that are often idiosyncratic, such as choosing evidence that fits an established belief. Typical statement: "I'd be more inclined to believe evolution if they had proof. It's just like the pyramids: I don't think we'll ever know. Who are you going to ask? No one was there." Summary: Reality cannot be known with certainty and knowledge claims are purely idiosyncratic.

Level 5: Beliefs are justified within a particular context using the rules of enquiry for that context, with the understanding that justification is context-specific or that beliefs are balanced against each other. Each approach has the effect of complicating and delaying judgements. Typical statement: "People think differently and so they attack the problem differently. Other theories could be as true as my own, but based on different evidence." Summary: Objective reality doesn't exist;there is only the subjective interpretation of data. Beliefs are justified only within a domain where legitimate interpretations can be made, but no comparisons can be made across domains.

Reflective Thinking (Post-Conventional)

The reasoning typified in these levels reflects the epistemological assumption that one's understanding of the world is not "given" but must be actively constructed and that knowledge must be understood in relationship to the context in which it was generated. An additional assumption is that some interpretations or knowledge claims may be judged as more plausible than others. Thus, while absolute truth will never be ascertained with complete certainty, some views may be evaluated as more reasonable explanations. This view presumes that judgements must not only be grounded in relevant data, but that they must also be evaluated to determine their validity. Criteria used to make such evaluations include, for example: conceptual soundness, coherence, degree of fit with the data, meaningfulness, usefulness, and parsimony.

Levels 6: Beliefs are justified by comparing evidence and opinion on different sides of an issue or across contexts, and by constructing solutions that are evaluated by personally-endorsed criteria, such as one's personal values or the pragmatic need for action. Typical statement: "It's very difficult in this life to be sure. There are degrees of sureness. You come to a point at which you are sure enough for a personal stance on an issue." Summary: While objective knowledge is not possible, some claims can be judged as better founded than others. There are principles of enquiry that are generalizable across domains.

Level 7: Beliefs are justified probabilistically using evidence and arguments;conclusions are defended as representing the most complete, most compelling, or most plausible understanding of an issue available to date, based on the current evidence. Typical statement: "One can judge arguments by how well thought out the positions are, what kinds of reasoning and evidence are used to support it, and how consistent the way one argues on this topic is as compared with other topics." Summary: Interpretations of the world can be synthesized into claims about the nature of the world. Therefore, knowledge must be constructed. We need to build coherent explanations.

The higher levels of Reflective Judgement incorporate non-absolute/ relativistic thinking. This is a unifying feature of Postformal methods of higher-order thinking: problem finding, dialectical reasoning, relativistic operations, reflective judgement, and trialectic reasoning. Reflective thinking is related to measurable personality traits: thinking introversion, response bias, altruism, autonomy, complexity, and theoretical orientation.

The goal of Mind Development is Epistemic Rationality. Unless a student is one in a million, the highest levels such as Trialectic Reasoning and the Metavert State will only come into operation with outside help, for which we particularly recommend the Mind Development Courses.

THE DIMENSIONS OF MENTAL GROWTH

There are eight parallel dimensions of mental growth that Mind Development has determined and all of our courses are designed to further development in each respect...

- First Dimension
- The ability to maintain attention over time to internal processes and external objects.
- Second Dimension
- An increase in the power of voluntary mechanisms of inhibition, manifesting themselves in diverse ways.
- Third Dimension
- An increase in the access of memory or awareness to verbal and voluntary processes.
- Fourth Dimension
- The ability to deal with a universe of objects, ideas, words and hypotheses logically and serially and derived from this, the power to access randomly from a spatial or temporal sequence. This is the specific quality of the left hemisphere and, by and large, this quality is over-rewarded in the present culture.
- Fifth Dimension
- The ability to superimpose dimensionality on the concrete situation, so one does not so much deal with events, but events in context. This is referred to as the power of synthesis - the special power of the right hemisphere.
- Sixth Dimension
- A decline in emotional dependence on other humans, which is manifest as a growing awareness of the body-image. A decline in affective dependence leads ultimately to a transcendence of belief systems and morality systems, which are rooted in emotional dependence on significant others. In the sixth dimension there is an increase in both Field Independence and Inner Directedness. Note: a block to growth along this dimension manifests as a body-mind duality, susceptibility to hypnosis, and a repressive Superego.
- Seventh Dimension
- An increase in speed capacity of the central nervous system (*i.e.* the frequency range of brain rhythms).
- Eighth Dimension

- An increase in Cognitive Autonomy. This is the cognitive component in autonomy - one's ability to think for one's self. This would not normally occur until late adolescence, after Formal operational thought has been established. Only after acquiring cognitive autonomy can a student reach the fully individuated state of Ego Autonomy.

Development in the above dimensions is open ended. With suitable tools, barring brain damage, development can occur until a student is on his death bed.

A change in quantity of these eight dimensions, when a critical threshold has been reached, will usher in a change in quality, manifest as a jump to a higher Stage of Ego Development - a student will move along to the next substage of Formal or Postformal Operations, until ultimately he reaches the Metavert State that is beyond Postformal Operations. In this way, the Eight Dimensions of Growth are like the accelerator in a car and the Stages of Cognitive Development described at the beginning of this chapter are like the gearbox.

As well as progressing further on the Stages of Cognitive Development, a student who develops their mind in the dimensions just described, will also progress on the equivalent levels of Reflective Judgement, on Loevinger's stages of Ego Development, on Kohlberg's stages of Moral Development and progress on theirSpiritual development and in overcoming the Superego. Furthermore, this will correspond with an increase in cognitive intelligence (IQ) and emotional intelligence (EQ).

Each of these progressions are the result of the mind acquiring a greater facility in perceptual and representational thought: in short, to be able to better handle mental complexity. Benjamin Bloom recognized a scale of mental complexity that covers the range from Pre-operational to Postformal Operations:

1. *Recognition:* Remembering and labeling
2. *Knowledge:* Recalling facts
3. *Comprehension:* Understanding important concepts
4. *Application:* Using what is known in a variety of situations
5. *Analysis:* Understanding the whole through an examination of the constituent parts
6. *Synthesis:* Making something new out of separate ideas
7. *Evaluation:* Judging the value of an idea, concept, or project

Wisdom is the result of exceptional self-development, including Ego maturity and Postformal operational thinking. Postformal development is associated with the ability to think both objectively and dialectically, and to be able to accept and integrate inherent contradictions and alternative truths. The Postformal mind is also able to integrate the various aspects of the psyche (including recognition of all the aspects of self such as Superego, Id, Shadow and Anima). The previously hidden parts of the psyche contain unrealized potentials;for example, by retaining his masculinity but also now integrating his feminine traits, adopting an androgynous gender role, a man can benefit from both the masculine and feminine qualities, and the tempering effect each has on the other. Furthermore, higher levels of Ego maturity are associated with greater recognition of negative aspects of self;self esteem does not suffer from acknowledging those aspects of personality or mental skills that need positive developmental work.

Unresolved personality issues can certainly have a profound effect on IQ. Lester Gelb tells the story of a young boy who had been the victim of poor teachers and exploitive foster homes, and as a result he was depressed and 'unmanageable.' He clearly felt isolated and misunderstood, but no-one was listening. His IQ was 79 at age 11. After Lester's acknowledgement of the appropriateness of his anger, the boy's attitude was transformed and he was ready to accept educational opportunities. His IQ had risen to 129 by age 17 and he went on to make a successful career.

The techniques of Mind Development are one of the best ways to stimulate intellectual development after the age of twenty and to achieve Individuation: a strong and mature Ego that is capable of metacognition, Postformal operations and beyond.

COGNITIVE FIXITY AND FLUIDITY

Cognitive fluidity is a term first popularly applied by Steven Mithen in his book The Prehistory of the Mind, a search for the cognitive origins of Art, Religion and Science. The book describes how a limited primate mind has evolved into modern human mind by combining different ways of process knowledge and using tools to create a modern civilization. By arriving at original thoughts, which are often highly creative and rely on metaphor and analogy modern humans differ from archaic humans. As such, cognitive fluidity is a key element of the human attentive consciousness. Let us examine the primitive mind, going right back to the Stone Ages. There were three Stone Ages: the Paleolithic, Mesolithic and Neo-lithic;three epochs that were universal and of sufficient magnitude that they could change the way the human mind operates.

The term Paleolithic or Old Stone Age refers to a prehistoric era distinguished by the development of the first stone tools. It covers the greatest portion of humanity's time (roughly 99per cent of human history) on Earth, extending from 2.5 or 2.6 million years ago, with the introduction of stone tools by hominids such as Homo habilis, to the introduction of agriculture and the end of the Pleistocene around 20,000 BC. The Paleolithic era ended with the Mesolithic, in Western Europe, and in areas not affected by the Ice Age with the Epipaleolithic (such as Africa). During the Paleolithic Stone Age, man developed a Swiss Knife Modular Mind. (He was in a state of Cognitive Fixity).

He had a number of self-contained, domain-specific solutions to the problems of survival, that were fast and inflexible. These were applied in a fixed way, without appraisal by general intelligence, therefore little progress occurred over thousands of years.

By 20,000 to 18,000 BC the climate and environment had changed, starting a period of transition that we call the Mesolithic or Middle Stone Age. The forest vegetation retreated, to be replaced by steppe. The hunter-gatherers would have had to modify their way of living and their pattern of settlement to adapt to the changing conditions. During the Mesolithic Stone Age, man had a Bicameral mind and started to develop Partial Cognitive Fluidity.

This was a transitional phase between Cognitive Fixity and Cognitive Fluidity in which the mind was Bicameral in operation: the experiences and memories of the right hemisphere of the brain are transmitted to the left hemisphere via auditory hallucinations. Cognitive functions were divided between a right hemisphere center which appears to be "speaking," and a passive left hemisphere which listens and obeys. Similar to that of a modern-day schizophrenic, rather than making conscious evaluations in novel or unexpected situations, the person would hallucinate a voice or "god" giving admonitory advice or commands, and obey these voices without question;one would not be at all conscious of one's own thought processes per se. The Bicameral mind gave rise to the phenomenon of shamanism and later, starting in about 10,000 B.C., religion.

The Neo-lithic or New Stone Age, began about 10,000 B.C. in the Middle East. The Neo-lithic way of life included farming, herding, polished stone axes, timber longhouses and pottery. The Neo-lithic era ended when metal tools became widespread in the Copper, Bronze or Iron Age - depending on geographical region. During the Neo-lithic Stone Age, man started to develop the modern mind with full Cognitive Fluidity, a process that has continued until the present day - an awakening from the Bicameral Mind! The Bicameral mental model was replaced by the conscious mode of thought, grounded in the acquisition of metaphorical language, self-awareness and introspection through development of the left hemisphere. Cognitive fluidity generates imagination, the capacity for symbolic thought, and the creative ability to generate complex mental symbols. The Ego arises from the brain's cortical cognitive fluidity. Elements of the Bicameral mentality remain in primitive people and "psychics."

Between about 4,000 B.C. to about 1,200 A.D. the entire world was theocratic: the world was explained in terms of the will of personified deities. *According to Auguste Comte, theocracy developed in three stages:*

1. Animism - Regarding natural phenomena and everyday items as worthy of religious worship, perhaps with godlike qualities. This

Naturalistic outlook is a form of pre-conventional spiritual intelligence, which aligns with Concrete Operations.

2. Polytheism - Explanation of the world through the influence of many gods.
3. Monotheism - Attributing all to a single, supreme deity, resulting in systems of government in which priests rule in the name of a God. This becomes the convention, the Normative outlook. The Monotheistic stage started with the Jews at about 4000BC: Christianity, and Islam came much later of course. Prior to that time, societies were either Animistic or Polytheistic.

Through contact with the writings of Aristotle, Plato and other non-Christian sources of philosophy that were reluctantly tolerated by the Catholic Church, Western society gradually gained emancipation from theocratic thinking, and this lead to the Renaissance, scientific thinking and the Age of Enlightenment, and in the eighteenth century, the start of the modern era, leading to fully modern consciousness. Over the last 200 years, this has spread over most of the world, coexisting with the influence of fundamentalist, monotheist religious societies (Christian, Muslim, Jewish, etc). There also remain communities with polytheistic and animist beliefs.

Only those capable of thinking beyond Formal Operations, the educated and open-minded thinkers of the time, demonstrate an autonomous search for Existential (post-conventional) understanding and values beyond those dictated by a personalised deity. At the other extreme, the primitive Bicameral mind is totally under the control of the Superego, which is experienced as the voices of gods or demons. Bicameral man has very little ego, so he does not think as we do. The fact that a person can have a lobotomy (the removal of the frontal lobes), and retain a Superego, indicates that the Superego is in the right hemisphere, in the parietal lobe. Once the frontal lobes take over, because a person has reached full cognitive maturity, the voice of the Superego becomes weak or non existent.

In some primitive cultures, the Formal stage of operations is seldom reached since there are not the language and educational demands, and so a further intuitive phase of the Concrete Operational stage may become manifest, and the concrete cognitive structures may be sufficiently mature to operate intuitively. Concrete Intuition is a missing stage in advanced cultures, because due to the influence of education the students progress quickly from Concrete Operations towards Formal Operations, or at least, the education system attempts to achieve that;on the other hand, Concrete Intuition is the mental state of shamans and witchdoctors and the Dream Time of the Australian Aborigine. In the state of Concrete Intuition, they have special powers and savant abilities. When manifest, this state is also similar to certain states of hypnosis. In these states, the hypnotized subject has greatly increased physical strength, heightened perception and an extended field of memory. There is much similarity between the awareness of people at the Concrete Intuitive level and the "no-mind" state described in Zen literature.

In my opinion, people who are still in a state of Bicameral Consciousness have eidetic imagery (outstanding concrete memory) and operate (at best) at the level of Concrete Intuition, in which perception and memory are undifferentiated. Concrete Intuition is therefore the endpoint of development for people living in primitive cultures. The commonest form of outstanding memory in primitive man is topographical memory, or recollection of a particular place or route. It retains an image, complete down to the tiniest details, that enables primitive man to find his way with an assurance Europeans regard as astonishing. Similarly the native would know instantly if a member of their herd was missing, without having to count linearly.

Cognitive Fluidity (also termed Flexibility) has a direct impact on people's ability to adapt and respond effectively to new or unfamiliar problems, and this development was essential to move beyond a primitive way of life. Cognitive fluidity hinges on a readiness to direct attention to novel events, to think differently, and to change one's mental set to find new solutions for old problems.

Beyond the development of a theocratic worldview, where religion is the dominant force, the French philosopher Comte (facing at his time the ruins of the French Revolution) postulated that a society will develop through two more stages...

- After the Theological stage in which man blindly believed in whatever he was taught by his ancestors, comes the Metaphysical stage: a recognition that Man has universal rights, not dependent upon any deity. This is therefore the beginning of investigation from a point of view of autonomy, in which people start reasoning and questioning all that they have previously believed, even though they may not have much solid evidence to build upon. This stage is the beginning of a world that questions authority and religion.
- In the Scientific stage, further evidence is sought, so that people can find solutions to the social problems that remain, even despite the proclamations of human rights or supposed destiny that is the will of God. The scientific method would be applied to social, ecological and economic issues, as well as the physical. It is a Positivist outlook that in Comte's epoch helped to launch the subject of sociology.

In modern times, to be successful a person needs to be able to think independently, objectively and flexibly, to be able to interweave abstract and specific thoughts appropriately and skillfully. This has been described as a "Helicopter Mind." Hold an image of a helicopter in your mind that moves up (towards abstract) when a WHY question is asked and moves down (towards specific) when a HOW question is asked. You ask WHY questions to review an activity in terms of its purpose, value and desired outcome. You ask HOW questions to review activities in terms of their method, process and skills involved.

Particularly at times of stress, thinking tends to become more "black and white," rigidly attached to concrete specifics, like a man overboard holding onto a floating plank of wood. In this state, there is an inability to turn one's attention away from a dominant stimulus or to pay attention to more than one stimulus at a time, in order to benefit from verbal self-regulation and even verbal instructions received. It leads to an inability to change behaviour according to an intelligent response, and inability to formulate different hypotheses when solving problems. At an extreme, suicidal individuals suffer from cognitive rigidity, which leads them to believe that suicide is their only option.

Chronic stress is also closely tied with physical health problems. Such stress may be due to overwork or particularly difficult circumstances, but also may be self-imposed by inner conflicts between beliefs that are rigidly attached to and the evidence of objective reality, and many other such psychological factors. Such psychological stress is increased by cognitive inflexibility, preventing perception of the reality of problems, and the stress itself increases the inflexibility further. Health problems such as depression, diabetes, heart disease, hyperthyroidism, obesity, ulcers and possibly even cancer can result, and affect life expectancy.

At Mind Development, we have noticed that a significant number of students, such as retired taxi drivers, have been over the age of 60 when they started Mind Development, yet they have made significant gains in their studies. Some entered a new profession, and more than a few lived to be over 90. Mind Development may have contributed to their longevity. I believe that unless you are senile, you are never too old to start developing your mind, and there will be benefits all around.

Although Cognitive Fluidity/Flexibility is not measured by an IQ test, it is an important dimension of real world intelligence, and the same applies to Cognitive Complexity...

COGNITIVE COMPLEXITY

Cognitive complexity is a psychological characteristic that indicates how complex or simple is the frame and perceptual skill of a person. A person who measures high on cognitive complexity tends to perceive nuances and subtle differences which a person with a lower measure, indicating a less complex cognitive structure for the task or activity, does not.

Jane Loevinger's ego development theory proposes that individuals progress through a series of stages that reflect increased levels of cognitive complexity and ego maturity. Loevinger proposes that the level of ego functioning influences how an individual perceives and interprets personal experiences and interpersonal relationships. The personal ideals that are important to an individual may also be influenced by their cultural context: the larger social community and religious beliefs.

In 1994, Harvard University Professor Robert Kegan wrote the book In Over Our Heads, which demonstrates that human development is in part a response to the changing demands of social environments, that the skills required for living a coherent life in modern western societies are different from those required by simpler, tribal cultures. We become more complex as the demands of our environment require such complexity.

Robert Kegan summarized the incremental process of increasing complexity of the subject-object relationship, which he calls The Five Orders of Increasing Mental Complexity:

- *1st Level:* Fantasy, impulse, single-point of view, immediate, atomistic
- *2nd Level:* Concrete-operational, role-concept, durable category
- *3rd Level:* Traditionalism, role consciousness, reciprocity, trans-categorical
- *4th Level:* Modernism, abstraction, ideology, multiple roles, system/complex
- *5th Level:* Post-Modernism, dialectical, trans-ideological, trans-system/complex

When we are infants (1st Level), we experience a lack of differentiation between subject and object. In short, we are one with the world. However, as we grow, our capacity to distinguish ourselves from the exterior world develops. Kegan calls this process one of increasing "object permanence." In the overall trajectory up the levels, Kegan has noticed a fascinating trend in human cognitive development: at one stage that which is subjective in our awareness later becomes objective in our awareness. In other words, something that we are not aware of at Level 2 (because it is embedded in our subjective awareness), we later become aware of objectively... we can take a perspective on it, hold it as external to our own experience, and take responsibility for it, because we are no longer captive to it.

As we develop mentally, we become increasingly objective in our perceptions of the world, eventually resulting in the ability to entertain multiple points of view simultaneously and to synthesize them. We become capable of imagining many scenarios and possibilities, and our own personal perspective takes on a certain degree of relativity in relationship to the multiple perspectives of the outside world.

Persons who are capable of complex analytical thinking are able to differentiate a situation into many constituent elements, and then explore connections and potential relationships among the elements. They are more flexible and creative in their thinking. The more the elements constituting a situation can be differentiated and the parts considered in novel relationships, the more refined the problem-solving response and successful the solution. It is my opinion that a person's level of mental complexity is the common factor between Piaget's stages of cognitive development and Loevinger's stages of Ego development. One cannot reach a post-conventional level of Ego development, until one has reached the post-formal stage of cognitive development.

BEYOND POSTFORMAL OPERATIONS: MATURE INTUITION AND THE METAVERT STATE

The formal approach to consciousness, simplistically, recognizes identity as the fundamental element. It allows for a fixed, static, identifiable world. In a formal world we can know what to expect. In dialectics the resolution of two elements (thesis and antitheses) occurs due to contradiction or conflict resolving into a new thesis (and thus creating a new antithesis). The process goes on and on.

Moving beyond dialectic argument, however, we can look at the pros and cons of an argumenttrialectically. These two elements exist but are viewed in a qualitatively different way, and the resolution between them is through complementarity or cooperation, giving rise to a higher degree of insight. Students will get glimpses of this higher realm, a taste of true wisdom, just as they may have peak experiences that offer a glimpse into the transpersonal or spiritual aspects of their being, but serious work with the techniques of Mind Development will increasingly make this a daily experience and domain general, rather than just in a specific area of expertise.

Trialectic reasoning is the transitional phase between the fifth stage of Postformal Operations and the sixth stage of intellectual development, Mature Intuition.

When Postformal Operations have been internalized, practiced to the degree of effortless competence, on not just a domain-specific (one's area of expert knowledge and competence) but on a domain-general basis, a sixth stage of development then naturally follows, called Mature Intuition. Work on the advanced courses of Mind Development will be of invaluable assistance in this process. When this stage is reached, all significant cognitive structures of the first five stages have sufficient maturity to be utilized pre-reflectively or intuitively. The individual can then make use of his creative and intuitive skills to become a breakthrough thinker and leader.

This state transcends introvert and extravert orientations - it is 'Metavert' - the individual can chose introspective introversion or expressive extraversion, as appropriate to his circumstances and needs. He has no neurotic compulsions nor inhibitions regarding one or the other;he is essentially free of Superego control. He can focus internally or externally at will, rather than being driven by the conditioning of his experiences and upbringing.

One may ask the question, "Does all thought take place in words?" It should now be evident that it is a question of degree. When we are dealing with a low level of abstraction, concerning concrete objects, we may think entirely without words. As we ascend the ladder of abstraction, words form an increasing part of our mental content. It may appear, from superficial observation, that people operate non-verbally at high levels of abstraction. In most cases this is an illusion... some form of imagery is being used, as a surrogate language. There is, however, Intuitive Thinking. This is not thinking in the same sense;it consists of mental operations at high speed, often in parallel and outside the frame of consciousness. At the cognitive level of Mature Intuition, words are sometimes used;however, because of the speed of the process - typically the speed of thought exceeds 1,200 words per minute and continues subcognitively - and because the process occurs largely outside of awareness as an intuitive process, there is an illusion of non-verbal thought. We can't think in terms of the speed of inner speech anymore, because in this Metavert state, thinking is transverbal.

Thought, in the Metavert state of Mature Intuition is post-symbolic and post-reflective - it is beyond language and beyond the scale of Reflective Judgement given above. The Metavert does not have to think reflectively, he just knows - all the reflective judgements are being made at high speed beneath the surface of consciousness, an intuitional process. He has access to the contents of both the affective and the cognitive subconscious as resources for intuition.

The Metavert state of Mature Intuition is not a transpersonal state;there is no sense of union with the Infinite and God. One, however, is illuminated in a certain sense. In the Metavert state one operates at a higher harmonic of intelligence, that of Certainty.

Most of a Metavert's thinking is intuitive;by this I mean that one perceives, poses and resolves problems intuitively. Most of a Metavert's thinking is transverbal and visual;one is thinking in meanings rather than words;one only needs to think conventionally when one makes conclusions and in order to explain things to another person. One can do this easily, because one retains access to all the skills of Formal and Postformal thought, so much of one's experience at the Metavert level can be translated into words.

At this final stage of mind development the intellect is integrated with feeling and both of these functions are put on automatic. The remaining active thinking continues the level of the Ego or conscious self. However, the functioning of the Ego itself becomes witnessed - a higher and transcendent state of consciousness. One of the hallmarks of this state is that the self is not involved with the world. Thinking, feeling and perception can function below the level of conscious attention, just as muscular motor coordination is generally automatic and apparently unconnected to attentional processing. The entire brain literally runs in parallel, and attention ceases to be a bottleneck in any cognitive processes;attention moves to the witnessing meta-intelligence.

DYNAMIC CONSCIOUSNESS

'Dynamic' consciousness means an ability on the part of the person concerned to be in the appropriate state of attention for the task in hand. Much of the current New Age movement is held in thrall by the attainment of 'ideal' states of consciousness, in particular a static state of right-brain awareness combined with a predominantly Alpha (relaxed) meditative detachment. Whilst this state has objective existence, and is different from the states of awareness experienced by most people most of the time, it is nonetheless comparable to a still photograph from the motion picture of life, or a still point at the extremity of the swing of a pendulum. It is only an ideal state for operating in particular contexts, but as real life is not static, we are continually changing from one context to another, and we need to be able to adjust our state of consciousness to be optimal for each situation.

The true meaning of 'raised consciousness' is the ability to rapidly and under one's own volition, attain the most appropriate state of consciousness for any circumstances. The primary signaling system in the brain is the sensori-motor (first programme) centered in the lower brain and controlling energetic responses and feelings. This is common to all animals. The secondary system, peculiar to man, is mediated by the frontal cortex and it reflects the primary impulses in the form of symbolic representations that may be communicated. Our present level of awareness is mainly restricted to this second system.

Intelligence develops from childhood in the way outlined by Piaget, starting with the sensori-motor stage from birth. A pre-logical, intuitive stage follows this while the child learns how best to adapt to the environment. By the age of five, when he goes to school, concrete imagery enables him to think constructively, then from about seven years of age language and other symbolic left-brain means of analysis are developed. The further development of this stage, that of formal operations, seems to be cut off when active education ceases, and that fixes the current scenario as a status-quo. However, Postformal Operations may develop between 18 and 30 in about 5per cent of the population who are in appropriately stimulating environments. It is postulated further intellectual development would lead to an advanced intuitional state, that of mature intuition. This is the state of whole-brain synchrony we call the Metavert state.

BRAIN MATURATION

The human brain is not a finished organ at birth — in fact, another 10 or 12 years are needed before even a general development is completed. Structural maturation of individual brain regions and their connecting pathways is required for the successful development of cognitive, motor, and sensory functions. This maturation eventually provides for a smooth flow of neural impulses throughout the brain, which allows for information to be integrated across the many spatially segregated brain regions involved in these functions.

The speed of neural transmission is an important factor, and this depends not only on the junctions between nerve cells (synapses), but also on the structural properties of the connecting fibres (axons). Critical axon structural properties include their diameters and the thickness of the special insulation (myelin) around many fibres. Large groups of myelinated axons, which connect various regions in the brain, appear visibly as "white matter". Axons of the major pathways in the human brain, such as those of the corpus callosum (which connects the two halves of the brain) or the corticospinal tract (which connects the brain to the spinal cord and the rest of the body), continue to develop throughout childhood and adolescence. Postmortem studies suggest that axon diameters and myelin sheaths undergo conspicuous growth during the first two years of life, but may not be fully mature before adolescence or even late adulthood.

The science of intelligence testing is now over one hundred years old. So long a time, in fact, that test subjects (typically high school students in the nineteen fifties) can be retested in order to compare results from today to those of fifty years ago. The results? Most people get smarter as they age. Or, perhaps better said, they test higher, as much as ten points higher, than when they were in their teens.

New findings seem to contradict one of the most widely accepted assumptions about aging: that the human brain is at its most powerful between the ages of 18 and 26. Scientists have discovered that intelligence, instead of peaking in our youth, remains stable and, in some respects, gets sharper as we grow older.

Note: Myelination is an important process in the nervous system as it helps to increase the speed at which action potentials propagate along axons efficiently. More intelligent brains show faster nerve conduction, less glucose utilization in positron emission tomography, faster reaction times, faster inspection times, faster speeds in general, greater circumference and volume, smaller standard deviation in reaction times, greater variability in EEG measures, shorter white matter T2 relaxation times, and higher gray-white matter contrast with magnetic resonance imaging. Researchers at Oxford observed with brain imaging that, when people learn a new skill (juggling), the white matter in their brain increased. This increase in white matter is most likely due to myelination. In other words, the brain is capable of increase myelin in response to learning even into adulthood.

Our current level of maturation is such that the signaling rate of our secondary system has only about a quarter of the reaction speed of the primary system. This means that our peculiar type of human consciousness can only exist by actively inhibiting the lower, primary (limbic) system. When the secondary system is switched off, as in hypnotism and shamanic trance states, the primary system is accessible to the hypnotist and its animalistic powers cause the strange phenomena of shamanic ritual. But this is not self-directed power, the individual is 'out to lunch'.

Should a way be found to activate primary consciousness while we are at a normal level of integration, the higher centers would be swamped with input that could not be processed. Restricted to formal operations conducted logically and serially, we would be compulsively in desperate cope in present time and unable to inhibit responses to incoming stimuli selectively. This is the state that a Kung-Fu or Karate expert is able to attain momentarily, in order to deliver a blow with the full force of the sensori-motor system and with the level of accuracy possible in this heightened mode of sensory acuity. A fraction of a second would seem like several seconds at this speed of signaling - time would stand still.

"Close analysis of brain tissue and MRIs clearly shows that the brain's wiring develops until middle age and then begins to decline as the breakdown of myelin triggers a destructive domino affect. Our time at the peak is short indeed," according to brain researcher Bartzokis. "The challenge for science and medicine is to figure out how to extend the brain's peak performance so that our minds function as long as our bodies."

The idea that the brain continues to mature and develop connections well into adulthood provides some exciting possibilities for the practical application of neuropsychological studies. Not only are we developing an increasingly detailed picture of the activity within our brains, we also are learning more about what factors can negatively or positively affect the way our brains function. Some factors, very prevalent in a adolescent's life, such as anxiety, sleep deprivation, dehydration, and inactivity can seriously impair their executive functioning as adults, which plays such an important role in creating and maintaining goal-directed activity.

Research shows that the three parts of the brain that are most heavily involved in ADHD are the areas of the brain that also control motor activity. Due to the overlap between motor and mental control, activities that encourage aerobic exercise, strengthening, and stretching, stimulate the executive brain. Also, there is evidence that motor control can be improved through patterned programmed movements thought to be particularly beneficial for executive functioning, which include martial arts, yoga, dance, swimming, and drumming.

With the application of advanced Mind Development techniques, the higher cortex becomes more developed. There is both a better specialization and delegation of functions, and a greater degree of integration of those functions, with whole-brain synchrony of dominant wavelengths, so that the degree of inhibition of primary centers can be reduced. Ultimately the secondary system of higher centers can fully integrate with the sensori-motor mode of consciousness. With the mature intuition of developed Metaversion, the higher centers will be able to undertake many operations simultaneously in parallel;linear thinking will be complemented by fully developed lateralism.

Note: The speed of thought and abundance of creativity that accompanies Metaversion has superficial resemblance to the abilities that frequently accompany mania. Like the Metavert, a person who has become manic has overcome theSuperego;however, due to a lack of Ego strength and maturity he fails to make the transition to a higher stage of consciousness - a creative consciousness;he remains bound and driven by the instinctive impulses of the Id, which are no longer moderated by the Superego. A warning: when there has been insufficient cognitive development to build Ego strength, overcoming the Superego by the use of drugs - or by any other means that does not strengthen the Ego - can lead to Mania.

True wisdom is realized during this sixth stage of Mind Development. Mature Intuition involves determining and mastering one's epistemic beliefs, to go beyond metacognition into the realm of meta-metacognition.

This 'arch-faculty' of our highest-level self remains awake and aware of the unique subjective perceptions defining our person, and can manipulate our perceptions almost as though senior to them. Thus one's personal epistemology becomes a conscious process - one becomes the 'meta-programmer' of one's own mind - and one can apply the same, more objective intelligence to recognizing, defining and solving life problems.

ONTOLOGICAL INTELLIGENCE

Ontology is the flip side of the coin from epistemology. Epistemology is concerned with the process by which the knowledge of reality is ascertained, whereas ontology is a systematic account of the nature of what exists, including that of oneself and other entities. Ontological beliefs include issues of identity and represent an even higher level than epistemic beliefs - a sort of meta meta-metacognition.

Although largely unconscious, ontological belief systems that are held at the conscious level tend to include many beliefs held with strong emotion, because they have been found in past experience to serve the person well, to gain safety, control, esteem or rightness - to be 'top dog.' Such 'privileged' beliefs are near synonymous with a person's identity. A person will say: "I cannot change this belief without changing who I am." In the early days of Christianity, believers would allow themselves to be thrown to the lions, rather than embracing paganism and giving up their beliefs. Likewise, in Russia, people have been willing to face a firing squad, rather than pretend they are communists.

From a Mind Development point of view, a person's ontological beliefs delimit the range of epistemic beliefs available to him. In turn, a person's epistemic beliefs influence his metacognition and so on, all the way down the line. For this reason, ontological beliefs are the hardest to deal with.

Beliefs are central to our sense of who we are, our sense of self and identity. Some beliefs (both ontological and epistemic) are conscious and easily accessible, others are deeply embedded. Beliefs and therefore identity become habits. Beliefs originate in the cultures in which we are embedded. Beliefs define who we are - and who we are not. Our mental models determine our unconscious epistemology, our unconscious assumptions about the world and how we give meaning to experience. They can both support alignment with life's pattern and obstruct it. To flow with life's unfolding pattern requires us to become more conscious of our unconscious epistemology. If we can recognize the patterning running through our models of the world, we can use our mental modeling to undo and update some of its earlier work.

Ontological Intelligence may be described as the ability to recognize one's currently adopted identity and the reasons for its adoption, and the changes of identity that occur reactively or proactively in new circumstances, and the identities of the organizations of which one is a member;plus the willingness to transcend any egotistical barriers to effective listening, learning and reconsideration of identity issues.

Ontological intelligence precedes and is more fundamental that epistemological intelligence, as it is the being of the human being. It is the foundation for the individual's assumed roles in life, and as ontological intelligence develops, new boundariess and paradigms become available for the expansion of knowledge and skills, and expression of epistemological intelligence. Acknowledging the importance of an ontological framework for education shifts its primary intention and attention from knowing to being.

Because of limits in human mental capacity, the mind cannot cope directly with the complexity of the world. Rather, we construct a simplified mental model of reality - within a bounded or limited rationality - and then work with this model. We may behave rationally within the confines of our mental model, but this model is not always well adapted to the requirements of the real world, and does not enable us to understand what is truly going on.

8

Developmental Psychology in Adults

Developmental psychology is a branch of psychology that attempts to explain the development of humans over time, both in the micro sense, as they develop from babies to mature adults, and in the macro sense, as the culture itself evolves through the years and decades. It should be noted that it's difficult to make broad claims about developmental psychology because it is effectively an umbrella term used to describe a number of disciplines all focused on the same goal. These disciplines, however, are often quite diverse, and can seem rather dissimilar from one another in all respects except their shared purpose. This being the case, a good understanding of developmental psychology should take into account an overview of the various unique disciplines that make up the branch as a whole.

PIAGET'S STAGE THEORY

One of the foremost figures in developmental psychology is Jean Piaget. He is credited with being the first to elaborate a "stage theory" and to argue that all humans develop through a similar path, progressing through recognizable "stages", each with definable characteristics and psycho-social goals that must be met if one is to progress to the next.

One of the most interesting facets of the stage theory is its proposition that children learn by constructing knowledge through experience, as opposed to it being directly imparted by environment, or being innate and instinctual. Because of this, Piaget's theory has found a lot of support from those who feel it makes for a successful pedagogical approach. Indeed, many elementary schools and pre-schools around the country subscribe to Piaget's theory and put it into practice in their respective curricula.

Experiments conducted by Piaget help to support his view and to establish a certain responsibility on the part of adults in guiding the learning of developing children (as opposed, for example, to Watson's hands-off approach). These experiments typically involved the use of engaging in Socratic questioning to incite children towards greater understanding of their actions. Famously, he arranged candy into two lines;a long line with fewer pieces and a short line with more pieces. When children said that the longer line had "more" because it was bigger, Socratic questioning was used to take them backwards through the decision making process, after which they were able to apply this reasoning to other situations.

LEV VYGOTSKY AND SOCIAL CONTEXTUALISM

Another researcher in developmental psychology, Lev Vygotsky, also believed that adults had the responsibility of aiding in the development of children. Instead of a directly didactic approach, however, he favoured that adults only intervene in development during critical stages known as "zones of proximal development", when a child was nearing progression from one developmental stage to the next.

Importantly, Vygotsky would go on to expand this theory to encompass a broader perspective of society as a whole. Just as Piaget felt that learning and development underwent a transmission from adult to child, Vygotsky made the claim that development began on the social level and trickled down to the individual level over time. In other words, the predominant culture into which an individual is born has a profound effect upon that individual's values and thusly their development. Thus asserted, he went on to state that culture itself has a responsibility to play in personal development.

Vygotsky first put forth these views in a 1929 essay called "The Problem of the Cultural Development of the Child", in which he outlined his experimental methods. For the most part, this experiments focused on goal-oriented behaviour, such as a child learning to kick a mobile for the purpose of making it spin. The implication was that the stimuli and environment put forth by culture would determine the opportunities a child had to learn skills and how to place these skills into an overall hierarchy of values. Considered from a broad viewpoint, the implications could be staggering: consider how different, for example, a child brought up in poverty can be from a child brought up in insulated wealth and luxury.

BANDURA'S SOCIAL LEARNING THEORY

One of the most recent researchers to made headway in the field of developmental psychology is Albert Bandura. Originally sympathetic to the beliefs of the Behaviourists, Bandura departed somewhat from his early convictions after a series of experiments that have famously come to be called the "Bobo Doll experiments".

A "Bobo doll" is an inflatable toy designed to stand back up on its own using weights after being knocked over. After viewing a video of a colleague savagely attacking such a doll, children were found to be highly susceptible to repeating this behaviour, even without the promise of reward or the threat of a negative reinforcement. This seemed to be at least a bit at odds with

Behaviourism's assertions that conditioning is responsible for nearly all observable behaviour.

So what exactly was going on here? Bandura eventually developed a theory that development occurs through a process of "social learning" wherein behaviours are witnessed, retained, and ultimately re-enacted by children after observing the behaviours of adults. This theory of social learning has had a major impact upon Western society to the extent that most people now feel that observed behaviour has a profound impact upon child development. Witness, for example, the rating system that prevents children from accessing excessively violent films or video games.

Bandura and later followers also attempted to apply the social learning theory to the sphere of abnormal psychology as a way of explaining criminal behaviour. They explained deviance as a learned behaviour that the deviant in question performs in hopes that they can avoid pain or humiliation in some way. The claim is that in nearly all cases, deviant behaviour develops as an avoidance strategy after someone undergoes a traumatic experience involving pain or humiliation. They supported these claims with an in-depth analysis of American serial murderers that proved to be quite compelling.

EMERGING ADULTS: THE IN-BETWEEN AGE

Starting in 1995, psychologist Jeffrey Jensen Arnett, PhD, interviewed 300 young people ages 18 to 29 in cities around the nation over five years, asking them questions about what they wanted out of life. Despite stark differences in their social backgrounds and likely economic prospects, Arnett was struck by the similar answers he heard from his young respondents. They shared a perception of "feeling in between"—knowing they were pulling clear of the struggles of adolescence and starting to feel responsible for themselves, but still closely tied to their parents and family.

They also reported pondering their personal identity, a theme that surprised Arnett, who thought most would have settled that question as adolescents. Working from those interviews and examining broad demographic indicators, Arnett proposed a new period of life-span development he calls "emerging adulthood."Arnett, a professor of psychology at Clark University currently teaching as a Fulbright scholar at the University of Copenhagen in Denmark, coined the term in his book "Emerging Adulthood: The Winding Road From the Late Teens Though the Twenties".

He describes emerging adulthood as the time from the end of adolescence to the young-adult responsibilities of a stable job, marriage and parenthood and has made it the subject of a new APA book, "Emerging Adults in America: Coming of Age in the 21st Century," co-edited with Jennifer Lynn Tanner, PhD.

The book claims the phenomenon has only arisen in the past few decades in the United States in response to social and economic changes, and it urges continuing scholarship examining the nature of life and paths of development for emerging adults.

FIVE FEATURES OF EMERGING ADULTS

As Arnett describes it, emerging adulthood can be defined as an:

- Age of identity exploration. Young people are deciding who they are and what they want out of work, school and love.
- Age of instability. The post-high school years are marked by repeated residence changes, as young people either go to college or live with friends or a romantic partner. For most, frequent moves end as families and careers are established in the 30s.
- Age of self-focus. Freed of the parent- and society-directed routine of school, young people try to decide what they want to do, where they want to go and who they want to be with—before those choices get limited by the constraints of marriage, children and a career.
- Age of feeling in between. Many emerging adults say they are taking responsibility for themselves, but still do not completely feel like an adult.
- Age of possibilities. Optimism reigns. Most emerging adults believe they have good chances of living "better than their parents did," and even if their parents divorced, they believe they'll find a lifelong soul mate.

Arnett's research shows that emerging adults want a lot out of life—a job that's well-paid and personally meaningful and a lasting bond with a partner. Many might be headed for disappointment, he says, noting that most employers simply want someone who can get a job done and almost half of all marriages end in divorce.

"If happiness is the difference between what you expect out of life and what you actually get, a lot of emerging adults are setting themselves up for unhappiness because they expect so much," he says.

LARGER TRENDS AT WORK

Arnett says emerging adulthood is tied to larger historical social trends in American society, noting that 50 years ago, the median age for marriage was 22 for men and 20 for women. Now, the median age for marriage has climbed past 28 for men and edged above 24 for women. One reason young people marry later is that a much larger percentage of young people attend some form of college, creating a longer transition time between adolescence and adulthood, Arnett says.

Before 1944 and the passage of the GI Bill of Rights for returning World War II veterans, only a small percentage of high school graduates went to college, an educational experience mainly reserved for men. Now, a majority of young people get some college experience in one form or another, whether it's a four-year residential school or a community college.

Moreover, women now make up a majority of college undergraduates, and many want to build a career before they marry and have children, Arnett says. The development of the birth control pill helped drive the change, Arnett says. Decades ago, young people got married rather then face the risks of pregnancy outside marriage. Now, sexual relationships outside of marriage are accepted as natural by many people.

SOME PROSPER;SOME STRUGGLE

Another marker of emerging adulthood is heterogeneity, says Arnett, in terms of the sheer multitude of paths young people can take and their widely varying levels of success.

Given some emerging adults' struggles, Arnett sees the need for greatly expanded societal efforts to help them navigate the transition into careers and family. He believes such efforts would pay off, given the self-awareness people develop in their 20s and their willingness to change.

"If you provide them with resources, they're much more likely to say, 'How can I improve my life?'" Arnett says. He hopes the book and other efforts, such as the future development of a society for studying emerging adulthood, will build a community of scholars devoted to studying the period of development. Arnett and fellow scholars currently discuss ideas through the Emerging Adulthood Special Interest Group, established through the Society for Research on Adolescence.

The group organized two academic conferences exploring aspects of emerging adulthood and a third is planned for February 2007 in Tucson, Ariz. The question of why some emerging adults do well, why some struggle and what can be done to help more make a successful transition is taken up by several book contributors. Tanner, co-editor of the APA book and an assistant research professor in the School of Social Work at Simmons College, argues that the heterogeneity Arnett cites can be explained by the foundation laid in childhood and adolescence. As she describes it, how well an adolescent makes the transition through young adulthood into adulthood and becomes a fully independent person depends in large part on the right balance of the adolescent pushing for independence and parents and society giving the correct amount of support—not pushing too hard or holding back too much, she says.

Many emerging adults who face problems becoming independent have faced past challenges meeting developmental tasks for one reason or another, she says. "There are enormous costs to young people who are not equipped to 'plug in' to adult roles and responsibilities," Tanner says.

Jean S. Phinney, PhD, a psychology professor at California State University, Los Angeles, writes on emerging adulthood's different features in ethnic-minority groups. Both for cultural and economic reasons, many young people from ethnic-minority groups tend to take on adult responsibilities earlier, contributing to the family income and taking care of siblings, sometimes at the cost of slowing down their own schooling, Phinney says.

During emerging adulthood, ethnic minorities have to deal with the larger culture and figure out their own identity in the context of the larger society. For children of immigrants, that can be especially challenging, she says. "I think it can be harder for minorities who come from a culture where the expectations of what you should do are very strong," she says.

Another book contributor, Stephen F. Hamilton, PhD, a professor of human development at Cornell University, focuses on young people who can't afford college or who don't move into vocational programmes. Many in that group languish in the low-paid jobs of the secondary labour market, bouncing from one low-skilled, dead-end job to another, Hamilton says. "They end up doing this work their whole lives," he says. Hamilton thinks there's a missing institution in American life—one devoted to helping young people join the primary labour market of decently paid jobs with benefits and a chance for advancement.

THE FIELD

Developmental psychology is concerned with the study of changes in behaviour throughout the life span. Although, logically, equal emphasis should be placed on development during all stages of life, so far most research has dealt primarily with infants, children, and adolescents. Because of this emphasis the term "developmental psychology" is often used interchangeably with the older terms "child psychology," "adolescent psychology," and "genetic psychology."

These areas are distinct from one another, but it is impractical to discuss them separately. Child and adolescent psychology traditionally include the investigation of behaviour at, rather than across, particular periods of development, and genetic psychology involves a concern for ontogenetic as well as phylogenetic changes in behaviour. Underlying all the terms, however, is a concern with the emergence of behaviour in the human being, and, therefore, in this discussion no attempt is made to distinguish between the various approaches [seeAdolescence;Aging;Infancy].

In the growth of developmental psychology theoretical positions, practical needs, public awareness, and support of research have been closely interrelated. In various phases different forces have been dominant, depending on the psychological and social milieu of the time. The field, therefore, has been one of shifting emphases. It is necessary to review the historical background of developmental psychology in order to understand its current structure.

The Early Period (1880–1920)

Although for centuries parents and other adults had observed children and gathered much "common-sense" knowledge about them, the information was contaminated by the biases of the parent–child relationship and the goals and wishes of other observers. Interest in systematically investigating developmental changes in behaviour is, in fact, relatively recent. Research in this area received its initial impetus from the late nineteenth-century work in evolutionary biology. Charles Darwin, Wil-helm T. Preyer, and other biologists observed the development of human infants as a means of gaining further understanding of human evolution. After the publication of these observations, many baby biographies were published. They gave some indications of the changes that occur in the infant's repertoire of behaviour, although they were typically limited to a few cases and covered only a restricted age range.

The theory of evolution had a stimulating effect on other types of research, including that of the "founder" of developmental psychology, G. Stanley Hall. His belief in the theory that ontogeny recapitulates phylogeny resulted in his studying the behaviour of the individual child as a source of in-sight into the behaviour of man at earlier evolutionary periods. Many aspects of children's behaviour were observed, including play and social relationships.

Hall introduced the questionnaire method, marking the end of a period in which observation was the primary method of obtaining data;questionnaires came to be widely used for studies of children's thoughts, interests, and wishes. Soon labora-tory procedures were applied to children, but the early experiments tended to be little more than demonstrations that certain phenomena associated with lower animals or with adults also occur in children. These studies dealt with the traditional topics of experimental psychology, such as memory, learning, sensation, and perception. In many cases, studies originally using animals or college students were adapted so that children could be used as subjects.

Intelligence Testing

By 1890 there was considerable emphasis on objective observation and laboratory methods. Society was faced with the growing number of problems related to children that accompanied increased urbanization and expansion of public education. When, for example, the question of how to handle mental defectives in schools and institutions arose, groups of individuals in Great Britain and France began studies of how to assess and deal with such children. One of the most significant outcomes of these investigations was the development by Alfred Binet of a scale to distinguish between individuals of normal and subnormal intelligence. Whereas previous efforts to assess intelligence had been unsatisfactory, Binet's work in constructing tests, which involved complex verbal and adaptive functions rather than simple sensory or motor functions, yielded a successful scale. It was soon obvious that such a scale had broader use than solely distinguishing between normal and defective children. Further work by Binet and others, such as Lewis M. Terman, resulted in useful tests for "measuring" children's intelligence and investigating the effects of variables potentially capable of influencing intellectual development.

Psychoanalysis

During this period Sigmund Freud was developing a theory of psychic functioning that emphasized the importance of childhood experiences as determinants of later behaviour. Aspects of the theory were presented in 1909 to developmental psychologists and others at Clark University. Although Freud directed attention towards the early emotional life of children, his work had a minimal effect on early research in developmental psychology. Not until the 1930s, when developmental psychologists were no longer so strongly influenced by biological thinking, did the resistance to his views decrease and did serious investigations of his ideas concerning the effects of early experiences on psychological development begin.

THE PERIOD OF EXPANSION (1920–1940)

Research during the first two decades of the 1900s was aimed at providing a clearer delineation and categorization of children's behaviour. The research was highly empirical and not significantly influenced by theoretical analysis of psychological functioning. The work of this period, however, provided data necessary for the later development of systematic positions.

By the 1920s developmental psychology was rapidly becoming a visible and important area in psychology. The belief was widely held that the application of scientific methods to the study of children would lead to solutions of problems in education, pediatrics, child care, and treatment. Educators began lecturing parents on how to rear children. Clinics were organized to evaluate children's abilities and to advise parents on such matters as discipline, toilet training, and feeding. Nursery schools were established in most large universities and in many colleges and were quickly put to use as a source of subjects for psychological research. Most important, funds became available for the support of research.

The most notable donor was the Laura Spelman Rockefeller Fund, under whose auspices institutes devoted to research with normal children were established or extended at the universities of California, Iowa, Minnesota, and Toronto, and at Columbia University. The Fels Research Institute and the Yale Child Study Center also became leading centers for the study of children's behaviour in the United States. The Institut J.-J. Rousseau in Geneva and the Vienna Psychologische Institut were the most active European institutions for research in developmental psychology. The 1920s and 1930s were exciting and productive years at these institutes, but because the institutes were separated from departments of psychology, developmental psychologists tended to be isolated from psychologists interested in other aspects of behaviour. Only during the past few years has the relationship with general psychology been firmly re-established.

Divergent viewpoints on how environmental and biological factors influence behaviour resulted in a major controversy over the question of the contributions of nature and nurture to intellectual functioning. It was easy to take sides;it was much more difficult to accumulate information that withstood the tests of critical scrutiny. The controversy eventually ended in a stalemate, for although scores of studies were published, few survived the devastating attacks that were waged against their design, execution, and analysis. Solutions for the enormously complex issues that were being raised would have to await the time when developmental psychologists had more sophisticated tools and information at their disposal.

Behaviourism and its Critics

The introduction of behaviourism into developmental psychology in the 1930s marked the beginning of an era in which schools of psychology, each with its own theories, problems, and preferred methods, polarized the field. Previous research had been aimed at providing information about children's behaviour;now research was often directed towards establishing the validity of theories advanced by various schools. Behaviourism had an effective and vigorous advocate in John B. Watson. Edward L. Thorndike and Ivan P. Pavlov had provided a background of information and techniques in their studies of learning and conditioning in animals, which Watson was able to use to develop his approach to psychology. He espoused an extreme form of environmentalism and relied heavily on the use of conditioning as the means for modifying behaviour. His studies of infant behaviour and of the acquisition and extinction of fear responses in children became classics, and his belief that introspection should be superseded by objective observation and measurement of behaviour exerted a healthy influence on developmental psychology. It was not long, however, before advocates of other views responded critically to Watson's position.

Among the most vocal schools of critics were gestalt psychologists and psychoanalysts. Although at the time neither group had a large influence on developmental psychology, their views provided the basis for later work. Another critic who took strong exception to the associationistic view of American behaviourists was Jean Piaget. As a result of his training in biology, Piaget emphasized the adaptive functions of behaviour in maintaining an equilibrium between the individual and the environment. Piaget's views were elaborated into a comprehensive theory of cognitive development. The contrast between him and the behaviourists extended to all aspects of their work. Whereas the behaviourists utilized the experimental method in their investigations of simple forms of behaviour and emphasized the role of controlled experiences in the modification of behaviour, Piaget preferred the clinical method and chose to study the interaction of maturation and experience in the production of complex behaviour and higher thought processes.

Normative and Longitudinal Studies

The charting of the development of behaviour was not confined to cognitive development. Arnold Gesell at Yale and Charlotte Bühler in Vienna had begun extensive normative studies of child development. For nearly forty years Gesell maintained an active programme of research in the exploration of motor, adaptive, language, and personal–social behaviour from birth through adolescence. The normative information from these studies, along with the results of his investigations of feeding, sleep, and other topics, became a major source of guidance for mothers in many countries. Gesell, like Piaget, had a strong biological orientation. While other American psychologists were proclaiming the influence of the environment on behaviour, Gesell continued to show how specific types of experiences may have differential effects on behaviour, depending on the maturational level of the individual.

A series of longitudinal studies of child development was initiated in the early 1930s. The longitudinal method had not been employed extensively prior to this time, although such investigations as Terman's famous study of gifted individuals had demonstrated its productivity. At the University of California, Nancy Bayley began a study of the development of mental abilities in infants and children (1940), Herbert Stolz and Harold Jones began a study of somatic and psychological development during adolescence, and Jean Macfarlane began a study of personality development.

At the Fels Research Institute, Lester Sontag and his associates began a comprehensive longitudinal study of growth and development. All these studies are still being conducted;data are being collected, and old data are being analyzed in new and interesting ways.

Gestalt and Field Theories

Psychology began to be influenced significantly by the work of the gestalt psychologists, who, in turn, were influenced by field theory from physical science. The extension of the gestalt approach by Kurt Lewin had the greatest influence on research with children. During his years in Berlin and in the United States, Lewin directed a series of studies aimed at demonstrating the important role of situational factors in determining behaviour. Lewin's preference for an ahistorical approach to the analysis of behaviour led him and others to a careful consideration of the structure of the psychological field and the forces operating in it.

LATER DEVELOPMENTS (1940–1965)

The remarkable rate of growth in developmental psychology was seriously curtailed at the end of the 1930s. Many factors contributed to a temporary decline in activity. The normative, descriptive approach had lost its allure;it was no longer of interest to reaffirm the fact that behaviour developed systematically.

Other areas of psychology appeared to be more challenging, and the number of persons entering developmental psychology decreased. World War ii disrupted research programmes. Perhaps as important as any factor, however, was the withdrawal of supporting funds from the institutes and the general unavailability of new funds for research. For about fifteen years it became more and more difficult to initiate new research projects and, in many cases, to complete the analyses of data obtained from earlier studies. In 1938, for example, approximately 500 publications concerned with children's behaviour appeared;by 1949 the number had dropped to approximately 250. The general level of the work also began to decline;writings became more speculative and less dependent on original observations or experiments. Fortunately, the field did not disintegrate;there was enough activity at an appropriately high level to maintain the interest in research with children during the critical years.

The period of decline came to a halt in the mid-1950s, when interest in developmental psychology was reactivated. Since then, interest has increased at a rapid pace and there has been a revitalization of the area of study. Research with children has been greatly stimulated by the rapid and sophisticated advances in psychological theories, methodology, and instrumentation. Many of the theoretical positions in general psychology have direct relevance to the discussion of the emergence of behaviour and are readily applicable to developmental investigations. Funds became available at an unprecedented level to support research and training. In the United States, for example, in 1962, a national Institute of Child Health and Human Development was established to provide leadership in training of investigators and research in developmental sciences, including developmental psychology. More powerful statistical analyses have been adopted and developed. Computers have made possible many types of studies that could never have been carried out without rapid mechanical analyses of the data.

The descriptive approach in developmental psychology has been replaced by a variable-oriented approach. The adoption of systematic positions dealing with developmental changes in children's behaviour has led to an increased interest in determining children's responses to particular specifiable or manipulable variables and to a decreased interest in describing behaviour in naturalistic or controlled settings. There is a tendency for subsystems to be developed that deal with specific aspects rather than with whole domains of behaviour. The level of conceptualization has increased;concepts and processes now dominate thinking in developmental psychology.

There has been a redistribution of emphases among the various methods used in studying children. The experimental method has gained in popularity, primarily because of the opportunity it allows for the control of both independent and dependent variables. An experiment is no longer conceived merely as a controlled situation yielding quantitative data but as a method that permits the manipulation of the variables under study.

Few long-term longitudinal studies have been initiated;the problems involved in the selecting of appropriate measures at the beginning of the study, the maintaining of the sample of subjects over long periods of time, and the organizing of the large amounts of data accumulated in such studies have discouraged most investigators from undertaking more than four-year or five-year longitudinal investigations. Observations, interviews, and tests tend to be used less frequently than they were in earlier periods, but they are still employed when they are particularly applicable to the topic under investigation,

Although attention continues to be directed towards developmental changes in such areas as children's learning, motivation, perception, and language, new interests are developing. The rediscovery of Piaget's work and modifications in behaviour theory have resulted in a rapid development of interest in research in cognitive processes. Research in socialization has been stimulated by psychoanalytic and social learning theories. Studies of personality development have concentrated on specific aspects of behaviour, for example, anxiety, aggression, and dependence, rather than attempting to deal with such global problems as adjustment and emotional behaviour. Interest has been reawakened in the study of neo-nates, especially in their sensory, perceptual, and adaptive behaviour.

Cross-cultural studies, once in the domain of social anthropology, have been undertaken to ascertain the effects of different child-rearing practices on children's later behaviour. Studies of the ecology of behaviour have resulted in detailed analyses of children's behaviour in naturalistic settings.

It is doubtful that twenty years ago anyone could have anticipated the remarkable resurgence of interest in developmental psychology that has occurred in the past decade. More research on basic processes of behaviour is being conducted than in any previous period. Programmes designed to train psychologists for research in developmental problems are being initiated and expanded, both in departments of psychology and in research institutes. A strong interest in applied problems is not evident, perhaps as a reaction to the overcommitment to the solution of social problems that characterized earlier work in developmental psychology. There are indications, however, that the techniques and knowledge now being accumulated can be used effectively in attacking the practical problems of the developing child. As the interest in such problems increases, it may be expected that the gap in communication between developmental psychology and pediatrics, education, sociology, and other disciplines will begin to close.

9

Adult Development, Personality and Learning

GENES AND THE ENVIRONMENT

First, although it is beyond the scope of this chapter, a word is in order about personality genetics. Early evidence for the genetic bedrock of personality came from studies of monozygotic and dizygotic twins, some reared together and others apart. Many of these studies have examined the few traits that are said to represent the entire composite of personality. For example, Bouchard and Loehlin (2001) used the Costa and McCrae (1992) five factor model (FFM) and reported average heritabilities of 0.40 to 0.60 for all five factors.

Some claim that personality is a trait constellation established by genes alone. This is the "plaster" view of personality, with many of its adherents maintaining that endogenously endowed personality traits are "influenced not at all by the environment". Yet there is strong evidence of personality malleability, on both an evolutionary and an individual basis. Genes necessarily require that one "have experience with... tasks for the gene to manifest its phenotypic effect". Intellectual engagement and learning, intra- and interpersonal awareness, and the expression of artistic, musical, and other abilities likely have a genetic component. Genes are the bedrock, and their interaction with other genes, with the environment, and with a volitional human, permit expression.

The genetic code resides in DNA. Between 20,000 and 25,000 human genes convey instructions that produce proteins, with their activity mediated by RNA, by environmental interactions, and by other factors (many of which are currently unknown). These genes and their mediating agents variously permit genetic expression, augmentation, dampening, and silencing. Genetic expression is also mediated by one's internal and external environments. With respect to the adult's endogenous (internal) environment and functional intelligence processes, reduced gene expression due to DNA damage (*e.g.*, oxidative stress) occurs in the aging human brain. Recently, there has been particular interest in the apolipoprotein E genotype as a risk factor for cognitive decline. With respect to general intelligence and the adult's exogenous (external) environment, ongoing genotype–environment interaction continues throughout life to support and sometimes thwart intellectual maintenance and growth. It is estimated that this interaction contributes about 0.50 of the variance to intelligence. In adulthood, mature roles and responsibilities socialize adults to perform in consistent, non-erratic ways.

Therefore, personality is relatively enduring, made up as it is of many intersecting qualities that "cohere", even as they also evolve through the species' history, through genetic and environmental interactions, and through persons' experiences and interpretations of experiences. Thus, as important as they are, genes alone do not create personality.

In part, adult personality plasticity is due to interactions with important persons, contexts, and roles in (and before) mature life. In important respects, the malleability or "plasticity" position that counters the "set like plaster" view of personality sees humans (and their genes) as changing in response to interactions with a dynamic environment, even as the environment is altered by humans who act in and on it.

PERSONALITY ATTRIBUTES

The five personality traits (neuroticism, extraversion, openness to experience, conscientiousness, and agreeableness) of the FFM have been among the most influential in personality research since the early 1980s. However, to many, they seem too "tidy" and far too restrictive in representing the totality of personality. In their extensive meta-analysis of personality studies, DeNeve and Cooper (1998) unearthed 137 personality attributes. Ackerman and Heggestad's (1997) meta-analysis reported 19 personality attributes in 135 investigations. In a content analysis of four key personality journals during a five-year period, Cribb, Ozone, and Pipes (1992) reported more than 500 instruments in use, instruments that reflect a vast and overlapping array of personality attributes.

In this section I consider personality attributes more broadly than trait theory. I look to the principal reported reciprocal relationships between learning and personality development as these relate to work experiences. Included are the development of personality attributes into and through the adult work years, and the ways that paid work promotes such development and related learning. Although there are many personality characteristics, I consider only six attributes because these six have been shown to develop as a function of employment. These are autonomy, interpersonal competence (including organizational citizenship behaviour), maturity, conscientiousness, openness to experience, and intellectual flexibility. Some of the data discussed here are used in employee selection, training, and promotion decisions.

WORK AUTONOMY

In the worldwide, highly competitive economy, many companies have flattened their hierarchies and decentralized decision making. Worker empowerment, continual learning, and self-direction are vital, and independent judgement is now exercised throughout many U.S. organizations, even at bottom levels.

Much of the literature refers to various aspects of such independent judgement as work autonomy. Work autonomy means the personal freedom to perform functions and roles in unique ways. This is the extent to which persons are expected and have the impetus, freedom, and control over their jobs to individually determine how, when, and sometimes where work is performed (*e.g.*, Barrick and Mount, 1993;Simmering et al., 2003). Among other aspects, employees prioritize and self-pace tasks, allocate resources, determine work methods, plan and schedule activities, and telecommute. Employees are also groomed to function in autonomous work teams, learn independently, and mesh their various responsibilities with others within and beyond the organization. As is true in a number of other areas, a continual reciprocal relationship exists in personality'! work/learning and personality effects. On the front end of this equation, high autonomy predicts the kind of work persons choose, their actions on the job, and their effectiveness.

Work conducted under autonomous conditions then leads to greater autonomy and control, job involvement, a sense of responsibility for one's job, and work satisfaction. If Vernon, Jang, Harris, and McCarthy's (1997) claim is correct, autonomy is one of the least heritable of the personality attributes;therefore, environmental factors mold selfdirection and its positive results.

Clearly, paid work is inseparable from the society in which that work occurs. Nations' social structures and views of individual rights alter personal tendencies, if not personality itself. With respect to autonomy, in the United States, a sense of personal uniqueness, independence, and self-determination arise from constitutionally granted individual rights, worldview, and beliefs in personal freedom. Such views, as well as sociohistorical changes in those views, alter attitudes and the expression of autonomy. For example, in their longitudinal investigation of the influence of increasing individualism in the United States, Roberts and Helson (1997) studied women at four periods over 31 years.

They found that increasing individualism in the aggregate, particularly between 1960 and 1985, was associated with women's declines in adherence to norms and to increases in their autonomy, self-focus, self-assertion, and narcissism. In the years between 1958 and 1989, those women's autonomy increased and peaked concurrently with trends in the escalation and peak of societal individualism (autonomy).

Work effects were seen in, for example, a growing intolerance for glass ceilings and expectations that salaries would be gender-neutral. In part, women's assertiveness learning emanated from the feminist movement during those years;their work experiences of personal empowerment and autonomy then furthered such learning and their increased sense of autonomy.

Supporting evidence comes from other societywork comparisons. Through longitudinal studies in the United States and Poland, Kohn and associates (1997) found that adults' position in society, as well as the tendency of a society towards freedom (*e.g.*, the United States) or authoritarian constriction (*e.g.*, Poland) produces organizations that either sponsor autonomy among workers (United States) or restrict this inclination (Poland). These investigators define occupational self-direction as "the use of initiative, thought, and independent judgement in work". For workers, structural job conditions directly affect psychological functioning on and beyond the job. In particular, closeness of supervision and routinization (repetitive jobs) restrict autonomy. In turn, all three factors (closeness of supervision, routinization, and restricted autonomy) thwart creativity;they also thwart the autonomous learning that might improve jobs and the occupational context itself. The absence of work autonomy leads to distrust, "authoritarian-conservative beliefs," rigidity, and a non-change orientation. Personal distress is manifest in selfdeprecation, anxiety, decreased self-confidence, and suppressed job involvement. It seems that nearly all employers these days wish to have workers who are intensely job involved and committed to their work.

Well they should be, for job involvement defines high-performing organizations. Together, work autonomy and job control foster job involvement. For example, managers who are selfdirected perform better in job conditions of high discretion. Autonomous work conditions and job involvement also encourage ongoing learning. In effect, the overall context for workers and for the organization improves under conditions of autonomy. In the United States work autonomy leads to greater personal self-direction and other positive results on the job and shows transfer effects to non-work environments. Work autonomy leads to an agentic, "can-do" approach in off-work roles and responsibilities, an increasingly internal locus of control, improved subjective well-being, and greater learning beyond the job. For example, in their 10-year, timelagged study of male employees, Kohn and Schooler found that the men they studied learned from their jobs and work contexts and then transferred such learning tendencies and outcomes to situations beyond the job.

Workers tended to "develop personally more responsible standards of morality, to become more trustful, more self-confident, less self-deprecatory, less fatalistic, less anxious, and less conformist in their ideas". Studying men's work roles in the United States, Japan, and Poland, the investigations of Kohn et al. (1990) led to similar conclusions. Defining social class advantage as having "greater control over the means of production and greater control over the labour power of others", these investigators found that autonomy and occupational control conferred powerful advantages. Men with occupational control were more intellectually flexible and selfdirected.

They enjoyed greater than average opportunities for autonomy and, by association, for cognitive development, contextual mastery, and learning. Such men were also more valuing of self-direction for their children, a positive spillover effect for the next generation. Autonomous work validates the self to the extent that greater emotional stability, self-confidence, and agreeableness also result. In their longitudinal study of 910 workers in New Zealand, Roberts, Caspi, and Moffitt (2003) concluded that six interrelated work and personal qualities significantly predict such outcomes.

These qualities are (a) high autonomy, (b) greater than average occupational attainment, (c) complex work, (d) substantial work resources and power, (e) higher than average financial security, and (e) high work satisfaction and involvement. In addition to the powerful effects of work autonomy on employees' positive sense of self, on their concepts of power and effectiveness, and on their increased autonomy in and beyond the work environment, other effects are found. Many persons who function in selfdirected roles show consistent non-authoritarianism. They also work better in teams, and the recent emphasis on self-directed teams requires independence, continual learning, and cooperation, all of which are enhanced by organizational conditions of autonomy and empowerment. Clearly, some individuals function better in autonomous circumstances than others.

Among employees whose personalities function well in autonomous conditions, organizations supporting individual worker autonomy and autonomous teams tend to profit. Corporate profit is the direct result of enhanced worker motivation, learning and achievement, well-being, and positive affect. Autonomous work conditions lead to even greater worker self-direction, improved competencies, decreased dependency (Froman, 1994), greater effectiveness, increased cooperation, and heightened creativity.

INTERPERSONAL COMPETENCE AND ORGANIZATIONAL CITIZENSHIP BEHAVIOUR

Interpersonal Competence Ferris, Witt, and Hochwarter (2001) described an ineffective "genius," a person of great brilliance whose minimal interpersonal skills made that worker useless on the job. Anecdotes such as this pepper work lore. Yet until recently, the bulk of personality research related to employment has paid rather little attention to the importance of interpersonal competence, social cognition, and personal desires to be prosocial and helpful at work. Sociability (extraversion), agreeableness, warmth, friendliness, positive affect and caring to learn about others and about relational functioning are components of interpersonal competence. They show a relationship among personality, learning tendencies, and work precursors and effects.

The ability to appraise interpersonal relationships and correctly interpret the meaning of human interactions in a social context is a dimension of adult intelligence. The cognitive literature uses the term *social cognition*, whereas the personality literature (reflecting the influence of the FFM) uses the terms *extraversion* (sociability), *agreeableness*, and *openness to experience.*

These personality terms tap part of the construct but tend to exclude cognitive dimensions and personal interest in learning about and seeing from within the roles and perspectives of others. Instead, I use the term *interpersonal competence* to capture the broader array of talents and developed abilities that are critical to success in work environments. In general, interpersonally competent, sociable persons tend to select jobs that provide opportunities to learn and to share knowledge with others. This reinforces and maintains (or extends) their outgoing and learning tendencies. Greater work satisfaction results.

Increased positive affect, better work conditions, and potentially more profitable organizations are the result. Russell (2001), for example, reported a longitudinal study of 98 toplevel executives. Hierarchical linear modeling showed that "problem-solving" ratings were crucial in executives' early performance in those roles, but "people-oriented" ratings predicted subsequent longterm performance. Based on the predictive model he developed based on these and related findings, Russell (2001) concluded: "Utility estimates suggested that the system generated an additional $3 million in annual profit per candidate selected.... Findings imply that a model of executive performance must contain main effects for person (competencies) and situation (economic-industrial) characteristics".

In teams that require close, cooperative relationships among workers, agreeableness and helping tendencies correlate with team productivity. Agreeableness results in more effective team functioning because of increased group cohesion (Greene, 1989). Other factors also enter the equation. For example, in Barrick, Stewart, Neubert, and Mount's (1998) group-level study of 652 workers in 51 work teams, individuals' agreeableness, extraversion, emotional stability, general mental ability, and conscientiousness correlated with supervisor ratings of team performance. At the individual team level of analysis, in Neuman and Wright's (1999) study of 79 four-person work teams, agreeableness and conscientiousness predicted peer assessments of individuals' performance beyond cognitive ability and job skills alone.

Organizational Citizenship Behaviour One stream of research, organizational citizenship behaviour (OCB) focuses on the merits of positive, outward extensions of the self among workers at various levels in the organization. In effect, OCB addresses interpersonal competence in task and contextual performance. OCB is extra-role behaviour, that is, "behaviour(s) of a discretionary nature that are not part of the employee's formal role requirements, but nevertheless promote the effective functioning of the organization". Attributes such as courtesy, helping and teaching behaviours, good sportsmanship, beyond-the-job volunteering, compliance, and altruism are included in OCB. These qualities bind people together, sustaining personal connections and mentally healthy work environments and organizations.

The OCB concept includes personal tendencies and learned behaviours. Prosocial behaviours are widely cited as essential ingredients of workplace harmony and psychological health, collegial functioning, self-directed team efforts, and organizational effectiveness and productivity. Reviewing the OCB literature, Podsakoff and MacKenzie (1997) found that OCB's general mechanism in increasing worker and organizational performance can be seen as that which "lubricates" the "social machinery of the organization, reducing friction, and/or increasing efficiency" (p. 135). For instance, when competent, longer tenured workers voluntarily help new employees to learn the ropes, the newly hired become productive more quickly. This enhances the division's effectiveness.

In a qualitative study of the meaning of paid work to 53 older women, Altschuler (2004) gives an example of this prosocial tendency in the words of a study subject: "I don't take the attitude 'Well—it's not part of my job.' I just know that when you see the overall picture of what has to be done in order for the office to move smoothly, then... I cannot say 'Hey, I'm not gonna do this because I'm not getting paid' because that's just not in my nature". With respect to the rejection of such citizenship behaviour, Buchwald (2004) provides a tongue-incheek example in the context of a recent influenza vaccine shortage: "The government knew for months that there was going to be a shortage, but each health supervisor said: 'It isn't my department. Besides, I have to go to lunch' " (p. C2). When organizations foster prosocial, extra-role endeavors, workers tend to learn aspects of jobs beyond their prescribed functions. This promotes organizational effectiveness, satisfactory relationships on the job, and worker retention.

In the long run, prosocial behaviours by competent, longer tenured workers lead to modeling effects, to the contagion of "best practices" throughout and beyond the unit, to the release of managers' time for planning and other responsibilities, and to better cross-division functioning. Studying blue-collar workers in a paper mill, Podsakoff, Ahearne, and MacKenzie (1997) concluded that almost 17per cent of the quality and 26per cent of the quantity of employee performance was due to OCB activities.

In a study of 116 agencies in an insurance company, 17per cent of the variance in overall agency performance was interpreted as having been due to OCB actions. Prosocial, helping tendencies such as the viewpoint expressed by the worker in Altschuler's (2004) study are related to conscientiousness, agreeableness, and personal integrity. Schmidt and Hunter (2004) found that integrity tests are valid for all levels and types of jobs studied;they show an additional predictive validity of 27per cent over general mental ability for job performance and an additional 20per cent for training performance.

Prosocial, OCB characteristics are readily overridden by harsh, authoritarian work situations, by conditions that set one employee against another, and by threatening circumstances. Then compliance, altruism, and helping functions typically retreat. Conditions of high threat include organizational restructuring with its potential for job loss;domineering, mean-minded, or condescending superiors;the possibility of lateral employee transfers with little promise of advancement;and psychologically unsafe work environments. In the latter, workers' expression of their authentic selves is restricted, and personal freedom and genuineness are curtailed.

One learns armored self-protection instead of more about how to perform job functions genuinely and effectively. And in jobs or occasions that carry the burden of severe time pressures or harried deadlines (*e.g.*, emergency room triage care, news journalism), the time that would be required for warmth, personal engagement, and a prosocial extension of the self to co-workers is often abandoned.

Repeated waves of downsizing, declining organizational loyalty to employees, and unethical organizational practices (*e.g.*, the Enron scandal) have led to increased vigilance among workers and declining trust in corporate leadership and business practices. If prosocial tendencies in which workers help each other do not decline, prosocial actions directed to aiding organizational goals may show slippage. Workers believe that good citizenship behaviour travels a two-way street.

ADULT BEHAVIOUR, EGO DEFENCES, AND GENERATIVITY

Due in part to work experiences and employers' expectations for mature, responsible behaviour, the mental mechanisms of most adults become more mature over developmental time. In work and other contexts, young, less mature adults are more likely to use more aggressive defence mechanisms, such as projection and displacement. Adults of greater maturity tend to have learned impulse control, employing coping strategies that include cognitive reappraisal, sublimation, humor, physical exercise, and altruism. Ego identity becomes stronger as adults, through work and other responsibilities, move towards higher level defence mechanisms. Generative care for others and increasing insight into the self represent developmental progressions, manifest in part through mature defences.

In such development, adults reach out to the social world and move upward in consciousness. Vaillant observed that the mature ego defences of altruism, humor, anticipation, suppression, and sublimation are mechanisms of increased consciousness. These defences are developmental progressions from unconscious, less mature defences such as denial, displacement, and projection. Just as the higher level ego defences represent movement forward in maturity and upward in consciousness, they are also more socially centered than self-centered. This is Erikson's (1975) concept of moving "outward" towards others as one develops in maturity and generativity. The outward-moving development that Erikson described is associated with progression to higher levels of ego development as per Loevinger's (1976) construct. In that construct, ego development means increments in consciousness, impulse control, perspective taking, reflectiveness, and social development;all are attributes of greater maturity. Conscious and tacit learning are variously involved in each of these ego developmental constituents.

Responding to criticisms that stage models of development are of limited value beyond, for instance, measures of intelligence, Cohn and Westenberg (2004) conducted a meta-analysis of 42 studies of ego development using the Loevinger Washington University Sentence Completion Test. Data show that although ego development shares variance with measured intelligence, it does not reduce to intelligence. As is true of moral development and the development of insight and openmindedness, these authors conclude that "intellectual capacity may be a necessary but insufficient condition for reaching relatively high levels of maturity". Studies have shown positive correlations between higher levels of ego development and learning to respect diverse others, as well as between greater ego development and learning to empathically understand the needs of others.

When one looks to emotional maturity against activity level and vitality, developmental data show mixed findings. Most persons become more emotionally stable, socially dominant, agreeable, and warm during young adulthood. However, separating extraversion into social dominance and social vitality alters the view somewhat. Trends point to increasing social dominance from 18 years of age to middle adulthood and decreasing social vitality, linearly, during young, middle, and older adulthood.

From adolescence to young adulthood, declines in negative affect and neuroticism occur. Employment is prominent in these declines because paid work incorporates young adults into mainstream society. Work fosters contextual learning and mastery of the job environment. As Roberts, Caspi, et al.'s (2003) longitudinal study found, incorporation into the societal work world decreased young adults' negativity from ages 18 to 26. However, adolescents who are particularly high in negativity tend towards stormy and less successful entries into the work world. For them, maintenance instead of declining neuroticism is apparent into young adulthood. For many such youths, ill preparation for work, marginal status, limited learning, or work identity refusal lead to cynicism and ongoing negativity. As one would expect, emotional instability negatively predicts mature behaviour, goal-setting activities, conscientiousness, and a range of other desirable work behaviours. For example, men with disorderly work histories have shown less personality coherence, learning, and planning tendencies than persons with stable career histories. Adults with poor coping mechanisms are also less able to handle work difficulties and stress, tending to absorb stress effects. On the other hand, those with good coping strategies tend to focus on work tasks, problem solving, and learning instead of on their emotional responses, thus neutralizing or deflecting stress.

In addition to relationships among developmental maturity, learning, and the use of higher order coping mechanisms, cognitive development plays an important role. The use of more mature defences is undergirded by greater understandings of coping processes, higher levels of ego development, and greater cognitive complexity. Higher levels of cognitive and ego development are essential if one is to understand the intricacies of emotions and coping mechanisms in general. Such understandings are vital to gaining insight into one's own and others' behaviour, to efforts to see from within the perspectives and work roles of others, and to understanding various complexities in the work environment. Due to persons' tendencies to emulate behaviour and to absorb the moods of others, different work climates vary in their mental health and in what one might call group-level neuroses.

Data from Joiner and Katz's (1999) meta-analysis of 36 studies, show that "emotional contagion" explains some of this variance. In emotional contagion, moods are passed along from one person to another. At the group level, depressive moods arise from neurotic or emotionally unstable persons who alter the subjective well-being of those with whom they interact: "People tend from moment to moment to 'catch' other people's emotions as a result of mimicry, feedback, and resulting synchrony in social encounters". This involves negative learning, with social modeling accounting for some of the contagion. In particular, workers low in self-efficacy and high in cynicism tend to evoke "contagious modeling" in their colleagues.

In work groups with a preponderance of positive affect among individual members, the overall group affect tends towards positivity. Low work absenteeism occurs. Conversely, when negative affect is expressed by several group members, the overriding mood becomes negative. Members of negative groups avoid engaging in prosocial behaviours and have higher than average work absenteeism. New entrants to the group tend to "catch" the prevailing mood or tone, and to then behave according to its predominant affect. Agreeableness and positive affect vary with the extent of social support for agreeableness and positivity in the organization, and with the cooperative spirit engendered by the group and the larger structure. Clearly, though, some persons are more sensitive and permeable to mood influence than others, showing greater inclinations to absorb the affect of others.

Because many technologically advanced nations now have companies with plants and offices abroad and sometimes have an international workforce in their home-based businesses, it is useful to consider cultural variations in personality characteristics and mental mechanisms. In a study of 53 countries, Cook, Young, Taylor, and Bedford (2000) found national variance in levels of extraversion, neuroticism, psychoticism, and subjective well-being. Nations with a high gross domestic product and norms of cooperation instead of competition show higher levels of wellbeing among their citizens. Based on personality data from 39 countries, Steel and Ones (2002) found a high correlation between gross national product and extraversion, subjective well-being, and conscientiousness. Although it would be foolhardy to claim a direct correspondence between broad-brush national data and corporate behaviour, it is a mistake to claim no relationship between the two climates.

National attributes are bound to influence if not modify personality expression. As discussed, Kohn and colleagues (1983, 1997) have repeatedly shown that a nation's tendency towards autonomy or authoritarianism lead to organizations in those countries that sponsor either worker self-direction and learning or subservience, respectively.

Variance has also been found as a function of culturally based values and social norms. Staudinger and colleagues (1999) found differences in subjective wellbeing and personality dispositions between U.S. and German citizens. They interpreted their findings in terms of a heterogeneous, individualistic, and less structured (U.S.) society versus a more homogeneous, structured, social welfare state (Germany). In U.S. society, more numerous resources promote well-being and potentially the expression of a greater array of personality characteristics. In Germany, the researchers concluded, fewer personality characteristics are adequate to the task.

National variances are also found in the way citizens handle conflict. In Hong Kong and in the People's Republic of China, for example, learning the Confucian ideal of harmony is important. In those cultures, persons respond to conflict by using passive avoidance strategies. Individuals in the United States and some other Western cultures learn to confront conflict directly, using more pointed, sometimes aggressive strategies. This applies to work settings and other contexts. With respect to other situational influences, personality expression varies with the context and with having learned various norms and protocols. Stable tendencies, shown by "behavioural signatures," occur in situations with like motifs. For example, in the United States, adult demeanor is frequently consistent in the presence of similar authority figures such as a corporate president or judge. Yet contexts differ. Any number of adults have learned to be assertive but formal and guarded in contemporary work environments, whereas they are warm, nurturing, and caring in their home environments. Some are highly organized and conscientious at work but far less methodical and fastidious in the relaxed, safe harbours of their homes.

Particularly in work situations that carry expectations of cerebral power, many persons preferentially operate on the basis of cool, analytical thinking and rational, linear learning and reasoning. Once at home, limbic powers of love and tenderness override cognitive intellect. Many contemporary U.S. organizational cultures and work unit cultures, with their relative absence of psychological safety, provoke workers to suppress their authentic, otherwise coherent personality tendencies and the integrated expression of cerebral and emotional intellect.

Generativity and Gender In midlife, men and women typically move in opposite directions from each other and from their prior, gender-typical, masculine or feminine tendencies. Many men become less assertive and individualistic and more affiliative, nurturant, empathic, and introspective. Women become less nurturant and communal and more assertive and independent. Gutmann has interpreted this as a psychological shift, one of increasing cathectic flexibility as middle-aged persons, however unconsciously, learn to explore their previously dormant, unexpressed tendencies. "Men discover a hitherto unsuspected vein of nurturance and aesthetic sensibility;women discover tough, managerial, and competitive qualities that they can apply in a first career or in a career change, as from social worker to lawyer". Altered estrogen–androgen ratios at midlife and other as yet undetermined factors likely play a role. In all, the intersecting dynamics of psychological forces, biological factors, historical and cohort effects, contemporary work roles, and career advancement norms are causal.

Workplace findings have been inconsistent, particularly with respect to job promotion. For example, although the ideal workplace is widely touted as one that supports gender neutrality, not only is masculine behaviour frequently preferred, it has been found to preferentially lead to career advancement for both men and women. We have yet to answer Kirchmeyer's (2002) question: Does "high masculinity help the workers advance, or did their masculinity levels increase with advancement?".

If midlife gender expression moves in opposite directions among men and women, there are implications for generative functions. Generativity is a hallmark of maturity. From Erikson's (*e.g.*, 1969) generativity concept to more recent ideas, experts find that the middle and later years are prime eras for adults to teach, mentor, and bring along younger workers. Creating opportunities for young adults;grooming them for advancement and leadership roles;mentoring, coaching, and providing advice and informal counsel are all generative functions. The work literature is replete with studies and examples of sponsorship in general and of same- and cross-gender mentoring in particular, but we do not yet know the extent to which gender differences at midlife may have causal implications for mentoring. Certainly, multiple variables (*e.g.*, endogenous factors, cohort effects, advancement norms, saturation in prior roles) are involved. Adults create their own equilibrated lives.

For example, the women achievers in Helson and Srivastava's (2001) study learned to balance their ambition and power needs with abilities to nurture others. Yet at midlife, due to some men's turn towards nurturance and centering on others and some women's turn towards power and centering on the self (in some, due to previously subverted achievement needs), some men may be more effective, caring mentors than some women. Men may also experience greater satisfaction doing so. For many achieving, contemporary women, the phrase "been there, done that" rings true.

Conscientiousness

Numerous studies show that conscientiousness is the best predictor of high job performance and one of the best predictors of life satisfaction as well. Meeting one's obligations leads to self-worth and a sense of competence. Conscientiousness is an attribute that many persons bring to the job. However, conscientiousness also increases as a result of having learned to function competently in jobs and other roles that require and reward such behaviour. Responsible, work-oriented individuals show gains in maturity, learn more than their less conscientious co-workers, and tend to set and to plan towards more difficult goals.

Goal setting leads to goal commitment and attainment. Loevinger (1993) demonstrated correlations between conscientiousness and achievement. Adults at the higher levels of ego development are more responsible, learning and achievement-oriented, tolerant, and autonomous.

Most persons show increased responsibility during young adulthood. Much of this is due to entry into the workforce because job requirements demand responsibility, reliable and consistent performance, focused learning, and greater self-control. When women's and men's responsibilities include parenting, increased conscientiousness results from this as well.

Increasing conscientiousness and competence during young adulthood depend partly on baseline competence during adolescence. Analyzing data from three longitudinal studies, Clausen and Jones (1998) found that highly competent adolescents showed rather little personal change in this regard from early adolescence through the mature years. On the other hand, many of those who had been low in competence and conscientiousness in adolescence advanced significantly in such qualities later in life. Roberts, Caspi, et al. (2003) reported a longitudinal study of a subset of 910 working adults from the larger Dunedin Study, a New Zealand investigation of health and behaviour of an entire cohort born in 1972 and 1973.

Personality at age 18 predicted work experiences at age 26, and work experiences predicted changes in personality during those years. Furthermore, there were reciprocal relationships among personality traits, learning, and work experiences in that the very personality attributes that led persons to elect specific work experiences were the attributes that were altered by those work experiences and by the learning that was integral to those experiences. Those who engaged in higher status work as young adults became more self-confident by age 26. They acquired more responsible and stimulating work, moved into supervisory and managerial positions, and were more work committed and happier in their jobs than cohort age mates who remained in positions that provided little in the way of opportunities for increased responsibility, advancement, and success.

Developmentally, there is evidence of ongoing conscientiousness development into middle age. For example, Clausen and Jones (1998) reported that women who had begun to work outside the home as young adults and remained employed while raising their children were primary agents in their own self-development. Due to their continual paid employment, when compared with their stay-at-home peers, they showed cognitive commitment, assertiveness, greater learning and selfconfidence, as well as the ability to handle multiple roles responsibly. In a longitudinal study of 81 women at two time periods (at ages 21–27 and 27–43), Roberts (1997) examined whether work experiences influence personality. Personality changes were not found during the young adult years;however, between 27 and 43 years of age, working women scored higher on agency, a measure that includes ambition, confidence, and self-sufficiency. Those who were more successful at work also learned occupational norms and became more norm-adhering. Norm adherence is a marker for conscientiousness as well as for responsible, prosocial (OCB) behaviour.

Unfortunately, one difficulty among studies using one of the big five factor personality inventories and finding evidence of linear increases in conscientiousness (*e.g.*, Simmering et al., 2003;Srivastava et al., 2003) is that such studies do not reveal what conscientiousness means in the lives of individual subjects. This applies to some non Five Factor Inventory (FFI)-based studies as well. For example, in Helson and Roberts's (1994) longitudinal study of ego development in 90 women, increases in responsibility were found from age 21 to 43 and from age 43 to 52. But little information is available with respect to how these attributes were manifest.

High conscientiousness and goal commitment lead to enhanced motivation to learn and inclinations to engage in continual learning. High growth needs strength (the need to develop and to learn), high need for achievement, and an internal locus of control intercorrelate. These three attributes predict and are enhanced by highly motivating jobs, and they correlate positively with conscientiousness. However, overconfidence in one's ability can create difficulties. As Simmering and colleagues (2003) found, subjects who were both conscientious and inordinately confident tended to deceive themselves, believing that their performance was better than it was. This dual tendency thwarts ongoing learning. Conscientiousness, accompanied as it is with goal setting and high goal attainment, strongly predicts competent work performance. A reciprocal, conscientiousness-enhancing effect is also seen: Competence in work tasks and job contexts predicts more responsible work roles, learning, and the maintenance or extension of conscientiousness.

10

Adult Education and Development

After independence, we have advanced considerably in many fields including education, agriculture, industries, transportation, communication etc. But how far these have been for the poor people? We pleaded for 'Sarvodaya'. But now many have been brought under such programmes? How many have benefited from these? Were there middle men who exploited the poor people? Answer to such questions are all revealing. All these point to the urgent need for conscialtisation among the public. Only then will people participate willingly in the nation building activities. When we achieved independence only less than 15per cent of Indians are literate. As per 1981 census, literacy percentage rose to 36.17. May be now it is around 40 or so. Still we have more than 50per cent of world illiterate population in India. The NAEP, 20 point programme etc., launched massive time-bound programme but could not achieve excepted results. Though it was stipulated in article 45 of the Indian constitution, even in 1986, many children at school going age are outside the school and many dropped out even before completing primary stage.

To improve this situation, point 16 of the new 20 point programme envisaged a three point approach *viz.,* ensure hundred per cent enrolment at the primary stage completely avoid dropping out from primary stage and providing non-formal education for the age group 15. In the new education policy formulated in 1986, item 10 provides for expansion of education both formal and non-formal. There is emphasis on alternative strategies and multiple approaches in the field of education. Village level committee on education also has been formulated in the NEP. The Jan Shikshan Nilayas are supposed to be continuing education centres catering to people of all ages, of all occupations, of all beliefs etc. The strategies laid down in the action plan of NEP, through the different task forces setup for specific purpose is hoped to offer better educational facilities and more and more opportunities for the continuing education of the pupils, who are interested in it.

Adult Education has somehow been equated with Adult literacy in the Indian context. In developed countries, it is really the education of the Adult, irrespective of whether it is for the illiterates, semi-literates, literates, and the educated. Education has since been accepted as a life long process and one has to learn many things, even if he is highly educated, to cope with the demands of the times. So appropriate courses have to be developed to suit the different types of clientele and launched with necessary care and vision. At the Centre and in each state there are many departments and agencies providing for the development and the welfare of the people. Now the term 'Antyodaya' has come to stay. Even the most backward and the poorest man/family in an areas has to be brought to a considerable level through appropriate steps. However appealing a programme be, if introduced and implemented in isolation, the anticipated results will not be achieved. Hence integration and coordination of developmental activities are essential. This is what is lacking at present and has to be over come. All agencies/Departments interested in the welfare of the people have to put in their efforts in a coordinated way for ensuring maximum effectiveness.

A cadre of extension workers has been suggested for every locality. This could be the village extension worker of the development department, health workers of the health services department volunteers and promoters of National Savings Scheme and Family Welfare Scheme, National Service Scheme volunteers and the NCC Cadets from the colleges and Universities etc. However now-a-days there is a feeling that the adult education functionaries/Supervisors and Instructors of the University sector/Government departments/voluntary Agencies who are working with the community helping them to overcome the hitherto annoying circumstances, be dovetailed for the cause of overall developmental activities. As full time workers are needed for each community to coordinate and oversee allied programmes, the question has to be seen in the right perspective.

Planning commission at the national level, state planning boards, district development committee and block level development committees are in vogue. These are mainly responsible for planning developmental activities for a specified area and period of time. Then these are to be implemented with dedication by a team of workers—paid and voluntary—on priority basis. Certain lacuna exists in the implementation of such programmes. Block level coordination efforts are to be streamlined and implemented with the support and cooperation of all implied agencies. Voluntary agencies have a major role to play. In the field of adult education there are a good number of voluntary agencies. These may be given representation in the BDC's/DDC's etc. and entrusted with the implementation of developmental programmes in a particular area. Effective monitoring supervision and follow up activities are also to be built in.

In most of the extension blocks/community development blocks, functional literacy programmes have been launched. All such blocks have to be covered for the purpose of linking adult education with development. In Kerala we have an organisation, KANFED, which is the sole agency in the state for linking non-formal education with development. As such various measures have been taken and programmes launched with the sole aim of improving the lot of the poor people. Panchayat level units are in existence looking after developmental needs of the locality. People are coming forward to donate land and buildings for establishing regular development network in the respective areas. These, when consolidated will become a great force as the library movement in Kerala or the Kerala Shastra Sahitya Parishad, aimed at popularising science among the masses. Developmental activities should not be mere governmental/ departmental activity but should secure people participation.

Adult educators should ensure the necessary linkage between the world of alphabets, through making every one literate and the world of development. They may create proper atmosphere and ensure effective field work. This is how nation's prosperity can be ensured. The adult educators have to pledge for this, realising that it is part of their duty. Development is a process of attaining certain targets which are essential for the well-being of the community and thus prosperity. Let adult educators come to the forefront in discharging this duty.

ADULT EDUCATION

Adult education in a multilingual country like India is the greatest challenge to the linguist. Faced with problems of instant communication to be linked up with the standardisation and modernisation of the languages, the linguist is called upon to develop a strategy of literacy which can steer through the maze of languages, dialects, styles, registors and such other varieties. Most literacy workers have convinced themselves that the dialect has nothing to do with literacy. And yet when a farmer's literacy manual is written in 'Suddh Hindi' (Chaste Hindi) in Delhi and is not accessible to a farmer in Rajasthan or in parts of Bihar, they do not know what to do about it. It is not as if a linguist can solve all the problems of literacy. After all there is the Mahaboobnagar experiment in Andhra Pradesh where one of India's well known linguists was associated in a programme for producing instructional material in the dialect. But the result was unsatisfactory. By the end of the course, the learners could read (and write) Mahaboobnagar Telugu, but they could not read standard Telugu with facility. What, then, is the role of a linguist in an adult education programme ?

The Mahaboonagar programme clearly shows that unless adult literacy is functionally defined and all steps from the curriculum formation through apperception to self-actualisation are well integrated, adult education is bound to be incomplete. Unless reading the dialect is linked with the reading of the standard by a switch over mechanism, this problem cannot be satisfactorily solved. It is not enough to identify the needs and set the objectives, but it is necessary to structure experience through language in such a way that the competence in a language would be of a level which will not permit sliding back to illiteracy. Use of dialect in illiteracy is not an end in itself, but a means to attain necessary skills in the literary language in which sufficient reading material is available for him to maintain literacy.

Mahaboobnagar as well as similar experiences of the project run by the Council for Social Development, the Seva Mandir in Udaipur (Rajasthan), the Institute of Indian Education, Poona and Central Institute of Indian Languages, Mysore go to indicate that whether it is for motivation or for ensuring the functionality of the programme, material sensitive to local language use is more effective for bringing the learners quickly to the threshold of literacy. But this is not enough. Constant bridging at all levels of language is necessary to relate the local to the standard, which invariably is the high status language. The problem of literacy in case of language which have accepted another language as 'culture language' needs more serious attention. It is to be remembered that the purpose of literacy is not to develop the undeveloped languages and dialects, but develop the human potential through conscientisation. Therefore, a knowledge of language dynamics and language engineering becomes a must for a literacy worker in a developing country.

It is not as if the linguist can be eliminated if the problem of dialect is isolated. In a poona slum where the literacy worker asks the child tujhe vadil kay kartat and gets frustrated as the child does not understand, the problem is of a different order. Undaunted, the worker asks tujha bap ka karto and pat comes the reply daru pito ani aila marto 'drinks wine and beats mother'.

This forcefully brings out the distance between the slum language and the standard spoken language, the problem of comprehension and the problem of status and attitude build into the language use. Linguists, who make it their business to study the structure of varieties of spoken and written languages in different domains, must be treated as indispensable allies of literacy workers to solve such problems.

In a meeting of the Scientific and Technical Terminology Commission, there was a discussion about the word for 'fishing rod'. Although many languages have the word 'bansi', the pundits rejected it in favour of a more Sanskritised word 'akheta danda'. Many people are in favour of such Sanskritisms without knowing their implication. The choice of a high culture word, whether Sanskritic or Perso-Arabic, determines the style of writing. Since this has serious consequences for literacy, it must be understood by the material producer. Take, for example, the Oriya word nasika and nake 'nose'. The choice of nasika will require kuncana kariba while nake modiba in the sense of disapproval. This not only is a problem in collocation, but the style of writing itself would be determined as a result of such choices. Hindi danta cikitsa and dat ka ilaj illustrate similar problems as the above. Yet another dimension of the problem of language which has direct bearing on literacy is illustrated by the Tamil word which is written as patam, read as padam and spoken as pado or the Assamese word which is written as citi bach but read as siti bas. The language specific conventions of writing and reading need to be analysed and integrated in the literacy curriculum. The rules for moving either from the spoken to the written or from the written to the spoken have to be carefully worked out and graded before texts are prepared.

Telugu, where most textbooks and much of the printed material was written in the Granthika style presents another formidable challenge to those engaged in adult education. In spite of the decision to effect a phased change over to the SiÀa vyavaharika, the spoken standard style, the anomaly is bound to persist for some more time.

The literacy workers even though working in a small homogeneous dialect area have to keep these broader aspects of language development in view. Otherwise devoid of the continuing flow of reading material which is likely to be available in the standard language for years to come, the neo-literates are bound to lapse into illiteracy. Linguistic minorities pose a major problem to the literacy worker. In many cases people are to be made literate in two languages, the mother tongue and the dominant language. The linguists must stretch their ingenuity to develop the strategy of transfer, thus making it feasible to run simultaneous literacy in the home language and the dominant language wherever possible. Of course, those of the dominant language area may have to be made literate in either one o both the languages according to their choice. Facilities may be provided for this purpose. The West Bengal Committee for Eradication of illiteracy, for instance, has taken commendable steps in this regard. But very little research and experiment has gone in to making the other minorities literate.

Another peculiar problem is posed by linguistic minority communities who use a pidginised varieties of a language as contact language. The most important among these is the pidgin Naga, which is popularly known as Nagamese. This variety is not only a bridge among the mutually unintelligible Naga language speakers, but also a bridge between the various tribal language speakers and Assamese speakers. No literacy effort in this area can ignore the existence of this variety. The various tribal language speakers in the Koraput District of Orissa use Desia as a communication language in this manner. Similarly those in and around Ranchi in Bihar use Sadri or Sadni. Desia is a variety of Oriya and Sadri is a variety of Hindi. To what extent these intermediate languages can be exploited for furthering literacy has to be examined very carefully.

Problem of Santhali somewhat parallels the situation obtaining in the case of Konkani speakers. The Konkani speakers are spread in Goa, Maharashtra, Karnataka and Kerala. The Konkani language is written in four scripts, the

Nagari, Kannada, Malayalam and the Roman script. The Santhalis are mainly distributed in Orissa, Bengal and Bihar, though there are few thousands in Assam. The language consequently is written in five scripts, Nagari, Bengali, Oriya, Roman and the 01 scripts. The last is an indigenously developed script by one Raghunatha Murmu, himself a Santhali. Since the matter of script is an emotionally surcharged problem and the adoption of one or the other has many wider implications, literacy workers would do well to inform themselves about various aspects of this question with the help of linguists who have worked in these areas.

The above list is illustrative of challenges which literacy workers are likely to face. The various efforts at script and spelling reforms pose constantly renewed problems which need watching by trained linguists and their implications spelled out for the literacy workers. However, it is not only in the area of more language analysis that a linguist is relevant to a literacy programme. In the area of material production three major operations are envisaged in the years to come. Apart from writing materials which would presuppose language analysis, it is visulised that there will be need for translating and simplifying manuals and reading materials written by specialists. Many international agencies are called upon to send specialists to prepare manuals are either designed for village level workers in health and education or for voluntary organizations engaged in extension work. As the knowledge of English of the workers themselves in minimal, the texts need to be simplified. Take for example an instruction from a manual (v.1: 101) prepared by the Ministry of Health. "Schedule domiciliary visits to new acceptors of condoms at least one during the first two months and every six months after they have become regular users".

This sentence has so many variables that for a person educated up to SSLC level it is difficult to comprehend it in one reading. Even after reading several times the chances of confusion cannot entirely be ruled out. Texts such as these need to be simplified. However the question is not as simple as it sounds at the first instance. How the simplification of an agreement between the governments of UK and Rhodesia assumed different nuances in the hands of government writers goes to prove that a lot of expertise has to be brought to bear upon the problem. In Indian languages where prestige is often attached to the high style, texts have to be simplified to guide the inexperienced reader through graded steps into becoming an efficient reader. Here a parallel may be drawn with preparing textual material for purposes of second language learning. As in the case of learning a second language the learner is first introduced to the simple language used for native speaker he is guided to progress to greater complexities, in this case simplified language for neo-literate inexperienced reader slowly moves through simple language to greater complexities. Needless to say that the help of a linguist is essential in this operation.

Translations will have to be resoited to, as, for sometimes to come, the experts will write in English. Even if some good reading material is published in one Indian language it may have to be translated into other Indian languages. Translation is one of the most neglected fields in the country. Without going into the details of discussion regarding linguistics and translation, it may suffice to point out that with language belonging to four language families and many languages of doubtful affiliation, almost all structural and semantic complexities of translation one is likely to find in the tour of the world can be illustrated by Indian languages. Fourteen languages as medium of higher education, administration and mass communication should indicate the extent of translation needed in the country. Apart from the problem of vocabulary, the presence or absence of verbs in equational sentences, passive and gender concord, the different modes of relativisation, the differing case relations are few of the important areas which pose obvious problems in translation. What is important to understand in this connection is that a research base has to be created in all these areas if functional adult education is to be achieved in a meaningful way.

The preparation of instructional material is not independent of the curriculum and philosophy underlying adult education in any country. Lyra Srinivasan (1977) speaks of four curriculum models. The four models, the Information model, the Problem solving model, the Projective model, and the Expressive, the Creative or the Self-actualising model, from a continuum on the basis of maximal and minimal role of a teacher. Each model will dictate its own material and teacher preparation.

For example, when people speak in terms of textbooks and supplementary readers their thinking is essentially of the information model. The system in which the teacher engages himself in a one way communication of information where the textbook dominates the class, where education is not relevant to the important segments of living of the adult learner is incompatible with adult education. External incentives and pursuations may result in external allegiance to a programme but it cannot generate the necessary emotional and intellectual precondition for adult education.

The conventional thinking on the subject makes a distinction between adult literacy and adult education. Thus in a curriculum of 350 hours, 90 100 hours are given for literacy. This represents a gross distortion and misunderstanding of both literacy and education. First of all it must be understood that language is not taught in a vacuum. Unless the content of the language instructional material is closely knit with the needs and interests of the learners this itself may act as the greatest disincentive for them. Therefore, taking structures like lala tala la, lala la, tala la, selected on an ad hoc and random basis, and trying to generalise it for all groups of learners may not be the most efficient introduction of literacy.

Many perfer to use the primer prepared for native children for initial literacy. This thinking does not take into consideration the special psychological problem of an adult who either feels deprived, because of being bypassed by the school or has a low self-image, because of being a drop-out. He certainly resents when treated as a child. Secondly, a primer is a unit of formal schooling where it is structured differently with the curriculum. Thirdly, even the primers themselves are often not even properly designed for the children. For example, the first seventeen pages of the current Marathi primer contains mostly imperatives. Under these circumstances, no matter how convenient it is for the administrator from the point of sale of material, this is not the proper answer to adult education. The knowledge sought to be imparted in an adult education situation must be need specific and the medium of communication location specific. This would indicate diversification of instructional material. But even accepting this diversity as basis, to what extent the initial material can be generialised needs to be studied more throughly and scientifically. So far only assertations of various literacy workers for and against such claims are available. For example, when one claims that the same literacy manual is being used for small and marginal farmers, industrial and mining workers, urban service workers, workers in different trades, tribals, scheduled caste groups and women it has to be examined a little more carefully and should not be taken at the face value.

Literacy to be functional, language must be well integrated with content. If the aim of adult education is to impart a level of competence to the learner so that he can sustain his interest of his own without lapsing into illiteracy, then it is not enough to give a mere recognition and manipulation of scripts, reading of controlled texts and writing letters to the grand child about one's health and the village fair.

The adult learner must be made a competent reader with understanding of fairly complex structures so that he can read newspapers and make sense of various governmental forms and notifications. Very little research has gone into the officialise language of our country. The forms and notifications, even in English in many countries, are written in a language which need simplification in order to be accessible to the English knowing public. Many of our forms and notifications, which are not originally drafted in Indian language, but are translations from English, are not even comprehended by highly educated native speakers. Therefore, it must be understood that both the content and language must be graded to carry the learner through successive skills while maintaining their relevance and creativity. This presupposes a team work in which a linguist is an indispensable component.

When we think of adult education, often, it is considered to be connected with writing and reading. Since every body speaks a language, spoken activity is completely ignored in the scheme of things. It must not be forgotten that

India has a 2000 year old tradition of oral transmission of knowledge. In any case through dialogue it is not only possible to establish a personal bond between the teacher and the learners, but also lay the foundation of problem sharing and culture sharing. Very little research has been conducted about the structure of oral presentation in the formal class room, the radio and under more non-formal conditions. The research conducted by the Coimbatore Agriculture University tend to indicate that there is more similarity in the structure of the class room presentation and the presentation by the Radio. This may be because, the radio presentation is first written and then read. The linking of the oral structures to reading and writing must also engage the attention of linguists.

A question is often asked about testing those who pass through adult literacy programmes. In such situation the word 'assessment' should be used to include besides testing, such observation techniques as rating and interviews, class performance records, job records and evaluation of the total learning outcome to reflect developmental changes. This also requires formulation of the goals of literacy in a more meaningful manner. Functional literacy in terms of UNESCO norms was considered to be equivalent to education of the level of class V. But in the circumstances where the emphasis is on non-formality the specification of goals has to be spelled out in terms of skills, learner's confidence level creative interpretations of a stimulus, problem solving ability, etc. This is the only way to ensure fairness of assessment of both individuals and groups in a pluralistic society.

Terms such as motivations, animators, facilitators are being freely used in connection with adult education. Following the Indian tradition in this regard, some have even suggested a three-tier organisation where a motivator is the programme in-charge whereas the facilitator is the teacher. Those in-charge of adult education must ensure that the new lables are not used to either maintain status quo or smuggle in the formal class room authoritarianism. Malcolm Knowles developing the concept of Androgogy (Knowles 1971) describes it as the art and science of helping adults to learn. Androgogy has also been termed as 'A technology of involvement'. This involvement on the part of both orgnisers and learners is crucial to the success of an adult education programme. This is the biggest challenge before the educationists and linguists of this country today.

CURRICULUM FOR ADULT EDUCATION

Adult Education is human resources development. Human resources development is necessary so that people's affairs can be left in the people's hands. Take, for example, law. Because of the lack of awareness among the people about their rights, duties and opportunities, and because administration including administration of law is conducted in a language not accessible to the people, there was great dependence on law courts and lawyers. Ignorance of law resulted from ignorance of language and literacy. Litigation often resulted in the ruination of both the parties. The purpose of measures underlying the setting up of village panchayats was to reduce the dependence of people on the law courts. But, unfortunately, while this was generally accepted, no effort was made to reduce the production of lawyers. On the contrary, law schools went on multiplying and the production of a large body of lawyers built into the system the antithesis of delivering the legal care of people in their hands.

Prohibition can be taken as another example. While the social reformists give sermons about the harmfulness of drinking, the diehard economists point out the revenue accruing to the public exchequer from this source. Therefore, law against drinking continues to be passed while breweries continue to multiply. It may be that part of the money so accrued to the public exchequer is spent on providing succour to the families ruined by drinking. But this is like killing the neighbour's cow and, when he complains, presenting him with a pair of shoes made of the cowhide.

Economic resources planning divorced from human resources development results in a system which invests the affairs of people in the hands of managers, who are self-appointed through make-believe democratic procedures. The imperialists all over the world have prided themselves in developing the economic resources of underdeveloped countries. Even after their departure, the beneficiaries swear in the name of economic development and work vigorously to maintain the system. Both in the capitalist and the communist countries, one finds systems where the affairs of the people are run by a managerial class. The people everywhere need to be educated about education in all countries, irrespective of achievements of formal educational institutions.

In India, today, the scientific manpower is the third in the world. But this cannot be termed as human resources development. As exploitation of raw material in one country for being processed in and marketed by another cannot be termed as the economic development of that country, similarly creation of cheap exportable educated labour at great cost to the country cannot be called human resources development to the country concerned. Both in technology and education one must develop system appropriate to one's need. One does not make or buy big caps, one gets caps that fit. Similarly a country does not ape big technology, it must have technology appropriate to its needs.

Education can be human resources development when it brings out the perfection inherent in a learner. The learner can thus contribute his mite to the society of which he is a member, while expecting the society to fulfil his needs. Societies built on capital intensive economy develop a pattern of life where profit is shared by a handful of individuals or by a set of managers appointed by the State. Where capital is scarce such an economy is bound to create greater inequalities. A country with surplus population must develop its manpower resources and creates a labour intensive economy. Only then, can it expect full employment and establishment of a society based on distributive justice.

The Institutional education in a country like India has resulted in providing education only for a low percentage of the population. It is responsible, on the one hand, for the widening gap between a few well trained and millions of illiterates and, on the other, a large primary school enrolment and an equally large dropout, stagnation and wastage. It is inflexible, textbook-bound, non-competitive and largely irrelevant to the needs and aspirations of the society. Merely multiplying such schools is neither likely to ensure universalisation of education nor obliteration of adult illiteracy.

Thus it will be seen that adult education has a role different from the time and textbook-bound certified education imparted in the school. It is to make the adult learner aware of the factors which limit his opportunities of free development, thus enabling him to manage his own affairs. The alphabetic literacy, which is being most talked about in developing countries of Asia and Africa is only one of the means, however important it may be, for attaining this end.

In a country like India, the declining adult education is intimately connected with the declining autonomy of individuals and groups to manage their affairs. It is, therefore, important that the factors inhibiting literacy are examined with care.

The factors inhibiting literacy can be seen from different angles. If one takes into consideration the geographical factor one finds that the physical geography is responsible for disparate groups living in isolated areas. This is particularly true of the tribal population. Geographical factors which isolate one group from another also inhibit dispersion of linguistic elements facilitating standardisation. Thus geographical factors which restrict the scale of communication become a major contributing factor for illiteracy.

The linguistic factor is partly a consequence of the natural regions and partly of stratified society. Multiple languages divided into regional and social dialects, written and spoken, and formal and colloquial styles are a major deterrent to literacy, particularly when a foreign tongue enjoys the highest status in the society. Multiplicity of scripts adds a further dimension to this problem. The divergence of the language of education from the language of administration, on the one hand, and the language of mass communication, on the other, inhibits literacy. Bi-and multi-lingualism pose serious challenges to the students of adult literacy. For the linguistic minorities there may at times be need for literacy. For the linguistic minorities there may at times be need for literacy in two languages.

The linguistic factor is intimately related to the cultural factor. The Indian languages belonging to four or more language families indicate the diverse ethnicity of the people speaking them. In fact maintainance of multilingulism in India to a large extent is due to the will to maintain distinct ethnic identity of groups. The history of the development of Indian languages show that when a language or a variety of language, which becomes prestigious because of its being the career of all knowledge, is confined to a minority upper strata, simplified spoken languages emerge. They act as sluices which carry the knowledge so confined to the people in India, where even in early times literacy was limited. There is a long tradition of oral transmission of knowledge;social life and leadership was not linked with the ability to read and write. By and large the society which was illiterate was educated as a result of the oral transmission of the accumulated wisdom and there were even uneducated among the scribes, those know how to read and write

The economic and political factors which brought about a near complete break with the past tradition have played a major role in the accentuation of illiteracy. It has even resulted in the blockade of natural communication between the literate educated and the illiterate, thus converting the large mass of illiterates into uneducated.

Economically, with the British take-over of the country, the village self-sufficiency based on pursuits of agriculture and handicrafts, became the first casualty. With the imperialist policy trying to exploit the natural resources of the country and using them to the best interest of the British, very little was available for distribution among the local populace. With the scarce resources and growing demand, only the sectors favoured by the rulers got the better of it and it resulted in the inequal distribution of resources. The society was divided between the privileged few and the underprivileged many. The upper class interest in the stratified Indian society and the interest of the economically privileged became one and both conspired to perpetuate an elitist rule. This led to the policy of illiteracy and ignorance even though there was external allegiance to education by all concerned.

The political factor also aided illiteracy. The centralised civil service was meant for the British. But what ever little was opened up for the Indians required rigorous and prolonged preparation and was only accessible to the privileged. With the advent of the British all Hindu, Muslim and Sikh educational institutions which provided grass root level literacy and education closed down but the secular education began mainly through the missionaries in an alien tongue which further inhibited literacy. As through the thousand year old literacy tradition was nullified by this process. The alignment of the church and the State at this stage resulted in (a) a small group of Christians separated from the majority of Indians divided by the worship of many gods;and (b) a small English knowing elite separated from the majority of Indian divided by the use of many tongues. This excessive learning on English naturally resulted in large scale illiteracy and limited education.

If adult education is to be attempted in a serious sense in the above background, then it will entail radical change of attitudes and existing educational programmes. Adult education can neither be effective through formal institutions nor would it succeed by institutionalising it. An adult literacy curriculum has to be built on the expressed needs of a community. The needs as felt by the Community and as observed by a trained social scientist together constitute the expressed need. To that extent adult education cannot be centrally directed and its curriculum cannot be uniform. However, the objectives need to be selled out and instead of trying to fit the objectives in a rigid time mould, time must be found for the attainment of the objectives. It is in this context that a core or minimum curriculum for adult education is suggested below. This may, however, be modified on the basis of experience of adult education workers.

ADULT EDUCATION IN THE PROMOTION OF SCIENCE AND TECHNOLOGY

The progress of any country depends on the advancement of Science and Technology. Science is a way of life;it is an outlook;it is search for truth;it is the enquiry for new practices and innovations;it is establishing validity of day-to-day life situations through cause and effect relationship or through statistical information. Scientific outlook is needed in the modern world. This is true of the child as well as of the masses. Scientific temper has to be developed among all citizens;this should start from the primary schools. Technological advances establish modern view points and make life more precise and fruitful. Ideas and ideals can be spread through oral culture and written culture.

Oral culture in prevalent even among the illiterate and the most backward sections of the society. Traditional behaviour cannot be changed all on a sudden. It requires proper motivation. It requires the acceptance or atleast the concurrence of all concerned. Knowledge and practices are transmitted to the generations through the family and peer groups. That is why traditional occupations remain the monopoly of a few. But when scientific advances take place, new approaches are evolved. These are taught in educational institutions such as Engineering College, Polytechnics, Industrial Training Institutes, Industrial Training Centres and Institutes of Technology. This leads to more of practical work, experimentation and verification of hypotheses. Here oral culture is not enough. Education comes in as a formal process. Non-formal approaches cannot be ruled out. This is an ongoing process in workshops all over the community, though at different levels.

Written culture becomes inevitable at this junction, to support practical know-how. In our country, even after 39 years of independence, nearly 65per cent of in population remain illiterates. It is rampant in North Indian States like Bihar, Rajasthan, Uttar Pradesh, Madhya Pradesh etc. which have very low levels of literacy. In some of these states the percentage of literacy among women is even less than 10per cent. With this lamentable situation of literacy, how can scientific temper be developed among the people.

Illiteracy is one of the major stumbling blocks in the promotion of science and Technology. People resort to various ways of life due to sheer ignorance. Their beliefs and customs are such that they observe them without questioning. The youth who try to question such unscientific acts are often termed as revolutionaries or extremists and victimised also. Even in this era, where most of the diseases could be cured, many die due to ignorance and consequent maltreatment. Even now there are groups of people who just pray for and do not treat the patient. It is believed that certain diseases occur due to the unhappiness or even anger of gods and goddesses. Without caring for environmental sanitation, people use unclean water and become victims of many diseases. This is where adult educators can do a lot.

They can, at the outset, create an awareness among the people on the need for scientific outlook and scientific pursuits. This need not necessarily be left to the health workers. This can be a part of the work of adult educators who are expected to mobilise the essential resources and adopt integrated approaches. They have to realise that all round development of the masses is their ultimate aim and for that education should become a vehicle. Literacy cannot be and need not be given as mere alphabets or words;instead, they should be made meaningful and presented in relation to life. For popularising science among the masses, concerted efforts are needed.

Voluntary groups/organisations are instituted for this. College teachers and students can give leadership and show the way. This can form a part of their curricular work or at least an extension component. School science teachers can also play a major role in creating scientific outlook and temper not only among children but also in the community. Such attempts are in progress in different countries. People's science movements have gained a sound footing in many states. The Kerala Shastra Sahitya Parisad (KSSP) has won ICSSR award for its meritorial work during 1985. The Shastra Kala Jatha has won it great reputation, not only in Kerala but also all over India. It organised an All India Jatha for the spread of scientific literacy through multiple media.

VOLUNTARY ORGANISATION OF SCIENCE

The KSSP is a voluntary organisation of science lovers. Besides college teachers, school teachers and university professors, a band of Doctors, Researchers, Social activists and students have joined the KSSP. Founded in 1957 the KSSP has grown into a very big organisation. It has branches all over the state and units in most of the schools and colleges. Children are inducted to scientific outlook from the primary classes. 'Balashastram' a monthly and `Eureka' another science journal addressed to primary school children are published regularly for this group. 'Shastrakeralam' is for high school pupils and 'Shastra gati' for college students.

All these appear every month and are read by a good number. Science Quiz Programme has become an approved programme of the Education Department though it began as a voluntary attempt of the KSSP. Similarly science fairs at which young students, present pieces of innovative experiments, have become not only a regular feature but they have really become `fairs' attracting people from all walks of life. Science clubs are organising a variety of programmes in Educational Institutions. The `Science cream series' which the KSSP published are so dear to the science students. The standard and vocabulary are different for different groups and as such a 'grading' has been attempted. The KSSP is also organising lecture series even in remote areas of the state for the masses. The most significant among the activities of the KSSP is its 'Shastrakala Jatha', which through its songs, street dramas, demonstration, etc. attract large audience wherever they stop, without prior notice. The KSSP has by now achieved a lot in popularising science especially among the masses. These activities have to reach the illiterate people also.

So more and more folk art forms are to be introduced. Better still would be to help people become literate. The KSSP is trying it indirectly, but they have to take up such programmes also as part of their regular activities. There are two other major agencies in Kerala. (1) KANFED (Kerala Association for Non-formal Education Development) which is trying to link Non-formal education programme with developmental and welfare programmes, all over Kerala and (2) Kerala Grandhasala Sangham, an association of libraries mainly engaged in the spread of reading habits thus providing opportunity or life long education. KSSP, can in collaboration with these two agencies, do better using the resources available with these agencies, avoiding repetition and ensuring necessary cooperation and coordination. Anyway, it is essential to create scientific awareness among the masses as a precondition to scientific literacy. Popularisation of science will follow and can result in scientific temper. Adult educators should consider it their responsibility to ensure scientific literacy along with basic literacy and functional literacy. At the stage of planning teaching learning materials and training programme scientific component has also to be taken care of.

In the primer, lessons of science, scientific temper and scientific advancements can be incorporated and even in other lessons, scientific approach can be ensured. In a recent WHO workshop held at Madras on 'environmental health and housing in rural and urban development strategies it was felt that a coordinated approach would yield better results than isolated attempts. Health, hygiene, modernisation, population education, legal literacy, science for the masses etc. should form part of a unified whole-a kit, it was suggested by the workshop. It has also been suggested that extension workers are appointed or deputed in each locality to render essential services. Adult educators have been tipped for this job as they are the torch bearers in the darkness. They alone can light candles as proposed by Welthy Fischer and keep the torch burning so that continuing education will result in the creation of a learning society.

The Departments/Centres/Units of Adult Continuing Education and Extension established in nearly 100 Indian Universities can widen their umbrella and incorporate 'science for the masses' as one of the activities and thus inculcate scientific temper among the students and teachers of the Institutions of higher learning. The scientific attitude and temper can be best-created by a group of scientists especially teachers and researchers taking it as part of their duty. Voluntary organisations can continue their work and new ones may be formed wherever found necessary.

The IUACE (Indian University Association for Continuing Education) has accepted 'science for the masses' as one of its new areas of work. At the state level, Departments of Science and Technology have been established. Attempts like biogas, smokeless choola, cheap latrines etc. are being launched by the Department. Voluntary activist groups are also emerging with the support of enthusiastic and scientists and researchers. Institutes for research and development have to be established and their research findings be disseminated to all concerned and used for nation-building programmes.

Adult educators can not escape saying that science is somebody elses realm of activity. It is also within the purview of the adult education. Hitherto this aspect was not fully recognised and utilised. At least in future, more emphasis has to be given to scientific aspects. It is good that at least now we are collectively thinking of promoting science and technology. If there is a will, there is a way. Let us sort out the strategies and plan our course of action. Every adult educator should feel it his duty to inculcate scientific attitude and scientific tamper among the adults whom they come across.

MASS PROGRAMME FOR FUNCTIONAL LITERACY (MPFL)

Yet another experiment aimed at eradication of illiteracy, 'started in May 1986 is heading for a collapse if not subjected to intensive care and treatment. It was in such a haste that Institutions of higher learning were asked to launch a mass programme involving NSS and non NSS students, all over India.

The State Resource Centres were asked to prepare large number of kits, which they did with great obedience but without vision and necessary skill and expertise. The time target—was taken care of but not the quality of the materials. This is not true of all SRC's but of atleast the majority. Had they been given enough notice and sufficient time, they could have done better work.

May 1st is an auspicious day. It is the May day ! It is a boon for the workers. But what is its sanctity for starting a mass programme involving student community? May and June are the mid summer vacation months. But in how many Universities are we having vacation during May-June? Many are having examinations during these months. There is no vacation so to say. Very few Universities which could start in May also were not adequately motivated to take up the task.

Yet another lacuna is that MPFL is launched along with the 'Centre Based Adult Education Programme (CBAEP). This programme as well as Centres/ Departments/Cells for Adult and Continuing Education Programmes are in vogue in 98 Universities, thanks to the untiring efforts of Dr. (Mrs.) Madhuri R. Shah, Dr. M.L. Mehta, Dr. S.C. Bhatia and others. 1985-90 being the second phase of the University involvement in adult education programme many colleges are actively engaged in this activity. But the centre Based Adult Education Programme will also be affected by the introduction of MPFL through back doors.

Where the Shoe Pinches?

Lack of coordination between the sections *viz.*, Education and Sports and Youth affairs of the Human Resource Development Ministry is hypothesised by many field workers. The MPFL is channelled mainly through the second one though the first one is also instrumental in its implementation. At the University level the UGC is sponsoring CBAEP, without any increase in the number of centres.

It also has requested the Universities to find out non NSS volunteers to involve themselves in the MPFL. While this is done on the one hand, the NSS Coordinator at the University level and the NSS Programme officers at the college level have been directed to enrol as many NSS and non- NSS volunteers, train them and implement the programme. Why this two fold approach? The Adult Education Programme officers in the colleges (some of them are NSS Programme Officers as well) are in a dilemma. The literacy kits prepared by the SRC and handed over to the State Adult Education Departments have been dumped in many colleges and they remain uncared for in some corner or the other. The Masters Training Programme envisaged in the MPFL has become a hoax, not to speak of instructor's (volunteers) orientation.

The prospective learners are to be identified by the volunteer himself/ herself. Two cards are expected to be filled in and submitted to the DAEO and the College level Programme Officer concerned. But how many such cards have been received during 1986-87? While the Kerala University Centre for Adult Education and Extension could organise 825 Adult Education Centres directly and through 34 affiliated colleges with an enrolment of about 23,000, it could muster only 1400 non-NSS volunteers from 30 colleges for the MPFL helping 1875 adult illiterates. The NSS sector might have enrolled a good number. However the targets are far away. Even among the enrolled, the results are yet to be monitored.

Meanwhile the Government of India Ministry of Sports and Youth Affairs has come forward with an appeal to enrol more volunteers and start the programme in May 1987 itself. The tall claim of enrolment of 1.3 lakh volunteers and making a sizeable number literate through MPFL have to be checked with 'real situations' and not with 'statistics' alone which always remain challenged by 'real workers'.

Unless we have the necessary political will and a uniform approach, eradication of illiteracy cannot be achieved. Multiple approaches are necessary but that should not be within one agency and in one institution. Proper incentives have to be worked out and adequate motivation and awareness has to be built up.

Involvement of students in this programme has to be made compulsory and as a prerequisite for receiving Degrees. Voluntarism will not help in this task. Short term centre based or even camp based programmes might deliver better results. A rethinking is urgently necessary in the planning, implementation, monitoring, evaluation, feedback etc., of the MPFL if real results are anticipated. In the interest of the nation this should be done before launching the 1987 programme, scheduled for May 1987.

PEOPLE'S EDUCATION SHOULD HAVE HIGHER PRIORITY

The development of even the most backward and downtrodden sections of the society should be the aim of any democratic country. This is now termed as 'Antyodaya'. This should be the policy of India, if we want to solve the problems of poverty and illiteracy. In India nearly two thirds of the population still could not read, write and comprehend even their mother-tongue. So also, more than half the population in India lie below the poverty line. Our five year plans aimed at improving the lot of the people have yet to attain the targeted goals, fully. There is marked improvement in many sectors, but they are not upto our expectations. Though there is increase in the percentage of literacy in India, there is increase in the number of illiterates as well. This is not only due to population explosion but due to other reasons as well. These are not acting in isolation. Thus the cumulative effect of a number of serious impediments minimise or adversely affect the development of the country and hamper its progress and prosperity. To ensure effective and real development, people should be educated, or at least made literate.

The illiterate who could not read and understand themselves are denied of the opportunities to act according to their likes and dislikes. They have to depend on others for writing letters filling in forms, preparing applications etc., and hence cannot be on a par with the others. Those who have only the spoken word to their credit, are not fully utilising the resources available to them. They have an inferiority feeling of their own and hence lead a discontented life. They are exploited by the others, especially the educated and are hence are anxious of their future. They lose optimism. They are doubtful about all developmental and welfare schemes. They look up to the Government for anything and everything. They are antagonistic to change of all kinds due to ignorance and bitter experiences.

The messages of 'small family norms', 'saving habits', 'values of life' are not accepted by the weaker sections of the society and especially the illiterates. Hence we have to educate the masses to ensure true benefits out of all plan schemes. Adult and continuing education are needed as priority programmes, but it is not so at present. While we spend crores on the formal system of education, we are rather reluctant in spending even 5per cent of the education budget for adult education. This is a pitiable situation over which people should not merely lament upon, but work out action plans and implement vigorously.

Unlike the advanced or affluent countries in India adult education is not the education of the adults but it denotes adult literacy. This is rather confusing to man westerners. Actually adult education should mean life long the educational opportunities for the adults to increase the horizons of their knowledge and to strengthen the capabilities. Out-of school education or own-time education as we perceive it, has to be offered to all the illiterate, the semi-literate, the literate, the highly educated etc. But we have not yet achieved adult literacy to a satisfactory level.

In India we should concentrate on providing literacy linked with functionality and awareness of all its citizens, with top priority for the productive age range of 15 to 35 and giving due attention and importance to the deprived and downtrodden sections of the society. Mere literacy is not enough continuing education facilities should also be offered to all. Hence them make use of their leisure hours profitably pursuing academic or vocational studies or equipping better in one's own profession. One cannot say that this is only of secondary importance. We have to prevent people from relapsing into illiteracy. The post-literacy stage thus becomes important. The neglect of the stage is non-excusable.

All educated persons should involve themselves directly or indirectly in the nation building process. Those who have interest and aptitude for adult education work can be tapped in for such work. Making some amount of social service/work inevitable for all graduates (before receiving their first degree), I think, will be ideal in the Indian context. The Universities and colleges have been requested to collaborate in solving the problem of illiteracy. But the response is not upto the expectations. It should be made obligatory on every institution of higher learning to make at least 100 persons literate every year. This, if continued for 5 years, will help in solving the problem considerably. The Corporations, Municipalities and Panchayats can do a lot in the area. They can find money out of their development funds or educational provisions. They should understand that without a learning society, all their attempts at developing the locality will be futile. A meeting of all local self government personnel under the chairmanship of District Collectors be organised and a time-bound programme and action plan for adult education should be evolved. Peoples' representatives should also be effectively involved in the discussions, planning, implementation and evaluation of the outcomes. Voluntary agencies of reputation should be given a place of pride in the implementation of this programme.

It is my firm conviction that only through proper education of the masses, can developmental programmes be implemented fruitfully. It won't be a waste, even if we fix top priority for peoples' education, to be followed by developmental activities. It should also be noted that social change is an inevitable phenomenon for which people have to be equipped. All kinds of social revolution-green, white or total revolution—will bear fruit only through the proper education and orientation of the prospective beneficiaries or participants. The State and Central Government should liberalise grant-in-aid rules so that local self government agencies can utilise other resources for adult education, which is a pre-condition for any development. Adult educators should even unite to pressurise the authorities concerned to do this, in the interest of the community.

PROBLEMS CONFRONTING ADULT EDUCATORS

For the successful implementation of the adult education programmes, frequent visits to the centres, constant dialogue with the instructors and effective monitoring and evaluation are needed. A jeep jatha was organised by the Centre for Adult Education and Extension in Karakulam and Anad Panchayats where 60 Adult Education Centres are directly run by the CAEE. The two day jeep jatha not only helped in evincing public awareness and support, but also in identifying the urgent needs of the community and the problems confronting them. Some of these were eye-openers to the team of 15 adult educators comprising of organisers, researchers, project officers, supervisors and social workers.

The jeep jatha which started from the University Students' Centre at 8 a.m., on 12-5-1984 reached Aruviyode Harijan Colony around 9 a.m. where 2 centres are run for men and women respectively. An emerging colony just outside the city limits, appeared remote and far from developed. The team was whole heartedly welcomed by a gathering of about 150 men and women. "Give us drinking water"—that demand came from all those who assembled there. They took us to a nearby well which was completely dry. The well was deep enough but there was no water. We were taken to two neighbouring places which used to be their solace, but that too had gone dry. Water supply has not reached that area yet. So the colony people had to travel at least 200 metres for a bucket of water. The people-are willing to extend manual labour but the walls couldn't be dug deeper due to mud and sand. But the adult illiterates are prompt in attending classes. They are half-starving, yet they are amenable to change. Which is the priority—dringking water or alphabets, they ask.

In a feeding centre attached adult education Centre-crowded to see us and talk to us. The attendance in that people is rather good, mainly due to the food supplied to the young-children. Mothers come with children and are taught health and hygiens, saving habits, first aid pollution, democracy etc., which they are eager to hear and learn. Their demand is that the quantum of food be increased so that mothers need not depend on the food supplied to their-children.

Though the target group is mainly of the 15-35 age group men and women of 50+are found in some centres, eager to learn the alphabets. They are more regular than the youth. But the elderly ones are short of sight and are looking forward to the welfare agencies for the supply of glasses. What they ask is whether there is some provision for 'glasses' for the old, in the scheme of adult education. A question yet to be answered.

When we reached a centre in the same Panchayat, we found that classes were run in the open in the shade of a jack tree. The ground is not plain and there is nothing to sit on. The learners squat on the muddy floor. The roller board supplie to the centre was rarely used due to lack of space for affixin the same. Such a pitiable condition was prevalent in the area. A Harijan Colony of recent origin other facilities were also meagre in the area. But the interest evinced was so high that the average attendance was more than 30. How to construct a temporary shed is their problem.

Though the State boasts of providing electricity in all its villages, we found many centres near which no electric post could be seen. In at least two places due to lack of money, electric connection could not be extended to the centre. Can't this be done as a gift to the learners?

In one centre we found children below 15 years also in the class. They told us that they found the adult education class more interesting than the regular school because of timing approach, variety, freedom etc. However these were only guest learners and not regular learners. On the first day we covered 20 centres within 11 hours and concluded the day visiting centre in a home for the physically handicapped, in the city area. Though not a literacy class in the strict sense, this centre was a non-formal education centre doing commendable work.

The journey was so tiring as it was through the village roads steep and dusty without even metal not to speak of tar. Anyway the members of the team were all rejoicing at the sight of the learners who are eager to continuing their learning even at to expense of their leisure time and work.

'On the 13th, as planned earlier, we marched to Anad Panchayat which has about 7000 illiterates compared to the 8700 in, 'Karakulam Panchayat. In either case women illiterates out number men. Centres are also mostly run by women air for women. Half the centres are located in Harijan colonies. The presence of the Panchayat President in the team-throughout the day was a morale booster. The Problems that were brought to our notice on the 12th were there again. May be this is the situation prevailing in all mofussil areas. On the 13th we covered 25 centres travelling 125 kms. Even after 8 p.m. learners were waiting for the team.

A cashew factory which reopened recently in Anad has posed problems for learners in some of the centres. Their timings overlap. Moreover, after the day's hardwork, with their hands unclean and a foul smell, find it difficult to attend classes. Only Sundays are free for them and they have a lot to do that-day. Having class for continuous hours will pose further problems. How to solve this? Will the factory owner be kind-enough to spare at least half an hour twice or thrice a week for their studies as in the case of worker's education?

Another serious problem posed was on the impact of the programme. Some learners who used to give their thumb impressions for receiving widow pension and other benefits are now denied of the same as they started signing their names. The change in signature has to be accepted by the authorities. This is a laborious task and time consuming. Can't the Project Officers be authorised to declare the new signature of neo-literates as valid and avoid unnecessary troubles?

Adult education programmes, to drive fruits have to be linked with developmental programmes and welfare schemes. Income generating projects have to be linked with adult and non-formal education programmes as well as incentives for functionaries and beneficiaries to be instituted. The needs and problems of learners have to be identified and programmes planned effectively linking these with all possible streams and ensuring proper coordination. The unnecessary and avoidable wastage-both of money and energy—has to be curbed for ensuring desired results. Lack of understanding and coordination among the different implementing agencies is yet another lacuna. Though State and District are not level worth the. Boards are being organised, they Mostly they are namesake and serve no purpose.

The recent changes in the norms of financial support are consoling to some extent. Provision of transport and adequate staff for effective monitoring and evaluation still remains a The accountability part also needs special attention problem of all concerned.

A Rural Convocation for Honouring Neo-literates

At a time when in the Kerala University, Convocations have—become an old story, the rural people of a local Panchayat, Karakulam, in Nedumangad Block neighbouring the city of Trivendrum had a unique recognition of receiving neo-literates certificates from no less a person than Hon. Speaker of the Kerala Assembly Shri. V.M. Sudheeran. More than 300 neo-literates (nearly 80per cent of whom were ladies) receiving their certificates in person, in recognition of their successful completion of 12 months intensive literacy campaign organised by the 'Centre for Adult Education and Extension (CAFE) of the Kerala University. Nearly 100 recipients were presented with a neo-literate book kit in recognition of their creditable performance during their discussions, field work and examination as judged through continuous evaluation and final testing.

The function was organised on 30-3-86 in the Karakulam Government Upper Primary School premises adjacent to the Panchayat Office. The local public cooperated with the CAEE authorities in erecting welcome arches, flower decorations etc., in and around the meeting place. The school hall and even the compound was fully packed with neo-literates, their family members and local people. The CAEE had organised street corner certification ceremonies during April 1985 for the neo-literates of 1984 batch. That was the first year of CAEE's direct involvement in eradicating illiteracy. Karakulam and Anad were the two panchayats adopted by the CAEE for intensive literacy campaign with a view to completely eradicating illiteracy, at least from the age group 15-35, by 31st March 1990. Nearly 800 illiterates were made literate during the first year In 1985 also centres were run in the same Panchayat for 12 months. Nearly 350 illiterate adults each were helped to become literate in these Panchayats.

With UGC's financial support, the CAEE has been instrumental in making nearly 9000 people literate through 12 colleges during the period 1980-1984. In 1984, the number of collaborating colleges rose to 22 and the centres organised to 590. The neo-literates of 1984 batch came to about 10200. During 1985 the number of colleges increased from 22 to 32 and the no. of centres from 590 to 780. Enrolment also increased considerably. But due to inordinate delays in the release of grants by the UGC, the results did not reach the targets expected, though the number of neo-literates of 1985 batch is also around 10,000. Thus so far the CAEE of the Kerala University has succeeded in helping around 30,000 adult illiterates not only in securing literacy and numeracy skills but also in improving their living conditions and in making attitudinal changes.

The CAEE has also launched 30 college level population education clubs and 225 Adult Education Centre level Population Education Clubs. These are organising a variety of programmes like seminars, discussions, exhibitions, medical camps, competitions, quiz programmes, drama festivals, film shows etc., for creating awareness among the people and college youth on the ill effects of population explosion and the need and importance of family welfare schemes. The CAEE has started 25 such Population Education Clubs in Anad and Karakulam Panchayat areas.

In the CAEE centres, a Primer prepared scientifically by the Unit itself is being made use of. A hand book on the effective use of the primer addressed to the Instructors is also supplied to all the Centres. The learners have learnt by heart the hit-songs in the collection of motivational songs entitled 'Janabodhanaganangal' published by the Literacy Forum, extension wing of the CAEE. There is effective monitoring work through the Supervisors. Each supervisor visits a centre at least once a month and gives necessary support, advice and leadership. Monthly meeting of the Instructors are used to clarify doubts, disseminate innovative trends and suggest ways and means for ensuring local support and cooperation. Thus the CAEE-centres are actually models to other agencies in the field. Certificates and Book kits were presented to the neo-literates by Hon. Speaker Shri. V. M. Sudheeran after a very encouraging and thought provoking speech. He pleaded for better financial allotment and status for non-formal education programmes. He criticised that developmental schemes are not reaching the real beneficiaries due to their ignorance, illiteracy and poverty. In his opinion commitment alone will succeed in the non-formal sector. He praised the Kerala University for undertaking such a genuine and commendable work.

While presenting the certificates Mr. Sudheeran interrogated the recipients on their motivation for learning, their achievements, learning time etc. The Television representatives covered the programme with emphasis on this interview. Dr. A. Sukumaran Nair, Pro-Vice-Chancellor presiding-over the function stressed the importance of education as an agent for human resource development. He stressed the extention role of universities and congratulated the CAEE for its meritorious work under the able leadership of Dr. Sivadasan Pillai.

Adv. Nafeesath Beevi, Former Dy. Speaker stressed on the need for Women's education. She presented certificates to the participants in the 10-day orientation course for rural women-organised by the Literacy Forum with financial support from the Central Social Welfare Board. As a follow up of this;programme it has been proposed to establish an 'Association for Women's Development at Karakulam with the 20 trained women as founding members.

Shri. Somasekharan Nair, Ex. M.L.A. felicitated the neo-literates and requested them to keep the certificates safer than their precious ration cards. Shri. P.I.A. Karim Reader in. Education, also spoke on the occasion highlighting the current importance of non-formal education.

In his welcome address Dr. Sivadasan Pillai, Director CAEE narrated the achievements of the CAFE during the short span of 6 years since its establishment in February 1980. The centre 'is rated very high among the 83 Universities in India which have centres/departments of Adult and Continuing Education, he said. He added that CAFE has been identified by the UGC as one of the five Units for Indo-Danish collaboration in Community education, one of the 12 'units' identified for UGC-UNFPA collaboration in the field of population Education and as one of the 12 centres selected for special support for audiovisual aids. The innovative attempts of the CAFE like preparation of- a training kit on 55 topics, supply of identity cards to all supervisors and instructors, preparation and supply of comprehensive monitoring registers for all the Adult Education Centres, preparation of proformas like observation schedule, monthly progress reports, instructor's profile, survey form, final evaluation schedule etc., have been approved by the UGC and recommended to the other Universities for adoption. The CAFE proposes to follow the area approach in starting the 780 centres approved for 1986. In Trivendrurn district, Nedumangad, Kazhakkoottam and Trivendrum rural. Blocks have been identified, he said. He also announced the formation of a People's Education Corp's (Janabodhana Sana) enlisting volunteers from among the students and the educated for fighting illiteracy on a voluntary basis agreeing to teach one, two or up to five, within the stipulated time.

It is learnt that the UGC, in recognition of the expertise and experience of Dr. Sivadasan Pillai, has put him as UGC representative in the University level advisory committee of all the Universities in the State of Karnataka. He is also an expert member of the advisory committees of Tamil University (Tanjore), Bharatidasan University (Trichy), Bharatiar University (Coimbatore), Gandhigram Rural University (Madurai), Madurai Kamaraj University, Calicut University, Kerala Agricultural University (Trichur) etc. He is also rendering expert advice and guidance to Delhi University and SNDT University Bombay in the implementation of their Post M.A. Diploma Course in Adult and Continuing Education. He is also attached to Madras University, SV University, Tirupati, Andhra University, Waltair, South Gujarat University, Surat, Punjabi University, Patiala, etc., in various capacities.

Out of the 13 Ph.D.'s so far produced by Dr. Pillai, 4 are in adult education. Currently 10 students are working for Ph.D. under his supervision and guidance of whom 6 are in the field of adult education. Having authored a number of books in English and Malayalam, Dr. Pillai is giving very effective leadership in the CAEE's activities. Dr. N.D. Joshi the only Project Officer attached to the CAFE is a specialist in tribal education and folk arts. The other posts of Asst. Directors and Project Officers are yet to be filled in.

The CAEE is currently housed in the Gandhi Bhavan at Kariavattom Campus. Only in Feb. '86 the new premises was occupied. Till then the CAFE was housed in the University Students' Centre Buildings. The 38th All India Adult Education Conference jointly sponsored by the CAEE, Kerala University and KANFED SRC was planned and organised effectively by Dr. Pillai as its Convener.

The CAFE has completed one UGC research project entitled "Identification of motivation and facilitating factors as well as barriers in the implementation of adult education programme in Kerala with special reference SC/ST and Women". Another study supported by the Directorate of Education,

Government of India is in progress. It is entitled 'Adult Education Programmes in Kerala—an evaluative study'. This study concentrating on 1983-84 programmes will be completed by the end of October 1986. Both the Projects are directed by Dr. Pillai. Still it is a pity that the CAEE is yet to be recognised as a research centre for inter-disciplinary researches.

Consequent on a week-long intensive workshop on 'Colleges in Continuing Education' sponsored by the UGC, 29 colleges and the CAEE have formulated proposals for launching continuing education programmes for the benefit of the weaker sections. The proposals are before the UGC for approval and financial support. When this is launched, it will attract more people to the programme, resulting in economic improvement and better life. Planning Forum has also become part of the activity of the 'Centre/Department of Adult and Continuing Education. The UGC has agreed to grant upto ₹. 4000 each to colleges on a 100per cent basis for organising such activities.

Newer areas which are being brought under the big umbrella of Adult and Continuing Education include legal literacy, science for the masses, environmental education, national integration etc. The UGC has recognised extension as the third and equally important function of all institutions of higher learning, along with teaching and research. Many Universities have by now established permanent statutory departments for adult and continuing education. Maharashtra and Madhya Pradesh are the states leading in this regard. Other states are being persuaded to follow suit. Kerala State which is providing leadership to other Indian States in many respects, it is hoped will not lag behind in the establishment of a statutory Department/Centre for Adult and Continuing Education in the University of Kerala. The long awaited Post M.A. Diploma Course in Adult and Continuing Education may also be established forthwith for equipping prospective functionaries technically and scientifically.

Appropriate incentives for students instructors, supervisors and college level programme officers have to be worked out and implemented. This would help in recruiting more and more volunteers from among students and e work of and whapproachlto the and follow whole programme, voluntary work will have to be given special significance and this can be achieved only through proper incentives.

Bibliography

Ajay Kumar Attri: *Adult Education*, APH Publication, Delhi, 2012.

Ajoy Chatterjee: *Adult Education and Rural Development*, Commonwealth Publication, Delhi, 2008.

Arun Bansal: *Adult Personality Development and Learning*, Pearl Books, Delhi, 2010.

B.C. Mishra and Santilata Patnaik: *Adult Attitude Towards Population Education*, Discovery Publication, Delhi, 2003.

B.P. Parashar: *A Textbook of Adult Education*, Dominant Publication, Delhi, 2005.

Bhawna Misra: *Adult and Social Education*, Mohit Publication, Delhi, 2003.

C.K. Pathak: *Adult Education : Millennium Challenges*, Rajat Publication, Delhi, 2003.

Digumarti Bhaskara Rao: *Adult Learning in the Twenty-First Century*, Discovery Publication, Delhi, 2004.

Farrukh Dhondy: *Adultery and Other Stories*, HarperCollins India, 2011.

H D Kamat and A David: *Adult Education*, Crescent Publication, Delhi, 2007.

Jagannath Mohanty: *Adult and Non-Formal Education*, Deep and Deep Publication, Delhi, 2002.

K V Singh: *Adult Education in India : Historical Perspective*, Vista International, Delhi, 2007.

L. Mishra: *Adult Education : (A Study of the Tribals)*, A P H Publication, Delhi, 2010.

Mercurio, Jed.: *American Adulterer*, Random House India, 2010.

Mubark Singh: *Adult Education in India : Some Reflections*, Kanishka Publication, Delhi, 2004.

N. K. Singh: *Adult Education*, Saurabh Publication, Delhi, 2010.

P. Adinarayan Reddy: *Adult Education : Role of Volunteers*, Sarup and Sons, Delhi, 2003.

P. Adinarayana Reddy and D. Uma Devi: *Current Trends in Adult Education*, Sarup & Sons, Delhi, 2006.

Prem Chand Patanjali: *Development of Adult Education in India*, Shree Publication, Delhi, 2005.

Prem Lata Sharma: *Adult Learning Methods*, Sarup & Sons., Delhi, 2006.

Rajender Singh Yadav: *Adult Education : Concept Theory and Practice*, Associated Publication, Delhi, 2002.

Rameshwari Pandya and Richa Kapoor: *Adult Education : Myths and Realities*, Authorspress, Delhi, 2010.

Rameshwari Pandya: *Adult and Non Formal Education*, Gyan Publication, Delhi, 2010.

S.P. Agrawal, Mithilesh Gupta, M.W.K. Sherwani and Meena Usmani: *Development of Adult, Continuing and Non-Formal Education in India*, Concept Publication, Delhi, 2002.

Sadananda Mishra: *Adult Education and Total Literacy*, Regal Publication, Delhi, 2008.

Saroj and S.P. Sharma: *Adult Education and Economic Reforms*, Vista Publication, Delhi, 2012.

Singh, N K.: *Adult Education*, Saurabh Publication, Delhi, 2009.

Sugan Bhatia: *Adult and Continuing Education*, Mittal Publications, Delhi, 2011.

T. Sharon Raju: *Adult Learners*, APH Publication, Delhi, 2011.

Turksen: *Adult Stem Cells*, Springer, India, 2003.

Index